Leadership, Legitimacy, and Conflict in China

FREDERICK C. TEIWES

Leadership, Legitimacy, and Conflict in China

FROM A CHARISMATIC MAO TO THE POLITICS OF SUCCESSION

M. E. Sharpe Inc.
Armonk, New York

Copyright ©1984 by M. E. Sharpe, Inc.
80 Business Park Drive, Armonk, New York 10504

Library of Congress Cataloging in Publications Data

Teiwes, Frederick C.
    Leadership, legitimacy, and conflict in China.
1. China—Politics and government—1949—1976—
Addresses, essays, lectures. 2. China—Politics and
government—1976- —Addresses, essays, lectures.
3. Mao, Tse-tung, 1893-1976—Addresses, essays, lectures.
I. Title.
DS777.75.T44 1983 951.05 83-15381
ISBN 0-87332-246-0
ISBN 0-87332-275-4 Pbk

Printed in the United States of America

To
KATH

CONTENTS

ACKNOWLEDGMENTS

This volume of essays owes a great deal to conferences on Leninist political systems held at The Australian National University in 1979 and 1981. These conferences, organized by T. H. Rigby and Robert F. Miller, led me to think systematically about many of the issues raised in the second and third pieces below, and Rigby's papers in particular laid some essential groundwork for my own analyses. At a later stage Michael Yahuda performed an invaluable service through detailed comments on the latter essays which sharpened my sense of the distinct Chinese dimension as opposed to the Leninist structural features of leadership politics in China. Graeme Gill provided not only valued criticism but also considerable guidance on comparative insights into Soviet politics.

I also thank a number of others who commented at various stages on one or more of the three essays: David Bachman, Gordon Bennett, Bernard Carey, Ross Curnow, Lowell Dittmer, Thomas Fingar, Tom Fisher, Michael Jackson, Pamela Tan, Wang Gungwu, and Gordon White. Sandra Gibbons provided helpful research assistance, while Sandra Donnelly, Wilma Sharp, and Sylvia Krietsch worked diligently on the various stages of the manuscript, and Margaret McAllister prepared the Index with brisk efficiency. Finally, I am deeply appreciative of the financial support of the Department of Government at the University of Sydney.

Frederick C. Teiwes

Sydney

ABBREVIATIONS

Organizations

CAC	Central Advisory Commission
CCP	Chinese Communist Party
CMC	Central Military Commission
JCP	Japanese Communist Party
MAC	Military Affairs Committee
NPC	National People's Congress
PLA	People's Liberation Army
PRC	People's Republic of China

Publications and Publishing Agencies

BR	*Beijing Review*
CB	*Current Background*
CLG	*Chinese Law and Government*
CNA	*China News Analysis*
CQ	*The China Quarterly*
FBIS:PRC	*Foreign Broadcast Information Service: People's Republic of China*
IS	*Issues & Studies*
JPRS	*Joint Publications Research Service*
MMT	*Miscellany of Mao Tse-tung Thought*
MP	*Mao Papers: Anthology and Bibliography*
NYT	*The New York Times*
PDA	*Communist China 1955-1959: Policy Documents with Analysis*
PR	*Peking Review*
RMRB	*Renmin Ribao* [People's Daily]
SCMM	*Selections from China Mainland Magazines*
SCMP	*Survey of China Mainland Press*
SW	*Selected Works of Mao Zedong*
USIS	*United States Information Service*

Leadership, Legitimacy, and Conflict in China

INTRODUCTION

The three essays in this volume address leadership politics at the apex
of the Chinese system. They raise a series of questions about conflict in
the most authoritative body, the Politburo of normally 20 to 25 men
(and since 1969 a very few women), and more broadly among the most
important leaders of China's various organizations who collectively
comprise what Mao Zedong once referred to as the 800 people ruling
China.[1] What are the sources of power and authority at the top? What
has been the nature of the relationship between the leader—most importantly Mao but also in recent years Deng Xiaoping—and his Politburo
colleagues? What tensions have emerged among those ranking elite
members serving under the leader? How do the fortunes of such figures
interact with the various institutional interests of contemporary China
and the massive bureaucracy as a whole? How have these various
aspects of Chinese politics evolved over the entire post-1949 period?

Inquiries such as these are, to a significant extent, necessarily speculative. The interactions of the highest leaders of any political system
are generally shielded from public view, and the problem is magnified
manyfold in the case of a closed system such as China's. Nevertheless,
speculation can be informed and conclusions, however tentative, tested
by rigorous analysis of what is known. Moreover, the problem varies
with the period subjected to investigation. Generally speaking, a fair
amount is known about the leadership politics of the 1950s. Rich and
detailed discussions of the problems facing Chinese Communist leaders
appeared in the official media of this decade, including detailed statements by top figures—statements sometimes identified as personal
opinions.[2] Further insights can be gained from the new sources appearing during the Cultural Revolution—especially various collections of
Mao's hitherto unpublished speeches and writings[3] and a deluge of
attacks on alleged ''capitalist-roaders'' within the elite. While the
latter source is often dubious at best, a careful comparison of such
attacks with contemporary documentation allows reconstruction of
elite conflict. It must be emphasized, however, that even for this period
such reconstructions are often very limited in what they can say about
positions adopted within the Politburo.[4]

Cultural Revolution "revelations" continue for the early 1960s, but the problem of analysis becomes somewhat more difficult owing to a decline in the amount and quality of contemporary official sources available for this period.[5] For the Cultural Revolution itself, from 1966 to 1968 much information is available from both official sources and unofficial Red Guard publications on the conflict-ridden and generally chaotic conditions of elite interaction. But while the activities of several key leaders, particularly Zhou Enlai, are known in some detail, the roles of other crucial figures, including Mao and Lin Biao, remain more elusive. The period following the Cultural Revolution culminating in Lin Biao's death in 1971 provides the most obscure case of leadership conflict in post-1949 China. The paucity of concrete information on elite differences in contemporary sources, the relative absence of detailed *ex post facto* "revelations" concerning Lin's crimes apart from his alleged plot to assassinate Mao, and the generally confusing and contradictory official explanations advanced after Lin's fall[6] all combine to make any analysis of this affair, including the one offered in the third essay below, even more speculative than for other cases.

The last years of Mao's life also involve difficulties of analysis, but polemics in contemporary official publications, internal documents which became available outside China, and "revelations" about the so-called "Gang of Four" following their fall provide the basis for an informed interpretation of the inner-elite struggles of the 1972-76 period. Finally, in the period since Mao's death the possibilities for analysis have been enhanced by more varied and frank official discussions of the issues and policy alternatives facing Chinese leaders and the development of a new "inside" source in the form of procommunist Hong Kong newspapers and journals,[7] but this has been offset to a degree by the Party's tendency to project a picture of elite solidarity, as had been the case before the Cultural Revolution. Thus, although in no period have the sources been adequate for a fully detailed picture of elite conflict, they nevertheless are sufficient to support the general propositions about Chinese leadership politics advanced in the following essays.

The first essay, originally published nearly a decade ago but not distributed in the United States,[8] focuses on leadership conflict and policy change in the pre-Cultural Revolution period. It was written at a time when, in the wake of the Cultural Revolution, a new model had come to dominate analyses of Chinese politics. Before 1966, reflecting Beijing's own stress on leadership solidarity, scholarly interpretation advanced a consensual model of elite interaction. Emphasizing bonds developed in the revolutionary period and what were believed to be homogenous values, this view depicted a leadership where conflict was restrained and a high degree of mutual loyalty existed between Mao and his ranking associates.[9] With the shock of the Cultural Revolution this model seemed no longer sustainable to most analysts, and in an effort to make sense of the turbulence and divisions then evident, many began to adopt a new model, an interpretation once again drawing sustenance from Chinese rhetoric—this time that of "two line struggle."

As discussed in the essay, the "two line struggle" model emphasized repeated conflict resulting in a polarized leadership. While few serious analysts adopted Beijing's dichotomy of Mao's "proletarian revolutionary line" against a "bourgeois reactionary line," other dichotomies abounded in the literature. Apart from the personalized Maoists versus Liuists, many instances amounted to relabeling the official version with social science concepts: mobilization/ institutionalization, revolutionary modernizer/managerial modernizer, activist/professional, equality/efficiency, etc. Of course, there were notable exceptions which did not adopt the "two line" mode of analysis,[10] while those following this interpretation often differed widely in general level of sophistication and on such matters as when the leadership polarized, how specific episodes were to be interpreted, and the degree to which Mao's power fluctuated. Nevertheless, in the early 1970s (and for several years beyond) the view of elite politics as a struggle between two clearly opposed conceptions of society and related policy programs permeated much of the literature, including the work of scholars sympathetic to Mao's China and those with more jaundiced attitudes.[11]

The first essay, then, was written as a critique of the "two line struggle" model and offered an alternative interpretation centering on Mao's changing role and shifting views as the key to Chinese leadership politics. Although this interpretation has been characterized as a "Mao in command" model,[12] it was never intended as quite that. As the text makes clear, it certainly did not argue that there was no serious disagreement with Mao's concepts. Nor, perhaps less clearly, did it contend that policy change was simply a function of Mao changing his mind. Mao acted in response to real pressures, and many avenues were closed to him, or deliberately not pursued by him, owing to societal, political, and administrative constraints. What the essay does depict is Mao as the unchallenged pivot of elite politics—a dominant leader. In this view, all other leaders were dependent to a significant degree on Mao's continued goodwill and, when sufficiently aroused, he was able to reorient not only major policies but also the overall direction of the regime.

Although the Mao-centered approach has not replaced the "two line struggle" thesis as a pervasive influence on analyses of pre-Cultural Revolution politics, from the mid-1970s, due partly to this and subsequent critiques[13] and more fundamentally to distance from Cultural Revolution rhetoric, the "two line" version has gone into gradual decline. Instead, competing for attention have been a number of more sophisticated approaches, including complex factional models, detailed analyses of conflicting bureaucratic interests, and emphasis on constraints created by social and economic conditions as well as the unintended consequences of previous policies.[14] Nevertheless, even in the 1980s, variants of the "two line struggle" model still appear.[15] The initial essay, then, is reprinted here partially because of the lingering influence of the "two line" interpretation, partially to reach the American audience which was previously excluded, but primarily in the belief that its analytic points about the nature of pre-Cultural Revolution leadership politics remain valid. It is presented in essentially its original form with only minor editing for reasons of style and, in some cases, to alter the nuance of meaning. In addition, a few explanatory notes (a to f) have been added where, upon reflection, I believe some clarification or amendment is required.

The second and third essays take the analysis of leadership politics up to the present. Thus they cover, in addition to 1949-1965, periods fundamentally different from those years. First, they examine the intense conflicts of Mao's last decade which, at least in the 1972-76 period, did involve something like a "two line struggle" of sharply contrasting programs—albeit one where Mao's position was not easily classifiable. Throughout this decade the Chairman remained a crucial part of the politial equation although, as argued particularly in the second essay, toward the end of his life he was significantly less dominant than at any previous time since the founding of the People's Republic. Finally, the analysis addresses a far different type of leadership politics in the post-Mao era where no leader has had the degree of authority or power of even the dying Mao of 1976. Although, as discussed in these last two essays, Deng Xiaoping quickly emerged as the generally acknowledged leader, a genuinely more collective pattern now developed with many ramifications for elite interaction as a whole.

The second essay in one sense takes up where the first leaves off. With Mao's dominant position before the Cultural Revolution established—a view confirmed for the subsequent period by Lin Biao's son when he remarked in 1971 that "the Chairman commands such high prestige that he need only utter one sentence to remove anybody he chooses"[16]—the second essay asks why this was the case. While granting Mao's political skills, ruthlessness and, at certain times, "divide and rule" tactics,[17] this analysis proceeds on the assumption that something more was involved—genuine authority and legitimacy. Recourse to such concepts is essential to explain the unchallenged nature of Mao's leadership even when his actions severely threatened entrenched interests and ranking colleagues. Two cases from the "Cultural Revolution decade" examined here make this particularly clear. First, Mao's ability to launch the Cultural Revolution against the interests of virtually all major institutions and a large proportion of the existing top elite, and the failure of key personal targets of the movement such as Liu Shaoqi and Deng Xiaoping to resist their removal from power, suggest obedience to the authority of the supreme leader. Then, ten years later, Mao's second ousting of Deng Xiaoping despite the fact that Mao was terminally ill and the great bulk of the elite had confidence in Deng and generally supported his prescriptions for China's future points to a similar conclusion. As before, there were social and political forces backing Mao, but those forces—without Mao—were far less powerful than the ones they temporarily bested. Again, Mao's ability to prevail is better explained in terms of other leaders accepting Mao's commands than by a more strictly political process of bargaining, persuading, and building a dominant coalition.

Relatively little of a systematic nature has been written about legitimacy in post-1949 China. Where such analysis has been undertaken, most notably by Chalmers Johnson,[18] the focus has generally been on the legitimacy of the *system as a whole* (or the Party/regime) in the eyes of the *population as a whole*.[19] The analysis offered here has a quite different focus. The legitimacy being examined is that of the leader. The crucial source of his legitimacy is not the population but the top political elite. While the legitimacy of the system and leader in the eyes of the people is relevant and considered in the discussion, it is argued that the acceptance of the leader's position and authority by the leadership group is the crucial factor for elite interaction. My concern, then, is why and to what extent top Chinese politicians have accepted an individual as their legitimate leader.

This inquiry begins with Max Weber's tripartite typology of charismatic, traditional, and legal-rational authority and also utilizes concepts developed in work on legitimacy in Soviet-style political systems.[20] While agreeing with most analysts that Mao's authority was essentially charismatic in character, the essay investigates the role of other legitimating principles, asks how these factors have interacted with the charismatic appeal over time, and seeks to determine the degree to which the Chairman's authority varied from period to period. A new set of questions is raised when the analysis is extended to the post-Mao era and the politics of succession. On what basis have various figures claimed legitimate leadership? To what extent have such claims been accepted within the top elite as a whole? How has the strong emphasis on collective leadership which emerged in this period affected the authority of the leader? And how has the attempt of recent years to shift the legitimacy of the system as a whole from charismatic to legal-rational grounds influenced leadership politics?

The final essay adopts yet another perspective on elite politics. Rather than focus on the dominant leader as in the previous essays, this investigation examines politics at the apex of the system from the point of view of other members of the Politburo. How did such figures protect or advance their interests in the presence of a dominant Mao? What strategies of political action did they adopt? To what extent can one identify patterns of behavior—i.e., prudential rules—that political leaders should follow in order to maximize their chances of success? In what ways were these rules altered by Mao's departure from the scene? And how do such prudential rules relate to the formal normative rules of the system concerning acceptable elite behavior?

The question of political strategies has been raised indirectly in many studies of Chinese politics, but only rarely has it been the center of inquiry. Where this has been done, the focus has generally been different or more restricted than that pursued here. For example, an influential study by Michel Oksenberg on the ways of getting ahead in the Chinese system deals with opportunities and career choices available to the Chinese people generally rather than to high-ranking leaders.[21] Other studies have examined the strategies of survival adopted by officials at various levels during the Cultural Revolution,[22] and still others have analyzed the strategies of Politburo-level groupings at specific times.[23] This essay, however, not only focuses on the apex of the system but attempts to generalize about the "rules" of maintaining or enhancing one's position at that level over the entire post-1949 period. As with the previous essay, it distinguishes among very different environments over time. After an overview of prudential rules during the relatively stable pre-Cultural Revolution period, it examines the far more turbulent 1966-1976 decade in terms of the strategies used first by Lin Biao and then by the clashing forces of the "Gang of Four" and the old-line Party and state administrators led by Zhou Enlai and Deng Xiaoping. By comparing these cases with the earlier period, the essay analyzes how prudential rules have been affected by changing circumstances, and also the crucial impact of the state of normative rules on that process.

Finally, the essay addresses the strategies of the post-Mao era—a period of succession politics but not of a succession struggle. As the analysis argues, Deng Xiaoping quickly emerged as the *de facto* leader—albeit of a far different type from Mao—despite the formal trappings of leadership initially bestowed on Hua Guofeng. It then discusses the options open to Hua in his efforts to retain his formal position, the types of prudential considerations restricting Deng in the exercise of his leadership, and the implications for leadership politics as a whole. Thus this concluding essay provides general insights into how elite politics has changed from the charismatically based rule of Mao to the more collective and constrained leadership of his successors.

I
CHINESE POLITICS
1949-1965:
A CHANGING MAO

The Cultural Revolution shattered the previous consensus view of Chinese politics—a view emphasizing a stable, unified leadership, the predominant authority of Mao Zedong, a close working relationship between Mao and his chosen successor, Liu Shaoqi, and the Chinese Communist Party (CCP) as the institutional embodiment of Mao's revolutionary values. In scholarly reinterpretations of the pre-Cultural Revolution period, a widespread tendency emerged which adopted, albeit with significant variations and modifications, concepts derived from Beijing's own "two line struggle" model of political conflict. The central assumption shared by proponents of this view is that Chinese politics was long marked by tension between two antithetical approaches. One, identified with Mao, sought modernization through mass mobilization and manifested a deep concern with the ideological purity of Chinese society. The opposing approach, ascribed to the gray Party bureaucracy and personified and led by Liu Shaoqi, was absorbed in the prosaic tasks of production and economic growth, wedded to rational strategies in dealing with China's problems, and obsessed with orderly development of the existing system.

According to the "two line struggle" interpretation, these different approaches may have been only potentially divisive in the early 1950s, but in the post-Great Leap period (after 1958)—or earlier some analysts have suggested—they began to harden into polarized positions. Fluctuations in Party policies are seen in terms of significant and often bitter conflict between advocates of each position in which the political balance has often been delicate, with Mao sometimes suffering severe losses of power. This essay questions the adequacy of the above view and presents a different interpretation of political conflict and policy change in China prior to the Cultural Revolution.*

Mao's Thought—An Evolving Dialectic

It is undeniable that leadership differences have been a factor in shifting Party policies in the pre-Cultural Revolution period. Nevertheless, it is also clear that Mao himself frequently changed his position both in terms of specific policies and by emphasizing different aspects of his intellectual outlook. This shifting of position derived in part from the very core of Mao's thinking, which depicts a world of constant flux in which the central problems, or "contradictions," change as society develops. Mao summed up this dialectical process as manifested in the general direction of Party policy: "When one opposes the right, the left [deviation] is bound to emerge; and when one opposes the left, the right [deviation] is bound to emerge."[1] Thus, a never ending process of adopting new measures to correct inevitable mistakes was required, however temporary each adjustment.

From another, nondialectical perspective, the shifting emphasis in Mao's outlook can be viewed as the result of dynamic tension between a series of contradictory elements, with first one aspect then another in ascendancy. The changing weights attached to the various elements were only loosely linked to "scientific" analyses of trends in society, with other factors such as the overall political situation, Mao's general mood, and his evaluation of colleagues often crucial. In any case, the various strands of Mao's thought were used to justify strikingly different policies. Mao, moreover, recognized the possibility that others might select portions of his writings to promote conflicting positions:

> I cannot determine when we should publish these words [of mine which question the assertions of the radical left] for the leftists and broad masses of people do not welcome my saying so. Maybe we should wait until I die when the rightists come to power, and let them do the publication. The

---

*The interpretation which follows is not in all particulars incompatible with individual examples of "two line struggle" analysis. My aim is to provide a coherent interpretation which may or may not conflict with such interpretations on specific points, but which challenges some common assumptions: the polarization of the leadership around dichotomous positions, shifting policies as primarily reflecting continuing conflict between those positions, and significant variations in Mao's power.

> rightists may attempt to use my words to hold high the black
> banner. . . . At that time, the rightists may prevail for some time by using
> my words, but the leftists may also organize some of my other words to
> overthrow the rightists. . . .[2]

It can be argued, then, that divergent tendencies in Mao's thought, whether due to Mao's rigorous analysis of a given situation, his personal preoccupations of the moment, or the efforts of others to apply his thought to problems at hand, go a long way in explaining shifting CCP policies. Thus it is necessary to examine in some detail the contradictory aspects of Mao's overall intellectual framework, both in terms of specific dualities and the evolution of his thought in the 1949-1965 period.

Subjective and Objective Forces. A basic ambivalence in Mao's thought, and in Marxism-Leninism generally, concerns the role of subjective and objective forces in history—whether the economic base determines and restricts the possibilities for political action or whether changes in the political superstructure can bring about basic social and economic changes. The voluntarist strain embodied in such concepts as "man over weapons" and "politics in command" was particularly deep in Mao's thinking. It maintained that regardless of unfavorable material conditions, once the subjective factor of human willpower is fully mobilized there is virtually no obstacle which cannot be overcome. As Mao wrote in 1955:

> In a few decades, why can't 600 million paupers, by their own efforts, create a socialist country, rich and strong? The wealth of society is created by the workers, peasants, and working intellectuals. If only they take their destiny into their own hands, follow a Marxist-Leninist line, and energetically tackle problems instead of evading them, there is no difficulty in the world that they cannot resolve.[3]

Yet Mao's faith in subjective possibilities was tempered by a marked caution, an insistence on realistic assessments of objective conditions, both political and economic, and on adjusting goals and methods accordingly. It should not be forgotten that in terms of revolutionary strategy, Mao accepted that no quick victories were possible, and he argued for flexible, moderate policies and for conserving forces until the time was ripe for action.[4] This same realism normally marked Mao's pre-Cultural Revolution actions, surfacing even during periods when his basic aim was to speed up the pace of development. Thus in early 1956, in the context of unexpectedly rapid advances in agricultural cooperativization, Mao warned of "'left' adventurism" and declared, "What cannot be done should be deleted from our plans so that they may rest on a solid reliable basis."[5] While there was no necessary incompatibility between Mao's attention to objective constraints and his belief that in certain circumstances the subjective factor can significantly alter material reality, there was a profound tension between the attitude which said virtually anything is possible and the one which cautioned that a great deal is merely wishful thinking.

Spontaneity and Organization. Once Mao's predilection to rely on the subjective factor is recognized, it becomes clear that his thinking was marked by further ambivalence concerning how this factor was to be brought into play. How much emphasis should be given to the spontaneous creativity of the masses and how much to organized Party leadership? A striking statement on the potential of mass creativity appeared in Mao's 1955 editorial notes to the collection *Socialist Upsurge in China's Countryside*:

> The masses have boundless creative power. . . . *They can organize themselves* and concentrate on places and branches of work where they can give full play to their energy; they can concentrate on production in breadth and depth and create more and more welfare undertakings for themselves.[6]

Mao's deep faith in the masses, whom he often viewed as naturally inclined to support socialism,[7] was reflected in his emphasis on democratic discussion, decentralization, and tapping local initiative. Moreover, Mao expressed fears that organization might become so oppressive as to stifle mass creativity.[8]

Mao's faith in the masses, however, was in conflict with his deep misgivings over where spontaneous activity might lead. Not only did Mao assert that "without a strong leading group to organize their activity properly" the masses cannot sustain activism,[9] he further viewed the people as prone to capitulate to "spontaneous capitalism" and other "evil winds" in society.[10] In a hardheaded analysis, Mao observed that only a small minority of the masses are even "relatively active," while the great majority are wavering "middle elements."[11] Thus, despite misgivings about the potentially stifling aspects of leadership, up to the Cultural Revolution Mao recognized the preeminent role of organization. As Stuart Schram has noted, in the revolutionary period Mao came down heavily on the side of order and discipline.[12] After 1949, Mao was careful to link the creativity of the masses to firm organization, even when he criticized leadership for lagging behind the masses.[13] Only in the Cultural Revolution did Mao temporarily place mass spontaneity above organized leadership, and then he moved back from the brink of anarchy.[14] Yet while leadership was clearly the dominant factor of this duality in Mao's thinking before 1966, the contradictions between the two aspects had volatile implications for CCP organizational methods.

Red and Expert. Although Mao envisioned an ideal cadre who was both "red and expert"—both politically pure and professionally competent—there clearly was a tension between the two priorities. Mao's advocacy of "redness" involved more than a desire that cadres have a high degree of commitment to CCP objectives. It also encompassed a rejection of narrow professionalism apparent in Mao's comments on education:

> This university education of ours! We suspect that from primary to university education, although sixteen, seventeen, or twenty years, [students don't have a chance] to see rice, peas, wheat, cereals, and millet. They do not see how workers work, how peasants plow, and how business is done. . . . I have told my children: "Go to the countryside and tell the poor and lower-middle peasants. Tell them that your father said, 'The more we learn, the more stupid we become. Uncles, brothers and sisters, we have come to learn from you.'" . . . [15]

Despite contempt for the pretenses of the learned and distress at their high social status, Mao acknowledged the need for advanced knowledge, particularly in science and technology. Moreover, he further pointed out that excessive emphasis on politics can be detrimental to national development; in Mao's view, people who babbled about politics while lacking technical competence were objects of scorn.[16] For Mao the question was one of the proper balance between the two elements, and although in theory a synthesis was possible, in practice Mao's conflicting concerns contributed to shifting policies.

Selflessness vs Particularistic Interests. The vision of an egalitarian society is a staple of Marxism; the problem has always been to determine the degree of egalitarianism possible or desirable at any given point along the road to communism. Mao generally placed considerable emphasis on narrowing differences in society and motivating people by ideological appeals to the common good. Perhaps more significant was his concern regarding the negative effects that social inequality and the pursuit of individual or group interests

might have on the future of the revolution. This was particularly apparent in the 1963-64 polemics with the Soviet Union, of which Mao was a
principal author. In the celebrated article, "On Khrushchev's Phoney
Communism and Its Historical Lessons for the World," Mao painted a
gloomy picture of current Soviet society, a picture he clearly saw
relevant to trends in Chinese society:

> A communist society which preserves any classes at all, let alone exploit-
> ing classes, is inconceivable. Yet Khrushchev is fostering a new bourgeoi-
> sie, restoring and extending the system of exploitation and accelerating
> class polarization in the Soviet Union. A privileged bourgeois stratum
> opposed to the Soviet people now occupies the ruling position in the Party
> and government and in the economic, cultural, and other departments.
> Can one find an iota of communism in all this?
>
> . . . By propogating material incentives, [Khrushchev] is turning all
> human relations into money relations and encouraging individualism and
> selfishness. Because of him, manual labor is again considered sordid and
> love of pleasure at the expense of other people's labor is again considered
> honorable. Certainly, the social ethics and atmosphere prompted by
> Khrushchev are far removed from communism, as far as can be.[17]

Despite such preoccupations, Mao recognized the practical limitations on any efforts to combat inequality and selfishness. He often
advocated flexible policies making concessions to the particularistic
interests of various social strata and acknowledged the necessity for
providing material benefits to secure popular support.[18] More interesting was the view that individual and group interests are both natural and
proper, as in Mao's April 1956 speech, "On the Ten Great Relationships":

> All things have their common and individual characters. To have only
> common character is impossible. For instance, our common character is
> to meet here. After the meeting our individual characters will prevail—
> some of us will take a walk, some read, and some others eat. Each one of
> us has his own individual character. . . . So, every productive unit or
> individual must have its initiative and individual character which are
> coordinated with the common character.[19]

This tolerance of individuality was totally rejected by Mao only during
the Cultural Revolution, when even the slightest consideration
of self-interest was held morally damnable. Nevertheless, the fluctuations in Mao's attitudes on this subject created much uncertainty in the
pre-1966 period.

Although the ebb and flow of contradictory aspects of Mao's thought was present in all periods since 1949, significant changes of emphasis and overall outlook evolved in the seventeen years prior to the Cultural Revolution. Three major periods, each linked to identifiable phases in CCP policy orientation, can be delineated. In the first period, 1949 through 1957, CCP policies were basically modeled on the Soviet experience. A brief second period, 1958-1960, was inextricably tied to the unprecedented developmental strategy of the Great Leap Forward. Finally, from 1961 to 1965, Mao's preoccupation with the future of the Chinese revolution was indicative of an indecisive search for new directions within the Party as a whole.

1949-1957: Planned Transformation. During the first eight years of the People's Republic of China (PRC), Mao's thinking was marked by a basic optimism and confidence. Although he indicated that determined efforts were necessary to prevent retrogression,[20] Mao gave no indication of doubts concerning the inevitable march of history toward communism. In Mao's eyes, events were unfolding basically as planned, with major achievements attained. This was particularly evident in the socialist transformation of agriculture and industry in 1955-56. Focusing on economic relations in orthodox Marxist fashion, Mao hailed this campaign as a ''decisive victory'' in the struggle between socialism and capitalism and one that brought about a ''fundamental change'' in China's internal situation.[21]

Despite Cultural Revolution assertions that Liu Shaoqi advanced the notion of the ''dying out of class struggle'' at this juncture, Mao's views in 1956 were not far removed from such an attitude. Indeed, Mao later admitted that during the period of socialist transformation he had wrongly believed the bourgeoisie would be eliminated, leaving only a few remnants of capitalist ideology.[22] To be sure, with the benefit of the Polish and Hungarian events of late 1956 and the unexpected outpouring of criticism during the Hundred Flowers movement in spring 1957, Mao began to place increasing emphasis on the long-term nature of political and ideological struggle. On balance, however, Mao's attitude was relatively restrained and optimistic throughout this initial period. As he put it in 1957:

> To achieve its ultimate consolidation, it is necessary not only to bring about the socialist industrialization of the country and persevere in the socialist revolution on the economic front, but to carry on constant and arduous socialist revolutionary struggles and socialist education on the political and ideological fronts. . . . In China the struggle to consolidate

the socialist system, the struggle to decide whether socialism or capitalism will prevail, will still take a long historical period. But we should all realize that the new system of socialism will unquestionably be consolidated. We can assuredly build a socialist state with modern industry, modern agriculture, and modern science and culture. This is the first point I want to make.

. . . .

Recently, a number of ghosts and monsters have been presented on the stage. Seeing this, some comrades have become very worried. In my opinion, a little of this does not matter much; within a few decades such ghosts and monsters will disappear from the stage altogether and you won't be able to see them even if you want to. . . . [23]

Mao's optimism was further reflected in his judgment that the campaigns undertaken in 1957—Party rectification and the Anti-Rightist struggle—had resulted in a basic victory on the political and ideological fronts.[24] While class struggle may not have been exactly dying out, it was certainly under control and the outcome never in doubt.

Although frequently calling for the harnessing of subjective forces to achieve ambitious goals, throughout the 1949-1957 period Mao normally advocated careful attention to objective limits and planned, phased development.[25] Even when subjective factors were especially stressed, as in the agricultural cooperativization movement, organization was still clearly preeminent over mass spontaneity. Thus, despite some rhapsodizing over popular creativity, Mao concretely called for detailed, methodical leadership:

Fight no battle that is not well prepared, no battle whose outcome is uncertain: that was the well-known slogan of our Party during the past revolutionary war. It applies equally well to the work of socialist construction. If you want to be sure of the outcome, there must be preparedness, full preparedness. A great deal of spade work must be done beforehand if you are going to set up a group of new agricultural producers' cooperatives. . . . The main thing this work includes is (1) criticism of wrong ideas and summarization of experience gained in work; (2) systematic and repeated publicity among the peasant masses of our Party's principles, policy and measures in agricultural cooperation . . . and on the basis of this comprehensive plan working out an annual plan. . . .[26]

Mao also placed a high priority on technical competence. Although his bias against overly elaborate education surfaced in this period,[27]

Mao put major emphasis on learning science and technology from the Soviet Union.[28] Moreover, in advocating political education in the universities Mao spoke of this as added to the regular course of specialized subjects, thus showing no qualms about expertise as such.[29] Finally, the Mao of the early and mid-1950s, while concerned with inequalities and pressing for measures to combat them,[30] was sensitive to the legitimate interests (in his terms) of individuals and groups, and he sought to strike a balance between them and the interests of society as a whole.[31]

In sum, a relatively moderate Mao emerges from an examination of his statements in the 1949-1957 period. While sometimes to the left of many of his colleagues on specific issues, at no time did he play the role of a radical ideologue.[a] Mao apparently saw himself as steering a middle course between deviations on both the left and the right,[32] making comparatively minor shifts as the occasion demanded.

1958-1960: Crash Transformation. The Great Leap Forward, which Mao identified with to an exceptional degree,[33] marked a significant change in his overall outlook. Mao remained optimistic in this period, but it was no longer the assured optimism of confidence in the tested Soviet model. Instead, it was a far more radical optimism which anticipated rapid breakthroughs and unprecedented achievements. Mao expressed this attitude in January 1958:

> I have observed this nation of ours for seven or eight years. I see great hope in our nation. Especially during the past year, it can be seen that the national spirit of our 600 million people has been more bouyant as compared to the past eight years. . . . [We] have clarified our problems and understood our tasks. We will catch up with Britian in about fifteen years. . . .
>
> . . . .
>
> Now our zeal has been bolstered. Our nation is one with ardor and there is

---

[a]A partial exception appears to have occurred toward the end of 1955 and in early 1956. A post-Mao inner Party report by Liao Gailong, "Historical Experiences and Our Road of Development" (October 25, 1980), translated in *Issues & Studies*, November 1981, p. 88, traces the origins of Mao's "leftist" thinking to his late 1955 "Prefaces to *Socialist Upsurge in China's Countryside*," and a careful reading of these and other statements of this period does suggest a subtle shift in the direction of radicalism. It should be noted, however, that Mao's position when launching the speedup of agricultural cooperativization in mid-1955 was distinctly more moderate (see below pp. 32-34), that even during the high optimism at the turn of the year he continued to warn of "leftist" excesses (see above, pp. 12-13), and by spring 1956 he retreated to a more balanced view.

a fervent tide now. Our nation is like an atom . . . and after the fission of
the atomic nucleus of our nation, thermal energy will be released which
becomes so formidable that we will be able to do what was beyond our
ability before. . . .[34]

Although growing problems with the Great Leap strategy and communes tempered Mao's optimism, his outlook remained hopeful. According to his summary of the situation on the eve of the July 1959
Lushan Conference, "Achievements are great, problems are considerable, and the future is bright."[35]

While Mao's optimism waxed he showed little preoccupation with
class struggle on the political and ideological front. He did not alter,
initially, his judgment that a basic victory had been won on that front.
Instead, he saw a "permanent revolution" moving on to new tasks:
"Beginning this year [1958], we must, even as we carry forward and
complete the socialist revolution on the political and ideological fronts,
shift the emphasis in the Party's work to the technical revolution."[36]
Only when the Great Leap met major opposition at the highest levels of
the Party at Lushan did Mao speak of class struggle as a prolonged life
or death process, one that would continue for twenty to fifty years. At
the same time, he remarked that in the past he had not spoken about
class struggle caused by reactionary ideology left over from old
times,[37] a statement not literally true but one indicating that he had not
previously *emphasized* this problem.

Before expectations for the Great Leap dimmed, Mao elevated the
subjective factor to unprecedented heights. A clear indication of this
was his changed attitude toward what he termed the "poor and blank"
character of China—its underdeveloped economy and low standard of
culture and science. In 1956 Mao saw this as both a weakness and a
strength: a weakness as an objective limitation to China's development
yet a subjective strength since poor people desire change, and "a blank
sheet of paper has no blotches and the newest and most beautiful words
can be written on it."[38] By 1958, however, Mao dropped all reference
to the weaknesses inherent in "poverty and blankness" and stressed
solely the positive aspects.[39]

In terms of the nature of subjective forces Mao similarly gave unprecedented emphasis to the creativity of the masses—but not at the
expense of leadership. This is indicated in Mao's comment following
his September 1958 tour of the country:

During this trip, I have witnessed the tremendous energy of the masses.

On this foundation it is possible to accomplish any task whatsoever. . . .
Nevertheless, in the country as a whole, there are a few places, a few
enterprises, where the work of mobilizing the masses has still not been
properly carried out, where mass meetings have not been held, and where
the tasks, the reasons for them, and the methods have still not been made
perfectly clear to the masses or discussed by the masses. . . .[40]

For all the innate energy of the masses, here Mao still assumed without
question the crucial role of organization in mobilizing the masses and
explaining Party policies to them. Yet this was to be a profoundly
different type of organization from that of the earlier period. It was one
shorn of bureaucracy, one that could be linked directly to the people. In
work methods, careful planning was replaced by *ad hoc* adaptation to
rapidly changing circumstances, an approach Mao depicted with a
Hunanese folk saying: "There is no pattern for straw sandals; they take
shape as you weave them."[41] Only leaders acting without rigid precon-
ceived notions would be able to combine effectively with and give
shape to the creativity of the masses.

In this period Mao envisioned a synthesis of red and expert; he
attacked both "empty-headed politicians" and "pragmatists who lose
their sense of direction." Nevertheless, his new formulation involved a
distinct shift in emphasis toward the primacy of redness; as he put it,
"Ideology and politics are the supreme commander, they are the
soul."[42] This attitude was further expressed by denigrating formal
learning; in 1958, Mao said he could no longer tolerate the awe and fear
with which bourgeois professors were regarded and declared his aim to
"show that the lowly are most intelligent while the elite are most
ignorant so as to expropriate the capital of the cocky senior
intellectuals."[43] While technical competence still was necessary, Mao
saw this as a competence found in the common sense of the workers and
peasants rather than in the specialized knowledge of the pampered
university elite.

The Great Leap and commune policies also marked an increased
emphasis on egalitarianism and ideological appeals in Mao's thinking.
When he did give cognizance to individual material needs, it was more
owing to a pragmatic need to correct extreme excesses in pursuit of
egalitarianism than out of a sense of the proper role of individuality.
Moreover, Mao felt that after excesses were curbed there would be
continued progress toward a decidedly more egalitarian society.[44]

The Mao of the Great Leap period was motivated by a vision—a
positive vision of a rapidly developing economy, of a technological

revolution energized by mass creativity linked to bold, flexible leadership, and of a society where inequalities were being eliminated with unprecedented speed. Mao had rejected his earlier tendency to balance left and right in favor of a new left synthesis.[45] Although he referred to himself as a "middle-of-the-roader"—"center-leftist" would have been more accurate—Mao no longer warned of left and right as equal dangers to be avoided.[46] Even when he appealed for greater realism in late 1959, Mao's sympathies were clear:

> Compared with the high key sung by everybody at the moment, what I have said is certainly low key. My aim is truly to mobilize our enthusiasm in order to increase production. If reality is at a higher key and loftier goals are attained, I shall be regarded as a conservative. I shall be grateful for that and feel extremely honored.[47]

As his vision faded, Mao clung to the hope that his radical goals would still be realized.

1961-1965: Transforming Individual Consciousness. The failure of the Great Leap Forward, together with the earlier shortcomings of the Hundred Flowers movement and the worsening Sino-Soviet split, apparently led Mao to some deep soul-searching and a rejection of his former optimism. His thought began to crystallize around one central concept—protracted, violent class struggle would continue throughout socialist society:

> It can now be affirmed that classes exist in socialist countries and class struggle definitely exists there. . . . We must recognize the protracted nature of the existence of classes, recognize the struggle of class against class. We must also recognize the possibility of the restoration of reactionary classes. It is necessary to heighten our vigilance as well as to educate the youth, cadres, the masses, the middle and basic level cadres, and even the veteran cadres. Otherwise, a country like ours may head in the opposite direction. . . . Hence, from this moment on, we must talk about it every year, every month, every day, at conferences, at Party congresses, at plenary sessions, and at each and every meeting, so that we may have a sounder Marxist-Leninist line in regard to this problem. . . .[48]

Here Mao saw the outcome of the struggle in doubt. Gone was the confident faith in inevitable progress toward communism; in its place appeared the notion that retrogression to revisionism was possible, indeed perhaps even probable,[49] in China. Thus, in the years preceding the Cultural Revolution, Mao became increasingly preoccupied with the problem of how to prevent the degeneration of his revolution.

Initially, however, Mao recognized that the work of government must go on. At the Tenth Plenum in September 1962, he declared that work and class struggle were "two different kinds of problems" and that "our work must not be jeopardized just because of class struggle."[50] Yet it was clearly unrealistic to expect that everyday governmental affairs could be insulated from class struggle given Mao's far-ranging view of the nature of class conflict.

Mao was increasingly preoccupied with the subjective factor in this period, but in a vastly different sense than during the Great Leap. He did not slight objective realities but instead emphasized the need for greater experience to master those realities.[51] His concern with the subjective was reflected in the sense that ideological preparation was inadequate, that far-reaching efforts to revolutionize the superstructure were necessary before the problems of developing the economic base could be tackled. Thus Mao brooded over shortcomings of individual morality and the need for a profound transformation of social attitudes:

> Corruption, law-breaking, the arrogance of intellectuals, the wish to do honor to one's family by becoming a white collar worker and not dirtying one's hands any more, all of these stupidities are symptoms [of historical and political conditions].
>
> . . . .
>
> The thought, culture, and customs which brought China to where we found her must disappear; the thought, customs, and culture of proletarian China, which does not yet exist, must appear.[52]

Given this outlook, it is not surprising that Mao's sharpest criticisms during this period were directed at those responsible for literature and art and education, the key battlefronts for the transformation of individual consciousness.

Although Mao championed the masses in the years immediately preceding the Cultural Revolution by calling for greater attention to their needs, he evinced no unusual faith in their creativity. Indeed in the critical fields concerned with shaping public attitudes, he viewed the problem as preeminently one of adequate leadership.[53] But while he recognized the need for leadership, Mao became increasingly hostile toward the "high and mighty bureaucrats [who] have not gone to the workers, peasants and soldiers . . .[and have] slid right down to the brink of revisionism."[54] While Mao had not theoretically rejected or even downplayed significantly the importance of organization, this antipathy to *bureaucratic* organization had reached epic proportions.

Mao's preoccupations were further elaborated in his comments bearing on the "red and expert" and egalitarian and individualistic dichotomies. Although the goal of "red and expert" officially was reaffirmed, Mao became increasingly skeptical of specialized expertise. He saw specialized knowledge as furthering esoteric disciplines rather than making concrete contributions to national progress.[55] Moreover, the accumulation of such knowledge "strangled talents [and] destroyed young people" by overburdening them with work and thus preventing their well-rounded moral, intellectual, and physical development.[56] Most pernicious, professional qualifications could serve as a rationale for sustaining privileged positions.[57] In addition to inequalities bolstered by specialized knowledge, Mao worried about rural-urban differentials, polarization into rich and poor in the countryside, and especially the gap between cadres and populace which he saw developing into an antagonistic class struggle.[58] Although during this period Mao neither called for the radical institutional forms of the Great Leap Forward, which sought to achieve an egalitarian society, nor demanded the ultimate denial of individuality, which came to mark the Cultural Revolution, he was deeply troubled by the threat he perceived to social justice.

In sum, in the years after the Great Leap a brooding Mao emerged, a man obsessed with a negative vision of degenerating revolution. There was no question where he saw the main danger—on the right, in bourgeois revisionism. But while the evils to be fought were clear to Mao, he gave little indication of having a strategy to defeat them. Mao seemed uncertain even of such basic factors as the potential role of the masses and the tolerable level of disruption of everyday work. This uncertainty, together with his deep foreboding concerning the future, provided the intellectual backdrop for Mao's launching of the Cultural Revolution.

Mao's Position in the CCP

Gauging the impact of Mao's shifting intellectual concerns on the political process[b] requires an examination of several key factors—

---

[b]This is not to suggest that Mao's views simply determined political outcomes, since it is clear that his outlook was in turn shaped by specific situations and that many aspects of the political process were beyond his (or anyone's) control. What is argued is that once a given situation created pressures for change, Mao's intellectual concerns were a critical factor in producing the political responses which emerged at the highest levels.

Mao's power and status within the CCP leadership, the norms of behavior which governed Mao's interaction with his colleagues, and the relationship betweeen Mao and the bureaucracy. After a discussion of these questions, we will examine the adequacy of the "two line struggle" interpretation of policy conflict in China before the Cultural Revolution.

The Predominance of Mao. Despite the attempt of Cultural Revolution materials to depict wide-ranging opposition to Mao, a careful reading of those materials supports the earlier consensus view of a Mao whose predominance within the leadership was firm throughout the entire 1949-1965 period. Clearly Mao's prestige had its ups and downs, but the evidence is overwhelming that his colleagues consistently regarded him as the ultimate authority. Reports of high-level meetings are instructive; while others were often referred to by the familiar "Shaoqi" or "Xiaoping," Mao was nearly always respectfully addressed as "Chairman Mao." Moreover, Party leaders clearly viewed Mao's attitude toward them and the general perception of that attitude as crucial to their careers. Thus Liu Shaoqi pictured himself as close to Mao.[59] Peng Zhen first attempted to win Mao's support for his handling of the Wu Han case—the incident which launched the Cultural Revolution—then subsequently sought to convince others that his views had Mao's backing.[60] And Luo Ruiqing feared Mao's distrust of him would harm his political future.[61] When Mao relinquished specific functions and powers, sometimes cited as evidence of his decline, he did so on his own initiative[62]—the sign of a confident leader. Indeed, Mao's authority was so evident to his colleagues that Chen Yi exclaimed, "No one can [dare to resist Chairman Mao] because Chairman Mao's prestige is too great."[63]

Mao's predominance could also be seen in his ability to intervene decisively and reverse policy. While this is not surprising in the case of the speedup of agricultural cooperativization in 1955, a time when Mao's revolutionary successes were still fresh memories, it takes on special significance in the post-Great Leap period when, according to many analysts, Mao's power was severely eroded. Two examples will suffice. The first concerns Mao's 1962 halting of the retreat in economic and rural policies. After various measures jettisoning the Great Leap strategy were affirmed with Mao's approval at a January 1962 work conference, Mao departed from Beijing, leaving the remaining leaders to cope with the situation. With new, more gloomy data available, Liu and others adopted even farther-reaching measures. Describing subsequent events in his first Cultural Revolution self-criticism, Liu recounted how he then went to "the Chairman's place to seek Mao's instructions." With various comrades putting forward "opinions opposing the general line," Liu said he "already felt very tense," so he "urgently requested that the Chairman return to Beijing."[64] Liu went on to say that when Mao returned to the capital, he introduced policies which turned the situation around and consolidated the collective economy. This account, in addition to indicating Mao's ability to alter virtually single-handedly the direction of policy, is also noteworthy for the obvious implication of personal authority in Liu's seeking out Mao for instructions and his urgent appeal that Mao return to Beijing.

The second case concerns the Sino-Soviet dispute, which intensely preoccupied Mao in the early 1960s. While most Chinese leaders probably shared Mao's belief that the Soviet Union had been an unreliable ally and dangerous signs of revisionism had appeared in the Soviet state, there is considerable evidence that at the very least Liu and others questioned the wisdom of total alienation of the Russians.[65] Nevertheless, the conflict intensified in the years preceding the Cultural Revolution. By 1965 the Japanese Communist Party (JCP) was engaged in an effort to mute the dispute in order to achieve Sino-Soviet cooperation regarding the escalating war in Vietnam. In early 1966 a JCP delegation visited China as well as other countries to pursue this goal. After intensive negotiations a communique making some concessions to the Japanese was agreed to by CCP leaders, including not only Deng Xiaoping and Peng Zhen—alleged "capitalist-roaders"—but also Zhou Enlai and Kang Sheng. When the communique was brought to Mao near Guangzhou by a delegation of these leaders, he reacted in anger against "You weak-kneed people in Beijing." No communique was issued.[66]

These cases, as will be shown, do not mean that Mao operated without restraints or that he always insisted on getting his way when differences emerged. They do suggest, however, that on issues which he regarded as vital matters of principle Mao was willing and able to enforce his views despite the serious reservations of his comrades.

Mao's Leadership Style.[c] At first glance, Mao's predominance is

---

[c]The following account does not adequately call attention to the erosion of Mao's democratic leadership style from about 1958-59, and especially from the dismissal of Peng Dehuai following Peng's critical comments on the Great Leap Forward at the 1959 Lushan meeting. I have analyzed this process at length in *Politics and*

hard to reconcile with such Cultural Revolution revelations as Liu's assertions that Mao was only an individual and had made mistakes;[67] Zhou Yang's objections to excessive emphasis on the "Thought of Mao Zedong" as vulgar and oversimplified;[68] and Chen Yi's claim that very few leaders had not opposed Mao at some point or other and there was nothing unusual or improper in this.[69] While it is undeniable that many disapproved of the Mao cult and felt he should be bound by Party regulations like anyone else, it is nevertheless striking that such views had ample support in Mao's own statements:

> On June 12 [1961], the last day of the Central Committee conference in Beijing, I spoke on my shortcomings and mistakes. I asked the comrades to report what I said to all provinces and areas. Subsequently, I learned that this was not disseminated in many areas. It seems that [many comrades felt] my mistakes could and should be concealed. Comrades, they cannot be concealed.[70]

> There is one point with which I disagree—that is, Zhang Zongxun said that he has erred because he did not study Mao Zedong's works carefully. This is not right; what he should say is that primarily it is because his level of Marxism-Leninism is not high.[71]

> [T]he leadership of the Party committees is a collective leadership; matters cannot be decided arbitrarily by the First Secretary. . . . The relationship of the First Secretary and the other secretaries . . . is one of the minority obeying the majority. For example, in the Standing Committee and the Politburo situations like this often arise: when I say something, no matter whether it is correct or incorrect, provided that everyone disagrees with me, I will accede to their point of view because they are the majority.[72]

These and other comments indicate that Mao had developed a leadership style which emphasized democratic norms. As already noted, this

---

Purges in China: Rectification and the Decline of Party Norms 1950-1965 (White Plains: M. E. Sharpe, 1979). The subsequent official analysis of the 1981 "Resolution on Certain Questions in the History of Our Party Since the Founding of the People's Republic of China" came to a similar conclusion: "During this period, . . . [Mao's] personal arbitrariness gradually undermined democratic centralism in Party life . . ." (*Beijing Review*, No. 27 [1981]). It is important to emphasize, however, that in the 1958-1965 period Mao's autocratic tendencies were muted to a significant extent by his sporadic efforts to reaffirm traditional democratic practices.

did not prevent him from enforcing his views on crucial questions, but it did indicate a desire to solicit candid opinions and stimulate debate within the Party and a willingness to accept the views of others under certain circumstances. To a substantial extent, of course, Mao's colleagues expected this as a matter of right. Yet it is important to emphasize that this style was crucial in maintaining Mao's prestige. Mao could command loyalty in large part because his associates could expect, within flexible limits, that they would not be cast into political oblivion for speaking their minds. As Chen Yi observed, Mao's tolerance and magnanimity and his refusal to wreak vengeance on those who had wronged him in the past gained invaluable respect for the Chairman.[73]

In this context, the active debate in the early 1960s over the characterization and popularization of Mao's thought requires analysis. Cultural Revolution documentation strongly suggests that Lin Biao rather than Mao himself was the main protagonist on the ''Maoist'' side of the argument. It was Lin who advanced such concepts as Mao's thought being the ''peak'' of Marxism-Leninism, depicted Mao as a ''genius,'' and popularized the little red book of Mao's quotations.[74] It is less significant that Mao eventually explicitly rejected most of Lin's inventions[75] than it is to note that other Party leaders could base their opposition to the Mao cult on both Mao's long-standing leadership style and his contemporary statements.[76] To be sure, a reassertion of their own status as Party leaders was involved, but this was something which had always been freely granted by Mao.

But as Mao's dissatisfaction with the state of Chinese society grew, so apparently did his distrust of longtime comrades.[77] In these circumstances, whatever his philosophical reservations may have been,[78] Mao apparently came to view the ardor of verbal support for his person and thinking as a litmus test of political loyalty. This test was ultimately proven wrong concerning some of those who passed it in 1965-66. It undoubtedly was equally flawed for many who failed it at that time.

Mao, Liu, and the Bureaucracy. The relationship of Mao Zedong and Liu Shaoqi from the 1940s to 1965 was a complex one that can be viewed from several perspectives. Certainly there were differences between the two men, not only in terms of specific policy issues but also in overall cast of mind. While it is a treacherous undertaking to delineate their respective outlooks given the changing nature of Mao's (and Liu's) thinking, it nevertheless seems reasonable to conclude that Mao was more preoccupied with class struggle, particularly in the ideological sphere, and held a more mystical notion of the masses, and Liu was more concerned with organizational detail. In general, Mao seems to have had a more philosophical bent than Liu—to be more given to reflection on the ultimate nature of things. Yet it should be stressed that, at least until Mao's increasing obsession with class struggle in the early 1960s, these were differences of emphasis, and generally narrow differences at that. As we have seen, Mao placed great importance on discipline and organization, was well aware of the limitations of mass creativity, and took a rather sanguine attitude toward class struggle until 1959 at the earliest. It would be erroneous to say the differences of shading between the two men contained the seeds of inevitable conflict. Only changed circumstances and the resultant evolution of Mao's thought created the conditions for Mao's rejection of Liu.

There is no better evidence of the compatibility between Mao and Liu than the close working relationship established between them in the early 1940s and the arrangements made in the 1950s (especially Liu's 1959 appointment as chief of state) to establish Liu as Mao's successor. While Mao did refer to Liu as his successor,[79] it is difficult to document that the choice was solely his.[d] Nevertheless, given the existence of other ambitious men in the CCP leadership, it is unlikely that Mao would have been unable either to designate someone else or, what would have been even easier, to avoid making any arrangements for the succession. Striking evidence of Mao's regard for Liu was his verbatim inclusion of Liu's views on organizational rules, Liu's acknowledged area of expertise, in the important "Sixty Articles on Work Methods," which Mao drafted at the start of the Great Leap Forward.[80] Moreover, Mao and Liu developed complementary roles in the running of the Chinese state. As Liu put it in 1961 concerning afforestation:

> Chairman Mao concerns himself only with important state affairs. It is enough for him to propose to turn the whole country into a big garden and forest land. He has no time to solve this problem. . . . Therefore, I have to tackle it.[81]

While Mao sometimes took a hand in concrete policy implementation

---

[d]In my view, Liu was at the same time Mao's personal choice and accepted by consensus within the top elite. This did not (see below) eliminate all maneuvering for position in anticipation of a post-Mao leadership that would inevitably be far more collective, but I do not believe such maneuvering would have necessarily led to a sharp succession struggle had Mao died before 1965-66. See the second and third essays in this volume for further discussion.

and Liu had an important voice in policy formulation, this picture of Mao as setting goals while Liu attended to translating them into action corresponded to much of actual practice. While this arrangement conferred considerable power on Liu, it also contained potential danger: if Mao's goals were not achieved, responsibility could be laid at Liu's doorstep.[82]

The timing of Mao's disenchantment with Liu is open to some interpretation. By Mao's own account, it was only in January 1965 when differences over the conduct of the Socialist Education Movement emerged that he realized his trust in Liu and others had been misplaced.[83] However, other statements indicate that Mao was disturbed by Liu's performance during the 1962 retreat in economic and rural policies,[84] and throughout the 1962-65 period his statements were sprinkled with dissatisfaction with the performance of the bureaucracy generally. Thus, while there is no reason to question Mao's version in the sense that his attitude toward Liu had *hardened* only in early 1965, it seems that his views had been changing since 1962.

It is important, in any case, to emphasize that Liu was not the bureaucracy incarnate. There were other ambitious leaders on the scene as well as a multitude of bureaucratic and local interests which had little common cause with Liu's interests as a political leader. Two interrelated tendencies of paramount importance appeared during the early 1960s: the progressive withdrawal of Mao from the operational side of government, and the growth of relatively autonomous bureaucratic actors. While Mao had always delegated a great many operational matters to his associates, following the Great Leap experience he was frequently absent from Beijing, leaving to Liu and others the responsibility of conducting major Party meetings and implementing policies. As a result, Mao was increasingly cut off from information and unable to influence important decisions, and he came to resent those he felt were ignoring him. It was hardly coincidence that Deng Xiaoping cited as his most serious mistake the "fail[ure] to make timely reports to Chairman Mao" and contrasted his behavior to that of Lin Biao who made such reports and sought Mao's instructions.[85]

What was involved in the early 1960s was not simply a lack of communication between Mao and other Party leaders. Mao's withdrawal from day-to-day affairs allowed key Party leaders to develop their own power and prepare for the post-Mao succession.[86] While Mao had seemingly arranged for Liu to assume the preeminent position, no arrangements could be immutable once he passed from the scene. Thus Party leaders, rather than forming a solid "anti-Mao" block based on a common bureaucratic-rational outlook, were potential rivals maneuvering for position. As long as Mao lived, moreover, the Chairman's support remained an important political asset. This was apparent in the conflict between Lin Biao and Luo Ruiqing. While Cultural Revolution sources have sought to picture this conflict as one between two antithetical military lines, and while there clearly were important differences between the two men, the evidence suggests that personal ambition as much as any other factor was the source of tension. With Lin frequently inactive owing to poor health, Luo, as People's Liberation Army (PLA) chief of staff, was in effective charge of military affairs. Yet Lin was Luo's superior and did from time to time issue directives of which Luo disapproved. The ambitious Luo, both chaffing under the restrictions to his authority and seeing an opportunity for promotion, allegedly sought to pressure Lin into giving up his power as minister of defense in 1964. Lin, however, had Mao's confidence and was elected first vice-premier in January 1965. Luo then reportedly said, "I never thought this man would again rise to power, [but] now I am convinced that I have to stick with [him]."[87] Although Luo's resolve in this regard was seemingly short-lived and conflict again broke out with Lin, the whole episode suggests the importance of power calculations in the dealings of Mao's associates with each other.

A similar inference can be drawn concerning Liu Shaoqi and Peng Zhen, from the perspective of the Cultural Revolution both "capitalist-roaders." In his self-criticism, Liu discussed his errors concerning the conduct of the Socialist Education Movement. He mentioned that a September 1963 directive on the movement—the "Latter Ten Points"—had been based on a report by Peng Zhen to Mao (an apparent effort to enlist Mao's support). A year later Liu decided this document was harmful and drafted the "Revised Latter Ten Points."[88] Although both documents were subsequently declared "anti-Maoist," they differed profoundly from each other in their assessments of the situation and in the measures proposed for dealing with it. While this undoubtedly reflected honest differences and new information which became available in the year from September 1963 to September 1964, it is plausible that the conflicting ambitions of the two men also were involved. At the very least, the case indicates important differences within the alleged "anti-Mao" camp.

The divergent tendencies of the post-Great Leap period reflected not only the competition of ambitious men; they also were the outgrowth of a complex bureaucracy where various units pursued their own objectives. As Mao complained in 1962:

> The Central Committee has some matters to discuss with the various provinces, municipalities, and various departments, but some departments don't discuss things with the Central Committee. . . .
>
> The various departments and committees on finance and economics have not made a report. When they don't ask for instructions before or report after, we have independent kingdoms, everything trying to be done at once, forced interpretations, no relations below with the masses. . . .
>
> We all know about foreign affairs. We even know what Kennedy is going to do, but who knows what the various departments in Beijing are going to do? I just don't know the situation in several major economic departments, I don't know how to get an idea. . . .[89]

The phenomenon of "independent kingdoms"—the pursuit of particularistic bureaucratic interests at the expense of the whole—was not new. According to Mao, this tendency developed shortly after "we entered the cities" in 1949,[90] but he began to speak much more frequently on the theme in the early 1960s. The intensification of the problem was related to a number of factors in addition to the secular trend of increasing governmental complexity. One factor was that in Mao's absence no Party leader wielded the same ultimate authority, and each tended to follow his own lead in the departments under his control.[91] Another was that despite some recentralization measures following the Great Leap Forward, a substantial degree of administrative decentralization continued to exist, and various local leaders seized the opportunity to experiment with their own policies.[92] Finally, the inability of the leadership to form a new consensus and clearly define new directions for the nation left individual bureaucrats with considerable room to seek their own goals. The net result was a bureaucracy which was not only sluggish in response to Mao's initiatives but also to a significant extent beyond Liu's control.

Patterns of Conflict

Before delineating the development of policy conflict in pre-Cultural Revolution China, it will be useful to examine the adequacy of the "two line struggle" concept through two case studies.

1952-1955: Agricultural Cooperativization. The debate over agricultural cooperativization in 1952-55 has been viewed by some analysts as an early manifestation of "two line struggle" between a Mao seeking rapid advances through mass mobilization and a cautious Party bureaucracy stressing orderly growth, with Mao finally overcoming his opponents with the support of provincial leaders. While Mao's July 1955 speech calling for a speedup of cooperativization did "settle the debate of the last three years,"[93] the nature of that debate was less clear-cut than the "two line" model allows.

The issues under discussion involved such matters as the rate of industrialization, the relation of technical reform (mechanization) to institutional reform (full collectivization), and the supply and control of grain, but the key question was the desirable rate of cooperativization. From 1952 to early 1955 the rate of cooperativization had been increased and then relaxed several times. This alteration of tempo was clearly linked to the debate among different views, but it also was consistent with the guideline Mao laid down for the gradual socialist transformation of agriculture in 1952—that it was necessary to avoid both right and left excesses.[94] In early 1955 the consensus of Party leaders was that the time had again come for consolidation, and the development of new cooperatives was temporarily suspended. Furthermore, a central Party meeting chaired by Liu accepted without opposition a proposal to disband a large number of recently established cooperatives.[95] This caution at the Center was reflected in the words and actions of provincial authorities at the time.[96] Shortly thereafter Mao intervened.

Mao did not merely call for a faster rate of cooperativization; he also laid down concrete measures to be observed in achieving that objective. As Kenneth Walker has aptly observed, "Far from taking an extreme position, Mao put forward a carefully reasoned and cautious policy for the institutional reform of agriculture. . . ."[97] While declaring the main danger to be the rightist error of being "stunned by success," Mao also warned against the left deviation of "dizziness with success." The essence of his approach was the concept of advance by stages—that peasants must first be organized into mutual-aid teams, then into lower-stage cooperatives where land was owned by individuals although managed collectively, and only then into higher-stage cooperatives, the fully socialist collectives. In terms of the rate of development, Mao's proposals were not radical. By the fall of 1954 the agreed Party policy had been a sixfold increase from 100,000 to 600,000 lower-stage cooperatives, a goal which was overfulfilled in early 1955. In July 1955 Mao proposed a doubling of the then existing 650,000 cooperatives to be achieved over a substantially longer time period, i.e., by October 1956.[98] Thus, although he called for a significant increase while many of his colleagues were advocating slower growth, Mao's proposals were well within the bounds of precedent.

Finally, in the course of implementing Mao's call, the Party bureaucracy both exceeded his targets and altered his policies in a leftward direction. From the time of Mao's speech until the end of 1955, China went through a cycle of the Center establishing goals, the provinces outstripping those goals, the Center revising its targets upward, and the provinces once again overfulfilling central targets. By the end of the year Mao's original target had been effectively advanced from 50 percent of agricultural households in cooperatives by spring 1958 to 70-80 percent by the end of 1956. The achievement of these goals meant discarding Mao's policy of advance by stages. More than a quarter of all peasant families joined cooperatives without prior organization into mutual-aid teams, and a widespread tendency to skip the lower-stage cooperatives altogether appeared. Mao apparently was not displeased with the result despite the violation of his directive. But to the extent that the speedup of collectivization was a success of mass mobilization policies, it was a success which the Party apparatus had as much claim to as Mao.[99]

The case of agricultural cooperativization reveals several things. First, the concept of a "two line struggle" between radical mass mobilization and a conservative bureaucracy is less adequate than the CCP's own early 1950s view of Mao and the Party attempting to steer a course between the Scylla of right conservatism and the Charybdis of left adventurism. Policy became a question of plotting the proper position on a continuum between the two extremes. Debate was over rates of development—a matter of degree—rather than fundamental approaches. Moreover, while Mao was indeed to the left of some of his leading associates in mid-1955, the bureaucracy quickly responded without any sign of major trauma by implementing a course even further to the left. And while it might be tempting to view this response as largely the work of provincial leaders as distinct from more conservative central bureaucrats, in fact provincial leaders had implemented the consolidation policies when they were in force. Clearly, individual leaders at all levels could shift positions out of conviction or calcula-

tion.[100] Whatever differences existed on agricultural cooperativization, they did not reflect antithetical views.

1958-1966: Agricultural Mechanization.[e] During the Cultural Revolution, a series of articles in the official press described a "two line
struggle" over agricultural machinery policy.[101] While the struggle
allegedly went back to the initial period after Liberation, its most
important phase took place from the early days of the Great Leap to the
start of the Cultural Revolution.

At the Chengdu Conference in March 1958, Mao put forward proposals calling for major efforts in agricultural mechanization, "the
basic way out for agriculture." The strategy Mao advocated emphasized the development of small and simple machines by agricultural
cooperatives (subsequently by rural communes) which would both finance and manage them. Liu and other Party leaders allegedly attempted to sabotage this program by a variety of devices. They blocked
dissemination of Mao's Chengdu proposals for seven years. Bo Yibo,
one of China's leading economic planners, claimed that Mao's emphasis on mechanization was incomplete as a guideline for the technical
transformation of agriculture. Most important, however, was the alle-
gation of reckless implementation of Mao's principles—a "'left' in
form but right in essence" ploy aimed at discrediting Mao's ideas. Tan
Zhenlin, the Party official responsible for agriculture, pushed the popularization of simple machines without regard for local conditions,
causing considerable financial losses and undermining mass enthusiasm. Liu and others, motivated by a desire to cut state costs, hastily
devolved control over tractors to the communes before preparations
were made to receive them. They then washed their hands of the matter,
provided few resources, abolished various higher-level departments in
charge of such work, and neither called conferences nor issued
directives. As a result, heavy damage to the commune-operated machinery occurred.

Next, Mao's opponents allegedly seized on the chaotic situation in
1961-62 to reverse Mao's policies and restore centralized control of

---

[e]Several years after the following was written, a major study of agricultural mechanization policy appeared: Benedict Stavis, *The Politics of Agricultural Mechanization in China* (Ithaca: Cornell University Press, 1978). Stavis' careful documentation supports the arguments advanced here, although at various points he adopts a
modified "two line struggle" approach (see pp. 183, 210). The central point is that
Stavis presents no evidence of concrete policy conflict between Mao and other Party
leaders over mechanization at any time before early 1966.

agricultural machinery. Tan Zhenlin drafted a plan which returned tractors to state-run stations. Other locally run projects, such as tool research institutes, were closed down as part of a general retrenchment. In 1964 Bo Yibo drafted a Third Five-Year Plan which didn't discuss mechanization and reduced investment in the agricultural machinery industry to 39 percent of the 1960 level. Mao sharply criticized and rejected this draft plan. Meanwhile, Liu and others pushed policies emphasizing large complex machines (including foreign imports), reliance on trained engineers rather than peasants to develop innovations, and modern research organs at the national and provincial levels. Liu's major schemes, however, were the agricultural machinery trust and the "hundred key counties" project. Through the trust, Liu sought both to increase central control by banning local Party committees from interfering in management and to supplant administrative methods with economic methods that emphasized profitability as an index of success. The "hundred key counties" plan sought to concentrate state investment in mechanization in 100 to 200 selected counties over a ten-year period and then to reinvest the recovered funds in other areas. This plan was another step in the direction of increased centralization and away from self-reliance on the part of local units.

Throughout this period Mao reportedly took a keen interest in agricultural machinery and "set forth a series of major policies for speeding up technical reform." But apart from Mao's rejection of Bo Yibo's draft Third Five-Year Plan, Cultural Revolution sources do not indicate what *specific* actions Mao took. In general, it seems his main concern was that adequate attention and resources be devoted to mechanization. Mao did endorse a specific position in February 1966, when he rejected the "hundred key counties" scheme and ordered publication of the achievements of a model brigade developed by the Hubei provincial authorities. The Hubei plan emphasized developing mechanization on a wide scale through the mobilization of local funds and resources. With this step, Mao clearly declared himself for self-reliance and against policies of centralization.

Several things stand out from the above account. First, individuals shifted their positions considerably over time. Thus the same individuals who were guilty of leftist excesses in 1958-1960 were charged with contrary deviations from 1961 on. Moreover, the various positions adopted by Mao's "opponents" both differed from one another and contained elements consistent with Mao's expressed concerns. For example, Bo Yibo's 1959 statement that Mao's proposals were "not complete'' was based on the view that electrification and chemical fertilizer programs as well as mechanization were required to solve fundamentally China's agricultural problems. Bo's position was to argue for greater state investment in agriculture against those wishing to monopolize resources for industry, a stance consistent with Mao's emphasis on agricultural development. Moreover, when Bo later called for cuts in investment in agricultural machinery, he apparently parted company with Liu Shaoqi, who viewed mechanization as a ''great undertaking'' and an ''imperative task,'' an attitude in tune with Mao's. Differences within the Party bureaucracy were also manifest in the Hubei plan which, by fostering decentralization, was compatible with the interests of provincial leaders.

The most important lesson to be drawn from the agricultural mechanization case concerns the method of argumentation—a method widely adopted in scholarly analysis of the post-Great Leap Forward period. Essentially, Mao's views during the Great Leap are taken as his thinking over the entire subsequent period in the absence of evidence concerning his concrete policy position. Thus the ''two line struggle'' becomes a struggle between the actual policies of various Party leaders in 1961-65, on the one hand, and Mao's 1958 position, on the other. While other leaders changed their views after 1958, no such flexibility is allowed Mao. The reemergence of some aspects of his 1958 proposals in 1966 suggests that Mao was strongly predisposed toward those concepts, but it does not prove that he was advocating policies based on such concepts in the intervening years. If he had, it is difficult to understand why Cultural Revolution materials, with the single exception of Bo Yibo's Third Five-Year Plan, did not cite clashes over specific policy proposals before February 1966. In sum, the ''Maoist line'' on agricultural mechanization in the early 1960s was more a specter from the past than a reality of the present.

The preceding case studies not only indicate the shortcomings of the ''two line struggle'' concept; they also reflect the changing pattern of policy conflict in the 1949-1965 period. A more comprehensive examination of this changing pattern is now in order.

1949-1957: Consensus on the Soviet Model. When the Chinese Communists came to power, only one example of how to build a socialist society existed—the Soviet Union. Although the Chinese altered the Soviet model in significant ways, Soviet precedent on institutional development and economic strategy was basically followed. As Mao later explained, ''Since we had no experience in economic construction we could only copy the Soviet Union, and our own creativity was small.''[102] This, of course, did not eliminate policy differences, but it tended to limit debate to the proper implementation of programs for which a broad consensus existed. The key questions became how fast should a policy be realized and what were the specific lessons of the Soviet experience for China. But why didn't differences on such questions strain leadership cohesion? To a significant degree the answer was the undisputed leadership of Mao. As long as power relations were well defined, little could be gained by exaggerating policy differences.

The question of agricultural cooperativization was one of the earliest major issues over which significant conflicting views developed.[103] As discussed earlier, a three-year debate on the subject centered on charting the proper course between right and left deviations. When the relatively leftist course adopted in 1955 resulted in rapid advances, Mao's initial response was to push for additional breakthroughs on the production front.[104] Yet by mid-1956, retrenchment was the order of the day. This decision undoubtedly followed serious debate over how to cope with imbalances appearing during the stepped-up production effort. It was clearly a decision which did not totally please Mao. As he put it in 1958:

> In 1956, something got blown away—the general line of ''more, faster, better, and more economical,'' the promoters of progress, the Forty Articles [on agricultural development]. There were three kinds of people, and three different reactions: one was regret, another was indifference, and the third was rejoicing that something had got blown away, the feeling that a rock had dropped to the ground, and from now on the empire would be at peace. Of the groups of people having these attitudes, the two extremes were small while that in the middle was large. Regarding very many issues in 1956, there were these three attitudes. . . .[105]

Mao plainly was one who regretted the turn of events in 1956, but this does not mean that retrenchment measures were taken against his will. As Roderick MacFarquhar has suggested, Mao may have been less confident about overruling his economic planners in 1956 than he was later, and he deferred to their judgment in an area where, by his own admission, he lacked competence.[106] In any case, Mao's major pronouncement of 1956, his April talk ''On the Ten Great Relationships,'' stressed balance and moderation and thus was in accord with the spirit of a more cautious economic approach.

The final source of major differences in this period was the Hundred Flowers movement, an experiment which met with opposition from both the Russians and leading CCP cadres.[107] Mao's attempt to enlist intellectual participation in Party rectification was both a challenge to important institutional interests and a departure from Soviet experience. The Hundred Flowers experiment can be viewed as one of the earliest efforts to evolve a unique Chinese path in response to inadequacies of the Soviet model. Although the Hundred Flowers policy was curbed in time and did not cause a serious leadership schism, the uncertainty generated demonstrated the dangers of ignoring Soviet practice.

1958-1960: Divisions over the Chinese Model. The Great Leap Forward was a far more profound effort to create a uniquely Chinese path of development, one without historical precedents.[f] Sharp differences were inevitable in a situation where, according to Mao, "we were unable to regularize [our] guiding principles, policies and methods . . . because our experience was not enough."[108] Differences first appeared in the formation stage and involved not only debate over details of the strategy but also basic opposition to so radical an approach. At the highest level, the Standing Committee of the Politburo, opposition came in late 1957 from Chen Yun, the Party's foremost economic specialist, who argued for a policy of material incentives to achieve a more balanced but slower rate of economic growth. Chen subsequently lost his major operational positions.[109] At the provincial level many leaders apparently felt the cautious measures of 1956 were more suitable to the existing situation than the proposed new policies, and significant provincial purges were conducted.[110]

But while there was significant opposition from the outset, Mao had powerful support within the Party apparatus. Liu Shaoqi was a particularly vigorous proponent of the leap forward policies and announced their official adoption at the May 1958 Party Congress.[111] At the provincial level, despite some doubters, many leaders enthusiastically supported and even helped shape the new strategy, perhaps calculating that its decentralization measures would enhance their own power.[112] Indeed, the Party apparatus as a whole vigorously implemented the Great Leap, with the result that "ultra-leftist" excesses appeared in great abundance.

---

[f]The Great Leap evolved as a number of pressures for change in developmental strategy converged by late 1957. The most important were: a growing realization that aspects of the Soviet model were unsuited to Chinese conditions, the questionable reliability of intellectuals as revealed by their harsh criticisms during the Hundred Flowers movement, and especially the sluggish performance of the economy— above all in the agricultural sector.

As 1958 wore on and shortcomings of the new policies became apparent, the stage was set for further divisions. In a series of meetings from November 1958 to April 1959, a wide range of policy adjustments were made to cope with emerging problems. Mao chaired these meetings and played an active role in formulating measures to ameliorate the situation. At first there was no sense of defeat in the concessions made; rather, Mao and his associates seemed to view this as an inevitable process required to consolidate a great success. By the spring of 1959, however, awareness of the number and scope of the problems created a less confident, more divided leadership. Some felt more far-reaching measures were necessary than those officially adopted. Others were critical of Mao for making too many concessions—thus giving some credence to Mao's misleading portrayal of himself as a "middle-of-the-roader."[113] The greatest dissent came from those who felt not enough concessions had been made and implicitly questioned the wisdom of the entire Great Leap program. This surfaced within the Politburo at the July Lushan Conference, with Peng Dehuai publicly voicing the dissenting view. Mao, with the support of Liu, retaliated by stripping Peng of his position as minister of defense. Significantly, however, the Lushan meeting adopted a number of measures which met the substance of much of Peng's criticism.[114] By this time, Mao, Liu, and other leaders were sanctioning additional concessions in a desperate effort to salvage the principles of the Great Leap.

1961-1965: Groping for New Directions. By the Ninth Central Committee Plenum in January 1961, the Great Leap policies had been effectively abandoned despite official insistence on their basic correctness. In 1961 and 1962 a series of measures were devised which fundamentally reversed national policy. At the January 1962 expanded Central Committee meeting, Mao explicitly endorsed many of these far-reaching measures, approved Liu Shaoqi's report, which admitted major errors, and himself acknowledged that "we bungled a lot in the last few years."[115] These undoubtedly were unpleasant steps for Mao to take, but he apparently saw no alternative given the deteriorating economic situation. Perhaps most significant was Mao's uncertainty over what was either possible or desirable:

[In 1960, Edgar] Snow wanted me to discuss long-term planning for the construction of China. I said, "I don't know how." He commented, "You are being too cautious with what you say." I replied: "It is not a matter of being cautious or not. I really do not know and do not have the experience." Comrades, it is true that we do not know. We truly are short of experience and a long-range plan. . . .

> In socialist construction we continue to grope our way without clear vision. . . . Taking myself as an example, there are many problems in the work of building up the economy which I do not understand. Industry and commerce, for instance, are things that I do not quite understand. I know a little about agriculture, but only to a certain degree by comparison and very little at that. . . .[116]

As we have seen, by the summer of 1962 Mao had called a halt to the further retreat which had been made since January. Yet the policies sanctioned at that time retained many of the concessions which had previously been made, particularly in the form of material incentives for workers and peasants.[117] Thus, while Mao had arrested the drift of policy, there is no evidence to suggest he advanced proposals to alter the moderate cast of CCP programs in 1962. While raising the slogan "never forget class struggle," Mao was unable to indicate concrete ways of applying it to many Party policies.

In the next few years, Mao was better able to define what was bothering him about Chinese society than he was to offer solutions to those problems. When addressing problems, Mao's statements tended to be either sweeping and impractical[118] or vague and tentative. Frequently in raising a problem, Mao did not prescribe comprehensive remedies but merely asked that the matter be studied and some action taken. Mao's approach was demonstrated at the September 1965 Central Committee work conference when he voiced great concern about political purity at the highest levels and asked his colleagues, "If revisionism appears in the Center what are you going to do?"[119] At most, Mao's performance in these years was one of identifying problems and prodding other Party leaders to do something about them. He indicated directions, but gave little detailed guidance on how to achieve his goals.

Mao's vagueness created problems as well as opportunities for other Party leaders. These men had considerable scope to develop a variety of policies in their own "independent kingdoms." But Mao's ambiguity was a problem in that he still was a crucial part of the political equation. Leaders who wanted to please Mao for their own reasons were frequently at a loss as to how to go about it. Thus Luo Ruiqing complained that "[Mao's] supreme directives are not easy to understand," while Hu Qiaomu observed that "the Chairman says something today and some other things tomorrow; it is very difficult to fathom him."[120]

In fact, many of the concerns Mao articulated did evoke a significant response from his associates and the bureaucracy. A new emphasis on rural health appeared.[121] Under Liu Shaoqi's guidance, more effort was placed on integrating labor with education, and educational opportunities for workers and peasants increased.[122] And in the literary field where Mao's barbs had been sharpest, a marked politicization unfolded in 1964-65.[123]

Yet for Mao, obsessed as he was with the dangers of revolutionary degeneration, such responses were halfhearted and inadequate. Indeed, he seemed to feel impotent in the face of a bureaucracy which, in his eyes, ignored him or resisted his initiatives. This is apparent in his 1964 comments to a Nepalese educational delegation:

> The school years are too long, the courses too many, and the method of teaching is by injection instead of imagination. The method of examination is to treat candidates as enemies and ambush them. Therefore I advise you not to entertain any blind faith in the Chinese education system. Do not regard it as a good system. Any drastic change is difficult [since] many people would oppose it. At present a few people may agree to the adoption of new methods, but many would disagree. . . .[124]

Clearly there was disagreement. Some undoubtedly felt that Mao's concerns were important but that his suggestions, when explicit, were impractical. Others probably felt that Mao was living in the past, and while it was politically necessary to retain his goodwill, China's future lay in directions quite different from what Mao envisioned. Resistance took the form of not only open disagreement but also the much derided tactic of "waving the red flag to oppose the red flag," i.e., advancing Mao's slogans while pursuing conflicting objectives. Yet in a situation where Mao was often unable to formulate a series of concrete policy proposals, even the most convinced "Maoist" had difficulty satisfying the Chairman.

Despite the existence of many divergent opinions, there is no evidence of a confrontation of two explicitly opposed lines. The performance of the bureaucracy and its leaders is best seen as checkered. On many matters where Mao had expressed concern, important action was taken; on others, the response appears largely verbal. Two sides where political figures could neatly line up did not exist; instead there was a variety of viewpoints, with Mao's concerns only one, albeit highly significant, element. It was only during the Cultural Revolution that many "capitalist-roaders" became aware that they had propagated an "'anti-Mao'' line.

Conclusion

The "two line struggle" view of pre-Cultural Revolution Chinese politics offers an exciting version of events, but it does not provide a discriminating tool for analyzing the realities of political struggle. Not only does it grossly oversimplify the complexity of bureaucratic interests and policy positions; it at once seriously underestimates Mao and overestimates the cohesion of other political leaders. Mao's associates had their own individual ambitions and ideas which made them potential rivals and led them to diverse positions. As for Mao, he was unique. The creator of a spectacularly successful revolutionary strategy, Mao stood above his colleagues, although he had sensibly fostered a democratic leadership style. His stature was such that as long as he lived, no matter how removed from daily operations or how ambiguous his positions, Mao remained a factor to which all others had to adjust. Only such a figure could attempt a Cultural Revolution.

II
THE LEGITIMACY
OF THE LEADER

For nearly four decades Mao Zedong was the *legitimate* leader of the CCP. As often stated but rarely analyzed, Mao's legitimacy had charismatic roots. To illuminate adequately the nature and sources of Mao's authority, Max Weber's other ideal types of legal-rational and traditional authority must also be considered. In fact, Mao drew on all three types of authority to sustain his rule. The pattern, however, changed markedly over time, with the alternative sources reinforcing the Chairman's charisma in some periods and conflicting with it to varying degrees in others. These same sources of legitimacy, moreover, have been apparent in the post-Mao CCP, albeit in a fundamentally altered mix. Thus Deng Xiaoping has emerged as the new legitimate leader of the Party without making charismatic claims. And although Deng has placed heavy emphasis on legal-rational principles, his leadership actually rests much more on considerations falling under Weber's traditional category.

Legitimacy is a crucial if elusive aspect of both political analysis and political life. Obedience, as Weber pointed out long ago, may have many sources, ranging "all the way from simple habituation to the most purely rational calculation of advantage," but a reliable system of obedience normally requires the additional element of belief in legitimacy.[1] That is to say, orders are accepted at least in part out of the conviction that they are in some sense just and proper and, in Weber's words, that disobedience "would be abhorrent to the sense of duty."[2] The focus is on the legitimate authority of the source of orders rather than the orders themselves; as Peter Blau observed, "Authority is distinguished from persuasion by the fact that people *a priori* suspend their own judgment and accept that of an acknowledged superior without having to be convinced that his is correct."[3] Thus while authority plays a key role in most political systems, in an important sense it must be distinguished from characteristic features of the political process—

pressure, negotiation, alliance building, compromise. Where an authority relationship prevails, as Blau suggests, a subordinate accepts the commands of a superior and acts accordingly. In a political relationship, the concerned parties bargain and come to an agreement reflecting their relative strengths, or one combination of actors forms a coalition to defeat competing forces. In the former case, the assertion of unchallenged powers is involved; in the latter the quest for support is central.[4]

The distinctive nature of exercising authority on the one hand and building political support on the other does not mean that the two processes are unrelated. Individual politicians seek support in order to obtain positions of leadership, and providing the process of accumulating support conforms to an accepted principle of legitimation, the successful contestant becomes a legitimate leader entitled to the office gained. (As will be seen below, the problem of withdrawing support and hence legitimacy from such a leader is a particularly difficult one in communist states.) This raises another distinction—that between legitimacy of position and legitimate authority. Legitimacy of position does not automatically translate into untrammeled authority; especially in legal-rational and traditional contexts, leaders are able to issue authoritative orders only on a circumscribed range of issues. Legitimacy of position, then, is a prerequisite to authority but does not guarantee it. Such position may or may not involve vast powers, yet particularly in communist systems even the most circumscribed cases contain the possibility of a gradual accretion of real authority.

Several further distinctions are central to this essay. First, the focus is on the legitimacy of the leader rather than that of the system as a whole. The two are obviously linked but still analytically separate. As the case of Khrushchev in the Soviet Union indicates, once a certain stage of institutionalization is reached, even dramatic changes of leadership have little impact on system legitimacy. Nevertheless, in other instances—particularly during the lifetime of revolutionary founding fathers like Mao—the legitimacy of the system and the legitimacy of the leader become virtually indistinguishable in both official claims and actual perceptions. Second, and more unique to this analysis, is the distinction among the top CCP elite, i.e., the roughly 800 rulers of China,[5] the mass of Party members and bureaucratic officials, and the general public. Each of these different ''constituencies''[6] has a somewhat different authority relationship to the leader. For example, as argued below, the deliberately fostered cult of Mao's personality was a much more potent source of legitimacy among the people and ordinary bureaucrats than with his leadership colleagues. Indeed, Chalmers Johnson has characterized Mao's rule by using Weber's concept of "Caesarism"—the suppression of leadership rivals by charismatic appeals to the masses.[7]

Here, however, the focus is on the legitimacy of the leader in the eyes of the top elite, what Weber calls the chief-staff relationship.[8] This is in the belief that the acceptance of the leader's legitimacy by his high-ranking colleagues is *the* crucial factor for survival in Leninist systems. While this has clearly been the case in post-Mao China, and post-Stalin Russia for that matter, it is a more problematic argument for periods of a dominant leader. But, contrary to Johnson, it is the contention of this analysis that in all periods of the PRC the leadership group conceded Mao's legitimacy (although not necessarily full authority at the end of his career) largely independent of his presumed hold on the masses. In fact, repeated failures over Mao's last two decades seriously damaged the legitimacy of both the system and the leader among major sections of the population (see below, pp. 62-63), while these same developments had a more limited impact on Mao's authority within the elite itself. While it remains a moot point whether Mao could have prevailed at various junctures by direct appeals to the populace in the absence of a grant of legitimacy by the elite, the willingness of the top elite to accept his leadership avoided such a test. In the post-Mao period there has been no question of direct appeals to the masses for purposes of gaining leadership.[9] For Deng Xiaoping and any future leaders, legitimacy has and will come from the elite.

The basis for this inquiry must remain speculative. Not only is legitimacy a preeminently heuristic device not subject to any precise measurement, but relevant empirical methods such as systematic interviewing of ranking figures are not available in the Chinese case. We can only crudely guess the degree to which personal ambition, fear, or sense of duty explains compliance to a leader's demands, while the "seldom simple composition"[10] of any political figure's belief in a leader's legitimacy is hardly subject to more than informed intuition.[11] Nevertheless, the extensive body of information on CCP leadership politics which does exist provides an adequate basis for investigation. Using this data, together with relevant literature on traditional Chinese and Soviet practice, the elucidation of authority patterns becomes possible.

The Bases of Legitimacy

The tripartite typology of legitimate authority was not meant to mirror the real world. Weber not only recognized that pure types were very exceptional in human history; he further emphasized the instability of the various forms (particularly the charismatic and legal-rational) and their tendency to be transformed into one another.[12] This flux notwithstanding, the basic categories of charismatic, traditional, and legal-rational can be clearly distinguished in CCP authority patterns. The crucial charismatic type can be further refined by taking into account personality cults designed to create fabricated or synthetic charisma for the leader.[13] In addition, political leaders often claim legitimacy on the basis of successful performance in official roles. Finally, it is indisputable that nationalism is a strong legitimizing force,[14] and room must be made for it in any overall analysis. The full schema can be outlined as follows:

I. charismatic
   a. revolutionary
   b. synthetic (personality cult)
   c. performance based*
   d. nationalist*
II. legal-rational
III. traditional

*Tenuous links to charismatic authority.

Figure 1. Types of Legitimate Authority

Charismatic Authority. According to Weber, charisma refers to the perception of "a certain quality of an individual personality by virtue of which he is set apart from ordinary men and treated as endowed with supernatural, superhuman, or at least specifically exceptional powers or qualities."[15] Charisma in its pure form only arises in periods of crisis when the unusual powers of the person in question are seen as providing the answers to the calamitous situation. Recognition of these powers carries with it a duty to obey, and the followers of a charismatic leader have *no* established rights *vis-à-vis* the leader in a relationship of complete personal devotion. Such a situation is inherently unstable, however, and as the crisis passes, the "routinization of charisma" sets in and the system of authority relations drifts in a traditional or legal-rational direction. The original features of the leader-led relationship (the absence of hierarchy, rejection of rules, repudiation of the past, unconcern with economic considerations) quickly give way to more regularized structures, and charisma itself becomes somewhat depersonalized in such forms as "hereditary charisma" or the "charisma of office."[16]

While communist movements have involved an unusual amount of personal authority, in no case has unfettered pure charisma existed. The case of Lenin is instructive. Although Lenin did not claim to be an infallible leader and his Bolshevik organization stressed precisely the insistence on strict rules and hierarchy which are anathema to true charisma, in practice he was convinced of his special theoretical understanding and often breached the rules in pursuit of correct policies.[17] Moreover, there was a real sense in which many of Lenin's associates regarded him as a charismatic figure and acted accordingly. The Marxist historian M. N. Pokrovsky, for example, reflected as follows on his experiences with the Bolshevik leader:

> There was above all, his enormous capacity to see to the root of things, a capacity which finally awakened in me a sort of superstitious feeling. I frequently had occasion to differ from him on practical questions but I came off badly every time. When this experience had been repeated about seven times, I ceased to dispute and submitted to Lenin even if logic told me that one should act otherwise. I was henceforth convinced that he understood things better and was master of the power denied to me, of seeing about ten feet down into the earth.[18]

This, however, was far from a universal response, especially in the pre-1917 period. Many in Lenin's own Bolshevik faction disputed with him bitterly on various major issues, sometimes outvoting him and on other occasions resigning from the Central Committee in disgust. Not only were Lenin's specific views opposed within the movement, but there was strong resistance to Lenin's tendency to try to impose his will. Where Lenin did prevail it was often owing to prolonged argument and pressure rather than acceptance of his authority *per se*.[19] Nevertheless, after the revolutionary success of 1917, Lenin repeatedly prevailed on key issues, usually after much debate, but in large measure because a majority of Bolsheviks, like Pokrovsky, capitulated to Lenin's judgment since he had been right so often during the Party's revolutionary crisis.[20] This was hardly an unquestioning grant of charismatic authority, as some Bolsheviks still opposed Lenin and others who fell into line had substantial sympathy for the minority, but it was a charisma based on repeated demonstrated success nevertheless.

Even this degree of charisma was difficult for Mao Zedong to obtain initially. Unlike Lenin, who was the creator of his organization, Mao was merely one of many energetic revolutionaries in the early years of the CCP. His skills as a theorist, always important for claims to preeminence among Marxists, were crude and stood him at a disadvantage among his fellow communists. The vicissitudes of his career in the early 1930s are well known, and it was more the failure of his opponents than any other fact which allowed him to escape semidisgrace during the Long March and begin his rise to the position of leader by the late 1930s and early 1940s.[21] But that rise was accomplished as Mao's colleagues within the CCP leadership began to recognize his "exceptional qualities."

What were these qualities? While in the strict sense it is the *perception* of imagined powers by followers rather than their reality or nonreality which defines charisma,[22] at least for close associates of the leader there must be some actual qualities that are demonstrated. Mao certainly had a political presence which encouraged deference among his associates. One aspect of this was his aloofness, whether genuine or staged for effect. One need not go as far as Lucian Pye's remark that after the Long March "witnesses began to sense in Mao . . . mystical powers and magic in his remoteness"[23] to appreciate that Mao's aloof posture as a great strategic thinker would impress other high-ranking CCP leaders. Linked to this was a common trait of great leaders—a vast reservoir of will. Henry Kissinger observed of the aged and infirm Mao, "I have met no one, with the possible exception of Charles de Gaulle, who so distilled raw, concentrated willpower."[24] But while aloofness, willpower, and related qualities such as coolness under fire undoubtedly inspired respect and not a little fear among close associates, these traits by themselves were not enough to secure charismatic leadership. As with Lenin, this required *demonstrated success at a time of revolutionary crisis*, and it is no accident that Mao consolidated his leadership as his policies of guerrilla warfare and "independence within the united front" gained ascendancy within the CCP in the late 1930s and produced a vast growth of communist power. However much Mao may have been helped by factors beyond his control (the American entry into the war, the incompetence of the Guomindang), within a dozen years strategies bearing his personal stamp led to an almost unimaginable victory which conferred on him a genuine revolutionary charisma.

Despite this grant of charismatic authority, the degree to which Mao's associates perceived "exceptional powers" should not be over-stated. It was certainly well known in the inner circle that Mao was no dialectical whiz, and his limitations as an administrator were plain to see.[25] While Deng Xiaoping's 1978 evaluation of Mao as only "70 percent correct"[26] perhaps reflected Deng's own recent bitter exper-iences, it is difficult not to believe that at all times Mao's closest collaborators had a clear sense of the limits of his "exceptional qualities." But this did not invalidate the charismatic claim, which was not concerned with Mao's performance of mundane tasks but instead focused on larger revolutionary issues.

Several significant ramifications follow. First, despite Weber's be-lief that pure charisma requires repeated demonstration and disinte-grates when the leader no longer provides successful answers,[27] in fact, the magnitude of a revolutionary victory such as that of 1949 is so great as to sustain the leader's charisma even in the face of major subsequent failures during the socialist era. This reflects not only the central importance of the fundamental revolutionary breakthrough in the Marxist myth, it also underlines a crucial aspect of charismatic author-ity. As a relationship between the leader and his followers, this author-ity has a representative aspect. In the case at hand, Mao embodied the goals and achievements which the top CCP elite had pursued for dec-ades. From this perspective, to have denied Mao's authority would have been tantamount to denying the meaning of a nearly lifelong commitment.[28]

Finally, the combination of demonstrated revolutionary success with continuing "revolutionary" tasks—i.e., the achievement of social-ism—creates a situation where the leader has special authority to define such tasks. Thus while as noted in the preceding essay[29] Mao often ceded to others responsibility for such specialized matters as economic planning, he retained for himself authority over the general direction of the revolution and, by the mid-1960s, even concluded that many of his leadership colleagues had forfeited *their* legitimacy by failing the revo-lutionary cause. What is especially relevant is that the top elite for a long time conceded Mao's right to make such determinations owing to his earlier success. And even during the last decade of Mao's life when the dominant group within the elite came to reject his vision, the charismatic legacy of 1949 was generally sufficient to prevent action against the Chairman.

The Personality Cult. If real "exceptional qualities" were at the root of the charismatic authority exercised by such leaders as Lenin and Mao, such authority has often been further bolstered by deliberate cults of the personality. In these cases the propaganda media attempt to create a sense of reverence and discipleship toward a remote figure who is pictured as having "exceptional powers." While there may be some basis in fact for the abilities ascribed to the leaders, cults typically create substantially fictitious qualities and often take on a quasi-religious air. If Lenin abjured a personality cult during his lifetime, his successors vied with one another to create a cult for their dead leader. Mao was less bashful, and a significant effort to contrive charisma for "the savior of the Chinese people"[30] emerged in the 1940s and later took on a particularly virulent form during the Cultural Revolution. And although lacking in fundamental ways the characteristics noted above, modest cults praising Hua Guofeng and latter-day Soviet leaders have appeared in recent times.[31] But the classic case of the personality cult was Stalin.

The Stalin cult is less interesting for its features of crude historical distortion, praise of nonexistent qualities, and general mysticism—all of which also existed in the Mao cult[32]—than for the significance it played in building up the Russian dictator's legitimacy. As with Mao, the Stalin cult began following his victory over inner-Party opponents. Although politically victorious, Stalin could hardly claim recognition within ruling Party circles for the same sort of "exceptional qualities" as Lenin. The contrived cult worked to bolster Stalin within the top elite in two ways. First, its major impact was on the general public and the broad Party membership, where a very substantial degree of charismatic authority was attained. This, in turn, became an important political factor inhibiting opposition to Stalin. How, after all, would one justify deposing "the initiator and organizer of all our victories"[33] even if one believed such claims to be shams? But perhaps equally important is the degree to which these claims were accepted within the top leadership itself. This was made possible by Stalin's brutal purge during the 1930s. The dictator's revolutionary peers, who knew from firsthand experience the falsity of the cult's claims, were largely eliminated; they were to a significant degree replaced by younger leaders who had been exposed to Stalin's cult before working closely with him. While it would be myopic to overlook the elements of sheer fear and Stalin's genuine contributions to "constructing socialism" and the war effort, it is arguable that the magical aura created around Stalin did contribute to a substantial number of believers within the top Soviet elite. The potency of even synthetic charisma is suggested by

Khrushchev's account of the reaction to Stalin's death:

> For years the propaganda agencies had been trumpeting . . . that Stalin was a genius, the friend and father of the people, the safeguard of the very air we breathed. . . . Then suddenly, there was no more Stalin. . . . [I]t was a great shock. Not only for the people, but for us, the others in the leadership, who had worked so many years at Stalin's side. Personally, I took his death hard. I wept for him. I sincerely wept.[34]

Mao was keenly aware of the political significance of manufactured cults. In a famous statement on the eve of the Cultural Revolution he remarked to Edgar Snow that perhaps the reason Khrushchev was unseated was "because he had had no cult of personality at all."[35] Yet within the upper echelons of the CCP the personality cult was a less useful basis for legitimacy than it had been for Stalin. While the political weight of the enormous reputation created for Mao within Chinese society had the same practical effect of inhibiting opposition as in Stalin's Russia, the cult was unlikely to add much to the genuine charisma Mao exerted among his colleagues. Indeed, as already indicated in the first essay and discussed further below,[36] the cult itself was an issue in Chinese politics, as many who did not challenge Mao's personal authority argued against the cult's exaggeration. Unlike the Soviet case, the key decision-makers within the CCP had dealt with Mao more or less as equals during the early history of the CCP and remained powerful leaders in their own right. While Mao had earned their loyalty by his genuine qualities and achievements, such long-time associates were unlikely to give credence to assertions of supernatural genius.[37]

Performance Criteria. As T. H. Rigby has observed, a characteristic feature of Marxist-Leninist systems is their orientation to goal or task achievement. The inner life of such systems is dominated by concrete tasks and specific targets. Moreover, the very legitimacy of Marxist-Leninist nations can be seen in these terms. Elaborating on Weber's notion of "substantive rationality," Rigby speaks of communist states as "goal-rational systems" where legitimacy is claimed, and to some degree granted, in terms of the ability to achieve declared goals. The supreme goal is "communism," a sufficiently vague concept to allow successive leaderships great leeway in giving it content. Nevertheless, certain socio-political forms (e.g., collectivized agriculture, state ownership of industry) and a general progress toward higher economic and cultural levels are clearly encompassed by the general goal which is constantly struggled for.[38] Since many of the specifics giving content to the broader vision are measurable, legitimacy therefore depends on visible progress toward declared goals, i.e., on the successful performance of specified tasks.

Task performance in state socialist systems can be linked to charisma in the sense that "exceptional qualities" assertedly are required to define the goals and provide concrete leadership for their achievement. Personality cults, for example, claim a direct relationship between the accomplishments of the Party and the inspiration of the leader.[39] But while a theoretical connection between performance and charisma is arguable, in actual fact the link is highly tenuous. As already argued, charisma is most likely to derive from the revolutionary struggle, and not from building up a socialist society after the seizure of power.[40] The tasks involved in the latter are usually less heroic, more dependent on specialized skills, and performed in an incremental manner rather than as grand strategy, particularly once the institutions of the new system are in place. The performance of such tasks is likely to affect charismatic authority only where charisma already exists for other reasons. Thus the subsequent analysis will argue that in some cases Mao's revolutionary charisma was further enhanced by post-1949 policy successes which seemed to confirm his reputation for "exceptional" insight, while in others, failures could only dent but not destroy that reputation.

Performance is also relevant to the legitimacy of communist leaders lacking charisma. Here the key factor is gathering sufficient political support to lay a claim to leadership. Once the leader is established, continued successful performance will deepen support and hence the sense of rightful possession of the leading post. On the other hand, repeated failure will undermine both the political support and legitimacy of even an established leader. Khrushchev is perhaps the classic case, as his numerous domestic and foreign "harebrained schemes" finally created a consensus within the elite that he had to go.

Finally, it should be noted in this context that some members of the elite might find the performance of various leaders not simply more or less successful but fundamentally illegitimate as a result of pursuing unacceptable "revisionist" programs. This indeed was the nature of the charges against alleged "capitalist-roaders" during the Cultural Revolution and remained a theme of radical figures over the entire 1966-1976 period. Yet while Marxist movements are inherently prone to such phenomena given their utopian objectives, in the Chinese case it has only been Mao himself and a relatively small leadership faction largely dependent on him that have applied this criterion to officials at the highest level. As suggested by the currents of disapproval during the Cultural Revolution, which will be examined below, the bulk of the elite had few doubts about either the revolutionary virtue of those under attack or the fundamental legitimacy of the system as it existed before 1966. In fact, as events after Mao's death demonstrated, it was the radical attacks made in the name of revolutionary values that were considered illegitimate because of their detrimental effect on the system's performance. While tension between revolutionary ideals and values associated with national development have marked Chinese politics both before and after the Cultural Revolution decade, only in those years was it central to questions of legitimacy. In the post-Mao period, the successful performance of more mundane tasks has become relevant to the leader's legitimacy in the indirect sense of maintaining support discussed above.

The Role of Nationalism. Nationalism does not fit easily into the Weberian schema. Although hardly dependent on rational rules for its potency, nationalism is often effectively used by constitutional leaders to bolster their policies and standing. Nationalism has often been virulently antitraditional, as modern Chinese history shows, but in other cases such as contemporary Iran, figures steeped in tradition have used it to enhance their legitimacy. And while many nationalist leaders have genuine charisma, nationalist appeals have also been manipulated by the most uninspiring types. Indeed, it appears that in most cases a degree of loyalty and legitimacy is conferred on a leader by the mere possession of the highest national office regardless of how that office was obtained. For at least some members of the community, a national leader somehow, to some degree, merges with the nation.

While nationalism defies satisfactory classification in Weberian terms, an argument can be made linking nationalism to both traditional and charismatic authority. There is an inevitable tie between national pride and traditional greatness. To the extent a national leader can identify himself with imposing figures of the past, as Stalin did with the most ruthless czars, he is likely to gain some nationalist appeal. Even in China where the CCP has rejected much of Chinese tradition as "feudal" and "exploitative," pride in the past is a tangible aspect of both official and popular attitudes. To put it simply, the very definition of the modern nation-state is rooted in the traditional past, and nationalism draws immense sustenance from the symbols of that past.

For the purposes of this essay, however, the link of nationalism and charisma in communist movements is more significant. In the Chinese case in particular, for the top elite the socialist revolution has been indistinguishable from national salvation. National humiliation at the hands of foreign imperialism drew the founding members and subsequent generations of CCP leaders to the cause of Marxism, and Mao's "exceptional qualities" were perceived as solving a national as well as a revolutionary crisis. The revolution, moreover, was pursued not merely to achieve socialism but also to make China "rich and powerful."[41] Mao further developed the nationalist element by evolving an explicitly Chinese strategy; his utilitarian view of Marxism as merely the "arrow" with which to hit the "target" of the *Chinese* revolution clearly struck a deep chord.[42] Most important, the charisma engendered for Mao by revolutionary success was in effect further heightened by national victory. Indeed, it was undoubtedly easier for the Chinese masses to respond to Mao as the conquering national leader than as the representative of an alien Marxism-Leninism.[43] For Party leaders and members there was no contradiction. Deng Xiaoping summed up the matter for all concerned many years after the fact: "Every Chinese knows that without Chairman Mao there would have been no new China."[44] Such recognition provided potent legitimacy indeed.

In sum, Mao obtained a significant degree of charismatic authority within the CCP elite as a result of the successes which culminated in the victory of 1949. As revolutionary practitioners, Mao's colleagues recognized his "exceptional qualities" in the sphere of strategy. As Marxists, their faith in those qualities was cemented by the founding of the promised socialist state. And as nationalists, they were emotionally drawn to the man who, in their eyes, made national rebirth possible and had virtually become fused with the nation.

Legal-Rational Authority. Theoretically, if not always in practice, legal-rational authority is incompatible with charisma. According to Weber, such authority "rests[s] on the belief in the 'legality' of patterns of normative rules and the right of those elevated to authority under such rules to issue commands."[45] However the rules were originally created, obedience is owed not to individuals but to the "law"; insofar as individuals can issue commands, it is a function of the office they hold under the accepted rules rather than of any personal qualities. Furthermore, any obedience owed to the holder of an office is strictly limited to the sphere of the office's jurisdiction as delimited by the rules, in contrast to the unlimited authority of the charismatic leader.

The ideal type of such authority is the appointed bureaucracy, a hierarchically organized administrative body entrusted with clearly defined tasks, subject to detailed procedures, and staffed by officials with specialized training. Such rational structures are not self-contained, however, and they are often linked to political authority of a charismatic or traditional nature. Indeed, bureaucratic agencies are inevitably restricted by other authorities which create the rules officials must abide by. Correspondingly, for Weber, presidents and ministers in constitutional systems are officials in the formal sense only, as they lack the narrowly defined tasks and specialized skills of the true bureaucrat.[46] Nevertheless, by extending Weber's concept, such leaders can be seen as having legal-rational authority by virtue of election to their positions according to established procedures, as well as by observing any limitations on their powers of office.[47] Ultimately, from the legal-rational point of view, the legitimacy of a leader is based on fidelity to the agreed selection procedures even if this is dressed up by such myths as the "popular will."

Communist regimes have many features of Weber's legal-rational authority system. Rules and constitutions exist and, most significantly, highly specialized hierarchical bureaucracies dominate political life. Fundamentally, however, such regimes are not based on legal-rational authority. As is well known, many aspects of formal documents bear little relation to reality. Even more to the point, the leaders of such systems have never been prepared to be strictly bound by their own rules, including those which were enacted in good faith. Given the tension between legal-rationality, on the one hand, and both revolutionary ideology and the pressure to achieve defined tasks, on the other, communist leaders have repeatedly swept away legal encumbrances which have been perceived as inhibiting the attainment of priority objectives.[48] In the Chinese context, moreover, the traditional view of just government as based on good men rather than good laws further undermines the force of legal norms.

The above notwithstanding, it is necessary to look at the CCP's specific rules of leadership before writing off the possibility of legal-rational authority in the Chinese case. On one major criterion the Chinese system comes off poorly: the position of leader has not been strongly defined in legal-rational terms. During Mao's lifetime the Party chairmanship was regarded as the office defining leadership above all others, but that was more a function of Mao holding the position than any constitutional authority vested in it. The five Party constitutions from 1945 to 1977 were silent concerning the powers of the office, while the most recent 1982 constitution unceremoniously abolished the post.[49] Where specific powers were vested in Mao, as in the 1943 Politburo decision to give Mao authority to make final decisions in the work of the Party secretariat, it was clearly a grant of power reflecting confidence in Mao's "exceptional qualities" rather than a consequence of any office he held.[50] In the post-Mao period, the relative unimportance of office has been even clearer, with the *de facto* leader, Deng Xiaoping, not even holding the chairmanship prior to its abolition and still listed as only number three in the hierarchy.

Limitations placed on the leader by official Party norms are more significant.[51] These norms, which are substantially based on Leninist principles of Party organization, have been enshrined in major legal documents and repeatedly emphasized in important Party statements. Although acknowledged since the earliest days of the CCP, these organizational norms were developed in particularly systematic fashion in the late 1930s and early 1940s as part of the consolidation of Mao's leadership. Of special relevance are two related principles: minority rights and collective leadership. Under the concept of minority rights, top CCP officials have a clear prerogative to argue their views vigorously within appropriate Party bodies without fear of punishment for winding up on the losing side. Moreover, even if one is in the minority, as long as one implements the majority decision one is free to continue to hold one's opinion and again advocate it at future Party meetings.[52] Things are not so simple in practice, however. An inevitable tension exists between the right to "reserve opinions" and the need for strict implementation; continued articulation of doubts inevitably undercuts the approved policies. Moreover, the insistence that the official line is ideologically correct is in basic conflict with the vigorous assertion of minority rights, since at least some questions are placed beyond challenge.[53] Nevertheless, in the pre-Cultural Revolution period and since Mao's death, minority rights have been frequently upheld by Mao and other leaders in an effort to secure the wide-ranging discussion necessary for an effective policy process. The implications of this for the leader are clear: he must tolerate the critical opinions of his colleagues even when they strike at policies dear to his own heart.

Collective leadership, of course, prescribes even more basic limits on the leader. If the majority is to rule, logically the leader must submit if he is in the minority. This requirement sits uneasily with the charismatic authority of the leader. In Yanan, for example, Liu Shaoqi observed that Mao "is the leader of the whole Party yet he also obeys the Party," but in virtually the same breath he declared that the Party Chairman "represent[s] the truth, so we obey [him]."[54] The way around the problem was a combination of the leader accepting majority views against his own preferences in some cases while securing a majority on matters of most importance to him. Thus Lenin, while never rejecting the principle and giving in on minor issues, got his way on major questions by cajoling, haranguing, and pleading with his colleagues, and even threatening his resignation when faced with particularly stubborn opposition.[55] For his part, Mao, too, frequently affirmed the collective principle, although by the time of the Cultural Revolution he clearly believed correct views overrode any procedural considerations.

Collective leadership, however, was only vaguely legal-rational in Chinese practice even in the best of times. This was not simply because Mao insisted on his own way on critical issues regardless of majority opinions, but also owing to the imprecise consensual definition of the process. Despite constitutional injunctions that "the minority is subordinate to the majority," there is little indication of the Politburo or Central Committee operating on the basis of votes. As we have seen, Mao himself interpreted the collective principle loosely: "provided that *everyone* disagrees with me, I will accede to their point of view because they are the majority."[56] In addition, while official statements emphasize that collective leadership must be combined with individual responsibility, as the case of the chairmanship shows, there is little indication of formal parameters on individual roles at the summit of the Party.[57] To a certain extent such problems are inherent to all systems practicing collective responsibility, but the more legal-rational variants, such as the Westminister system, generally have procedures for breaking deadlocks in cabinet and regulations defining the powers of prime ministers. In China, however, the "rules" of collective leadership have not only been vulnerable to charismatic authority but themselves reflect more traditional notions of consensus.

An even more basic inadequacy in legal-rational terms is the failure of existing procedures to come to grips with the dominant fact of political life—the competition for power. No regularized mechanisms for achieving leadership exist: while formal documents sanction elections by Party congresses and central committees, in fact such procedures only ratify decisions taken elsewhere. Of particular moment is the absence of any procedure to remove an established leader—in the traditions of the CCP and other communist movements leaders are expected to continue serving. As the case of Khrushchev in the Soviet Union demonstrates, the lack of such mechanisms can necessitate conspiratorial activity to remove a leader who had lost the confidence of the elite. This need not always be the case, as the example of Hua Guofeng suggests,[58] but without clearly defined rules of removal, any change of leaders will be questionable from a legal-rational perspective.

In sum, China is a weak legal-rational system, but various formal Party norms have been taken seriously by the elite as an indication of how the system and leader should operate. For many years Mao himself was a strong advocate of those rules, although he sometimes violated them in practice. With the Cultural Revolution, he determined that the struggle against "revisionism" took precedence over established procedures. As the following argues, from the point of view of the top elite, Mao's respect or disrespect for the rules added or detracted from his authority although his charismatic claims were never fully undermined. Moreover, the damage to legality over Mao's last decade was so severe as to lead to a renewed emphasis on legal-rational principles after his death, albeit an emphasis only imperfectly reflected in practice.

Traditional Authority. Tradition conceptually stands somewhere between charisma and legal-rationality. For Weber, traditional authority is based on a belief in "The sanctity of . . . powers . . . as they have been handed down from the past, 'have always existed.' "[59] Authority is vested in leaders selected on the basis of their traditional status, and obedience is owed to the *person* holding the traditionally sanctioned position. While traditional authority normally has roots in some past charismatic figure who established the prevailing pattern, it differs significantly from charismatic leadership, because tradition has also imposed definite limits on the leader. Obedience is owed the traditional king only so long as the traditional order is not violated; overstepping traditional bounds endangers the ruler's position as it can be used to justify resistance and rebellion. But while traditional prescriptions limit the ruler's freedom of action, his personal authority, unlike an official in a legal-rational system, also encompasses unspecified prerogatives, a sphere of arbitrary free grace where he can act as he chooses. The extent of this arbitrary sphere varies from one traditional system to another, and in some cases it is very extensive. Moreover, when any question of violating traditional limits arises, the burden of proof rests with those owing loyalty to the leader.[60]

In his writings, Weber noted the charismatic quality conferred on the Chinese emperor by the notion that his personal virtue crucially determined the well-being of the realm.[61] Charisma was particularly apropos of dynastic founders who were portrayed as awesome figures in traditional culture. Such charisma, however, was traditionalized after the establishment of a dynasty. Whatever "exceptional qualities" founders of dynasties may have had, the concept of a special relationship to Heaven was passed on to successors as a form of hereditary charisma, whereby the imagined qualities really rested in the *status* of emperor. Moreover, a sense of limits marked the imperial system. The best known of these, of course, revolves around the concept of the Mandate of Heaven. If an emperor ruled in a tyrannical fashion, his subjects theoretically had a duty to rebel[62] and depose him because he was not carrying out the trust of Heaven. But more important, and more central to our concern here, are traditional notions about the relationship of the emperor and his ministers.

Imperial officials owed personal loyalty to the throne. Such loyalty was limited to an individual emperor or at least to his house; in the orthodox Neo-Confucian view, nothing was more dishonorable than transferring obedience from one dynasty to another.[63] (Within a dynasty, loyalty could be transferred to a legitimate successor. Such succession had long been fixed in the eldest son of the empress consort, but in the Qing dynasty the practice of the emperor designating his successor evolved.[64]) Obedience, however, was mitigated by ethical considerations. Officials were not to be mere tools of the ruler but were to guide him according to traditional concepts of right and wrong. A righteous emperor was to heed such advice, and conventions of broad consultation and even of the throne accepting the consensus of court officials apparently existed in various periods. Most significantly, when an official detected unwise or unrighteous behavior in his monarch, Confucian tradition enjoined him to speak out and oppose the emperor's course of action, a practice institutionalized in the censorate. Righteousness, according to the classics, was the supreme duty of officals and far outweighed simple obedience. If the emperor were to persist in serious error and refuse to listen to the remonstrations of his officials, Mencius argued, they were then duty bound to disassociate themselves from the throne through resignation and withdrawal or, in extreme cases, to seek the monarch's overthrow.[65]

Although such ethical considerations receive strong backing in the classical tradition, it would be misleading to overemphasize them with regard to either imperial practice or the actual legitimacy of the throne. First, ethical Confucianism was in tension with official court principles. From the time of the early Han these principles emphasized that political authority was centralized in the hands of one man, the emperor.[66] This centralization reached quite extreme forms by the time of the Ming and Qing. Moreover, even the ethical tradition tacitly acknowledged the relatively untrammeled authority of the throne. For despite Mencius' assertion that there were cases where officials should dethrone the emperor, the classics generally emphasized a more passive course of criticizing an erring ruler *at grave personal risk*. According to Confucius, "The determined official never forgets that his end may be in a ditch or a stream; the brave official never forgets that he may lose his head."[67] This call to martyrdom implies a political authority for even the unrighteous ruler. Officials may, indeed should, protest unjust behavior, but they must also accept the harsh retribution of the throne if it is forthcoming. Rebellion was not a real option for those serving at court; any challenge to the Mandate had to come from outside. In effect, then, the imperial system involved a very large component of Weber's sphere of arbitrary free grace despite all the ethical considerations governing the relationship of ruler and official. Just officials could remonstrate with the emperor or even leave their posts, but they could do little more.

What is the relevance of all this for authority relations in post-1949 China? The CCP's explicit rejection of much of the Chinese past should caution against too readily seeking traditional explanations for contemporary developments. Indeed, analysts emphasizing continuities with the past are often reduced to drawing attention to similar phenomena without being able to demonstrate that the inner dynamics of the new system remain essentially traditional. Nevertheless, parallels are there, and they suggest that in many respects deeply embedded traditional values have played an important role in the politics of the PRC. Perhaps the strongest support for this view is found in the statements and actions of Chinese political leaders themselves. For example, as will be argued in greater detail later, traditional perceptions of the leader at least in part guided the actions of Peng Dehuai at the Lushan meetings in 1959. There, Peng allegedly responded to Zhang Wentian's observation that Mao was ruthless in dealing with people by noting that "the first emperor of any dynasty . . . was always ruthless and brilliant."[68] Furthermore, Mao himself commented that his personality cult may

have been exaggerated by the "habits of 3,000 years of emperor wor-
shiping traditions," while in the view of his successors, Mao's "arbitrary individual rule" was deeply influenced by China's feudal past.[69]
And the initial, if ultimately unsuccessful, effort after Mao's death to
picture Hua Guofeng as the late Chairman's personally chosen successor suggests at the very least a belief that traditionally justified legitimacy carried weight with the Chinese people.

The imperial tradition, then, has had some influence on authority
relations in post-1949 China. Traditional notions of the loyalty owed to
emperors, especially the founders of dynasties, reinforced the charismatic basis of Mao's hold over the elite. Even after Mao's death
reluctance to criticize him too harshly is at least partially explainable in
terms of the respect owed to ancestors and the practice of regarding the
merits of dynastic founders as outweighing their faults. Moreover, like
the personality cult, traditional factors probably constrained any in the
leadership who considered opposing Mao. As the post-Mao leadership
has argued, the propensity of a conservative peasantry to worship
authority long served to underpin Mao's rule.[70] Tradition cut two
ways, however. In addition to providing loyalty to the "throne," it led
to expectations of righteous behavior by the "emperor." When Mao, in
the eyes of leading colleagues, failed to live up to such standards, a
basis was created for the withdrawal of support though not outright
opposition. Similarly, in the post-Mao period those elements of imperial tradition calling on the ruler to consult and heed the advice of loyal
ministers has served as an even more potent limit on the authority of
successor leaders.

Finally, it should be noted that the utility of Weber's concept of
traditional authority is not exhausted by consideration of the legacy of
the premodern period. At least as important are the CCP's own traditions built up during its sixty-odd years of existence. Thus when organizational norms were systematically restated by the "Guiding Principles for Inner-Party Political Life" in 1980, this was hailed as "restoring the Party's fine traditions."[71] This was appropriate given the
rather loose nature of these rules from a legal-rational point of view.
Furthermore, former PRC residents indicate that under CCP rule personal influence based on prestige and qualifications carries more legitimacy than official power[72]—and within the Party such prestige derives
from participation in the revolutionary movement. Thus in the history
of Chinese communism status and seniority have been key factors in
authority relations within the Party. While, as argued above, Mao's

status went beyond tradition to involve large doses of charisma, the top elite which granted his authority was defined as much or more in terms of revolutionary roles as by post-1949 bureaucratic positions. Moreover, any contender for the mantle of legitimate leadership after Mao would inevitably lack charisma and thus require sufficient seniority in the Party to make his claims credible.

The Shifting Nature of Mao's Authority, 1949-1976

While Mao Zedong's legitimacy as leader was never challenged within the elite after the founding of the PRC, and his authority was seriously questioned only in his last few years, the bases of this authority shifted markedly over the entire post-1949 period despite some crucial continuities. Here, four distinct periods will be analyzed: (1) 1949-1958, when virtually all modes of legitimation reinforced Mao's authority; (2) 1959-1965, when Mao's behavior led to reservations on traditional and legal-rational grounds by ranking officials but no serious challenge; (3) 1966-1971, when the resort to unbridled charismatic claims destroyed legality and caused graver doubts within the elite; and (4) 1972-76, when limited challenges to Mao's authority appeared.

To understand this changing pattern more fully, a word on the legitimacy of the regime and leader in the eyes of the population is in order.[73] In broad terms, after enjoying a high degree of legitimacy in its first decade, the system suffered a series of shocks that caused the disillusionment of key groups in society so that by the time of Mao's death the basis was laid for what has since been called a "crisis of faith." For most of the 1950s a combination of factors including enthusiasm for building the New China, the sense that a new dynasty with the right to establish its own orthodoxy had come to power, and popular approval of both gradual increases in living standards and the emergence of the PRC as a major international actor provided substantial authority for the new order and its founder. The first major setback came with the economic crisis following the failure of the Great Leap Forward, a crisis so severe as to shake the faith of the peasantry in the Party and Mao.[74] Even more disillusioning were the consequences of the Cultural Revolution, which alienated a whole range of groups including intellectuals who suffered severe and often violent attacks, urban youths who were sent to confront conditions of extreme poverty in the countryside, and ordinary Party members and bureaucrats who could not fathom the rationale for internecine struggles within their units or credit explanations for such political turnabouts as the fall of Lin Biao. Finally, in Mao's last year, this cumulative erosion of legitimacy exploded in the Tiananmen riots and disturbances in other cities where Mao's rule came under direct attack during some of the most genuinely spontaneous political protests in the history of the PRC.[75]

1949-1958: Mutual Reinforcement. Mao's personal authority within the elite during this period was bolstered by a confluence of virtually all the types of legitimacy discussed above. The period began, of course, with the victory of the revolution, which provided the most intense confirmation of the essential basis of Mao's charisma—his role as the "exceptional" strategist who led the way to *communist* and *national* victory and liberation. This enormous reservoir of authority was further augmented by the Party's successes under his leadership in achieving the next set of goals the leadership set for itself—socialist transformation and economic growth. During the First Five-Year Plan (1953-57) the collectivization of agriculture and the socialization of commerce and industry were not only accomplished ahead of schedule, but a very respectable economic growth rate of 6 to 8 percent was attained despite continuing problems which eventually led to the dramatic innovations of the Great Leap Forward.

Mao's authority was enhanced not only by the overall performance of the new regime but also by his specific policy initiatives. While Mao on the whole tended to operate as a consensus leader in this period, those cases where he did play a uniquely forceful role generally furthered his reputation for "exceptional" judgment. Soon after the founding of the new regime, he apparently overrode the doubts of many of his top colleagues on the question of intervention in the Korean War, a move which for all its costs wound up establishing China as a force to be reckoned with in international politics.[76] As has been shown in the previous essay,[77] in 1955 Mao played a prominent role in forcing the pace of agricultural cooperativization with the result that official goals were accomplished much more rapidly than had been imagined possible. And while the Hundred Flowers experiment of 1956-57 was probably the Chairman's most significant miscalculation of the period, his timely shift to a crackdown on intellectual dissent through the Anti-Rightist Campaign undoubtedly did much to restore any lost prestige within leading Party circles.[78] Finally, Mao's judgment in pushing the Great Leap also seemed borne out initially. By the end of 1958, despite a growing awareness of shortcomings, it still appeared to China's leaders that totally unprecedented economic gains had been made.[79]

The one area of somewhat fluctuating impact during the initial period was the personality cult. Overall, there were ample efforts to add contrived charisma to Mao's growing stock. The earliest years saw a spate of articles attributing manifold abilities to the Party Chairman,[80] and his closest collaborators declared the impossibility of separating revolutionary victory from Mao's leadership.[81] Yet by 1956 the personality cult had fallen on hard times, most notably by the excising of the "Thought of Mao Zedong" from the new Party constitution. Despite many assertions to the contrary, this should not be seen as a defeat for Mao; it was clearly a response to the anti-personality cult atmosphere in the international movement created by Khrushchev's denunciation of Stalin, and Mao himself was an active participant in the decision.[82] Moreover, the matter-of-factness with which this reference was set aside underlines how peripheral the cult was for the Chairman's authority within top CCP circles. In any case, by 1958 a new round of public acclaim for Mao's Thought was initiated in conjunction with the Great Leap Forward.

In legal-rational terms, Mao's authority was also high throughout 1949-1958.[83] This was made possible by the substantial consensus on the Soviet model within the leadership for most of the period—a consensus which as we have seen (above, pp. 16-18, 36-38) meant policy debates centered on incremental adjustments while Mao generally performed a centrist balancing role by criticizing both the "right" and the "left." In such circumstances both minority rights and collective leadership were normally upheld. With only limited and temporary exceptions, those who argued minority views did not suffer politically.[84] Most significantly, there were no purges for policy reasons until late 1957,[85] and practically the entire Central Committee was reelected in 1956. While the lenient treatment of dissenters encouraged vigorous debate, collective leadership apparently also thrived. In cases such as the Hundred Flowers where Mao took the lead in initiating innovative policies, the evidence indicates he was able to muster a majority. More significant was the fact that Mao allowed his personal preferences to be overruled even in such major cases as the 1956 slowdown in economic growth. Furthermore, Mao initially obtained strong majority backing for the Great Leap strategy, although now the rules were infringed upon by purges of apparent provincial-level dissenters, and the consensual basis of collective leadership was weakened by significant divisions over the radical departure from the Soviet model.[86] Thus the "legal" basis of Mao's rule was generally reinforced by developments of the early and mid-1950s, although by the end of the period it was showing some signs of strain.

Finally, throughout the 1949-1958 period traditional factors gave additional support to Mao's authority within the elite. The charismatic authority Mao gained as architect of the revolutionary victory was echoed in the aura of founding a new dynasty. Moreover, much as Mao's observance of official Party norms enhanced his legal-rational legitimacy, his style of broad consultation, consensus politics, and magnanimous treatment of those who disagreed with him struck a significant resonance with the behavior traditionally associated with righteous emperors. In this earliest period of the PRC, tradition as well as legal-rational considerations reinforced the essentially charismatic basis of Mao's legitimacy.

1959-1965: Legal-Rational and Traditional Ambivalence. Apart from the collapse of the Great Leap Forward, the crucial event affecting Mao's standing in this period was the Lushan meetings convened in mid-1959 to cope with the increasingly perceived problems of that movement.[87] Mao's actions at Lushan, particularly his strong attack on Peng Dehuai after Peng's criticisms of the leap, both seriously violated Party rules and raised problems from a traditional perspective. By the time of Lushan, Mao had already caused discontent among his colleagues by cavalierly disregarding the principle of collective leadership. Mao's deep involvement in the administration of the Great Leap in early 1959 led to his issuing circulars and orders without proper consultation within the Politburo. In April of that year, Peng reportedly criticized Mao for "assuming command in person," while shortly thereafter Zhang Wentian objected to the Chairman's "individual style" in issuing a letter critical of Great Leap excesses despite the fact that he shared Mao's views. At Lushan, moreover, Zhang complained that "meetings of the Politburo [are] only large-scale briefing meetings without any collective discussion."[88]

These infringements, however, were minor compared with the blatant attack on minority rights that Mao's onslaught against Peng represented. While Peng's criticism of the leap forward was comprehensive, it was not extreme: it not only did not represent a personal attack on Mao (see below) but to a large extent was a response to the Chairman's emphasis over the previous months on the need to reveal the shortcomings of the new economic strategy.[89] Most important, it was a criticism wholly within Peng's rights as a Politburo member to state dissenting views on policy matters. The significance attached to these legal-rational considerations within the CCP elite was indicated by the widespread feeling that Peng had been unfairly treated, that he had merely exercised his legitimate prerogative. Even ''leftists'' who opposed the substance of Peng's views were appalled at the handling of his case. Thus Li Jingquan, who had argued with Peng at Lushan and earlier had even criticized Mao for being too pessimistic about the leap, reportedly exclaimed shortly after the meetings: ''Peng Dehuai mixed up the subjective and the objective, he only said a few wrong sentences. It certainly does not mean opposing us by [using] our shortcomings.''[90]

The developments at Lushan can also be seen in traditional terms—those of the proper relationship between an emperor and his ministers. As argued earlier, this is supported by more than mere speculation. Not only did Peng allude to Mao as the founder of the dynasty at Lushan, but the style of the critique in his ''letter of opinion'' to Mao bore more resemblance to a memorial to the emperor than to collective discussion: ''I am a simple man . . . and indeed I am crude and have no tact at all. For this reason, whether this letter is of reference value or not is for you to decide. If what I say is wrong, please correct me.''[91] And once Mao forced Peng's dismissal as minister of defense, historical discussions of past dismissals of righteous ministers took on special significance. While Tom Fisher's persuasive analysis raises doubts as to the precise intention of Wu Han's 1959-1962 writings about the Ming official Hai Rui and notably about whether they were perceived as attacks on Mao at the time,[92] it is likely that at least some Chinese leaders saw an analogy between Peng and Hai Rui.[93] What is significant in the Hai Rui analogy is not only the dismay expressed that a just official had been badly treated, but also the recognition that while such an official was duty bound to remonstrate he was still required to accept the throne's decision. Much as Hai Rui had no choice but to accept the emperor's edict, Peng Dehuai could only accede to Mao's demand and request the opportunity to go to China's countryside.

Peng's dismissal gained the support of Mao's leading colleagues despite misgivings within the elite over the violation of the rules. Ye Jianying recalled the event nearly two decades later:

> At the beginning, I, Comrades Liu Shaoqi and Deng Xiaoping, and
> . . . Premier [Zhou] all felt that what Peng Dehuai said was right. But
> later, after the Chairman had written a letter, issued an instruction, and
> talked for an hour or so, we all changed our attitude and came to side with
> Chairman Mao to attack the hapless Peng. . . . [94]

This capitulation to Mao's wishes can be seen as prudent politics. Mao had in effect drawn the line at Lushan: Peng or me. In any political contest along these lines Mao could be expected to win. Moreover, even if a Politburo or Central Committee majority had the fortitude to resist Mao within higher Party councils, the problem of how to sell this to wider publics long exposed to Mao's personality cult was forbidding. From this perspective, the potential instability of a direct clash with the leader must have seemed a far greater danger than the damage done to formal norms. Yet it would be wrong to overemphasize political calculation in the decision to back Mao: to a large extent Mao's authority was being acknowledged. Over and above those aspects of tradition which called for obedience, this was largely charismatic authority. But it was not charisma based on ongoing successes. As Ye's recollections indicate, the Great Leap policies which Mao had forcefully pushed were now viewed with growing skepticism by a far greater segment of the top elite than Peng alone; taken together with the failure of Mao's recent Hundred Flowers experiment, it represented a sharp blow to the Chairman's prestige as someone with the answers to current problems. Yet these failures paled by comparison with the dual victory of communist revolution and national liberation. However serious his policy errors and violations of official norms in 1959, Mao's colleagues could not separate him from the Party or the nation.

When the severity of the economic crisis was finally recognized in the early 1960s and fundamental policy changes were initiated, this process was accompanied by a far-ranging effort to restore inner-Party norms—and coincidentally to refurbish Mao's image as a just ruler. Mao himself was in the forefront of the effort. He not only advocated collective decisions but repeatedly called on his colleagues to exercise minority rights by speaking out without fear.[95] In this same period, however, the disconcerting issue of the personality cult heated up. With Lin Biao promoting Mao and Mao's Thought, other leaders became concerned that excessive emphasis on the Chairman's words would inhibit effective solutions to China's problems. Typically, the Chairman himself was ambivalent. In 1961 Mao reportedly backed the Central Committee propaganda department's view against drawing a parallel between his Thought and Marxism-Leninism, and three years later he declared "really great" Liu Shaoqi's warning about accepting "Mao Zedong's works and sayings as a dogma."[96] Yet Mao also made approving noises over Lin's efforts and concluded that claims concerning his [Mao's] thoughts contributing to championship table tennis performances were "full of dialectical materialism."[97] Thus the leadership was divided on the desirability of the resurrected personality cult while Mao wavered, but in any case the cult was unlikely to add to Mao's authority in the eyes of the elite as a whole.

In one important regard due respect was given to legal-rational and traditional considerations: the handling of the critical succession problem. In early 1959, after a period of considerable preparation, Liu Shaoqi assumed the position of chief of state, and his status as heir apparent was made abundantly clear in the following years.[98] Since there is little doubt that Liu was Mao's choice, his selection had elements of both hereditary charisma[99] and imperial succession. However, given that succession arrangements had been under way since at least 1956 and Liu's position as number two in the Party had been apparent for years before that, this undoubtedly was a decision made after the substantial consultation expected from upright rulers. Moreover, Liu's status as a major revolutionary figure made him an acceptable successor—if not necessarily everyone's personal choice— in terms of the CCP's own traditions. Finally, Liu's 1959 appointment was ratified by the highest state bodies and provided a major formal office to further bolster his claims. In this sense Liu was not only a "chosen" successor of proper status; he was a "legal" successor as well.

But despite his legal office and the apparent consensus on his designation, as events soon showed, Liu's position was dependent on the favor of the charismatic leader. As for Mao himself, by the eve of the Cultural Revolution his authority within the elite rested more than ever on the fundamental victory of 1949. The Chairman's charisma reflected both the Marxist revolutionary achievement and national aspirations, but it received only limited support from more recent events. If the loss of prestige Mao undoubtedly suffered as a result of the Great Leap failure had been partially offset by the recovery of 1962-65, it was well known that many of the policies which retrieved the situation had been designed by the Chairman's colleagues.[100] The revived personality cult did not enhance Mao within the top elite but instead provided a bone of contention. Traditional support for the throne presumably operated in the background to shore up Mao's position, but it was flawed by his unjust treatment of Peng Dehuai. And although official norms still functioned with some difficulty, the legal-rational basis of Mao's authority had also been damaged by his arbitrary actions at Lushan.

1966-1971: Legality Shattered, Charisma Triumphant. Mao's frustrations with pervasive problems of Chinese society resulted in a fundamental rejection of legal-rational norms during the Cultural Revolution. The weakening of legal procedures was apparent when the August 1966 Central Committee plenum, which ratified a major leadership reshuffle and sanctioned the extra-Party Red Guards, was packed with "revolutionary teachers and students" and seemingly excluded many *bona fide* members.[101] As the campaign unfolded, a sweeping attack was launched against long standing CCP norms. Opposition to Mao on any issue under any circumstances, and beyond that any deviation from a highly idealized version of Mao's Thought, was now judged culpable. The fact that such "opposition" may have been a majority view that the Chairman accepted at the time, or that a dissenting opinion had been an open exercise of minority rights without drawing any rebuke from the contemporary Mao, was simply dismissed out of hand. The newly dominant view demanded the unqualified obedience characteristic of charismatic authority. Lin Biao lectured his colleagues on this point at the August Central Committee meeting:

> We must regard Chairman Mao as the axis. We must do everything in accordance with the Thought of the Chairman. . . . In handling problems, the Chairman takes the whole situation into consideration; he is farsighted and has his own reasons, many of which are not understood by us. We must resolutely implement the Chairman's directives whether we understand them or not.[102]

This demand was linked to a further intensification of Mao's personality cult to an extent unprecedented in post-1949 China. While incessant claims of Mao's genius as the "greatest Marxist-Leninist of our era" together with distortions of revolutionary history virtually eliminating the contributions of most other leaders could hardly have enhanced his reputation within the top elite, the cult undoubtedly bolstered Mao's authority among the impressionable Red Guards, who were the cutting edge of the Cultural Revolution. Indeed, this synthetic charisma increasingly became the basis of Mao's legitimacy within society at large if not among Party leaders. While in reality the disruption of the period surely led to a net loss of authority for the Chairman among the public,[103] what authority remained was fostered by a cult with striking traditional overtones. In the Cultural Revolution, Mao was presented as the sole arbiter of China's course, not unlike the founders of imperial dynasties, and as a just leader doing battle with corrupt ministers, similar to exemplary rulers of the past. More pervasively, his image as the remote father figure fit the traditional ideal of a great emperor.[104] Thus an outlandishly magnified revolutionary charisma merged with traditional images in the personality cult directed at the Chinese people.

Meanwhile, a cult was also created for Lin Biao, but the decidedly charismatic claims made for Lin could not be separated from Mao. Lin's revolutionary achievements were built up to absurd lengths, but his key "exceptional quality" was the derivative one of being "Chairman Mao's best student."[105] Like Liu, Lin was Mao's personal choice—but without the broad consensus which marked the earlier succession arrangements. In contrast to the long preparations which had marked Liu's emergence as heir, Lin was suddenly thrust upon the Party as the new successor at the August 1966 plenum. The subsequent effort to provide legal trappings for Lin's position ironically indicated just how far removed it was from any legal-rational basis. The 1969 Party constitution not only named him the sole vice-chairman of the CCP, it also designated him as "Comrade Mao Zedong's close comrade-in-arms and successor."[106] Here legitimacy was vested in a person on the basis of qualities allegedly derived from the charismatic leader. Any authority derived from the position of vice-chairman was clearly peripheral to that fact.

The question of authority lies at the heart of the Cultural Revolution puzzle. How did a movement directly and severely attacking virtually *all* vested institutional interests (the PLA being only a partial exception[107]) and most of the top elite get off the ground? Why did Mao's major individual targets give up without any resistance,[108] while members of the elite generally only sought to defend reputations and avoid disgrace rather than coalesce to oppose Mao frontally? The unwillingness of Mao's top colleagues to stop the Cultural Revolution in the face of a determined Chairman was graphically revealed by the so-called "February [1967] Adverse Current." At that time a substantial number of Politburo members, including a majority of vice-premiers and vice-chairmen of the Party's Military Affairs Committee (MAC), expressed their dismay at the attacks on Liu and other leading figures. They passionately argued that loyalty was owed to veteran comrades who had devoted decades to the revolutionary cause but were now subjected to public humiliation by callow youths. The level of outrage was expressed in Tan Zhenlin's exclamation that "I should not have followed Chairman Mao . . . for forty years." Yet this group of veteran officials was unable to restrain Mao, and the powers formally vested in the Politburo were taken over by the recently established Cultural Revolution Group, where Mao's wife, Jiang Qing, played a key role. When the crunch came as the demands for curbing the Cultural Revolution were placed before Mao, the Chairman, as in 1959, again offered a choice of submitting to his will or engaging in a direct confrontation, and the old revolutionaries caved in.[109]

Undoubtedly many factors influenced the refusal to fight. The pre-viously noted fear that a direct attack on the regime's founder would severely damage the system served as a restraint. Another factor of some significance was the apparent belief or at least hope within lead-ing circles that, the vandalism of the Red Guards notwithstanding, Mao would ultimately act within the bounds of propriety toward long-standing comrades.[110] Other considerations included the fact that the course the movement would take was not clear at the outset, the implicit threat of military force given Mao's alliance with Lin Biao, and sheer timidity in the face of unprecedented developments. Yet certainly, as at Lushan, more than fear and calculation were involved. Liu Shaoqi, Deng Xiaoping, and the others undoubtedly felt a sense of duty as they stepped off the political stage. Once again, charisma based on the revolutionary *cum* nationalist victory of 1949—with its traditional overtones of founding a dynasty as well—carried the day. But now this charisma had to carry a much heavier burden—the fact that Mao's actions went directly *against* the objectives of building a strong social-ist society as they had long been understood. While many in the elite may have shared elements of Mao's vision at the start of the Cultural Revolution, it quickly became apparent that the new movement was wreaking havoc on the performance of the system. Severe economic losses, institutional paralysis, a weakened defense capacity, and wide-spread social strife were hardly the results to convince longstanding administrators of the great helmsman's wisdom. Nevertheless, support remained for Mao the charismatic leader. As Xu Shiyou exclaimed in 1971, ''I object to . . . the Cultural Revolution, [but] I would fight all the way to Beijing to protect you.''[111] That personal authority could withstand a clearly dysfunctional campaign of such magnitude is testimony to the profound impact of Mao's pre-1949 successes in the minds of those leaders who shared the revolutionary experience with him.

Although victorious, Mao's stock of revolutionary based charisma must have been comparatively low by the time the Cultural Revolution petered out in 1968. The subsequent effort to restore a semblance of stability may have alleviated some of the damge to Mao's prestige, but the Chairman was to receive another severe blow from the Lin Biao affair (see the concluding essay). Whatever the truth of allegations of assassination plots directed at Mao, the hard political fact was that Mao's ''best student,'' his personally annointed successor, had been shown at the least totally inadequate if not unimaginably villainous. Far from demonstrating the ''exceptional qualities'' needed to keep the Chinese revolution true to its principles, over the tumultuous Cultural

Revolution period Mao had only shown political naïveté in falling for the empty words of a sycophant.[112]

1972-1976: Traditional Resistance to the Leader. It took more than a year for Chinese politics to emerge from the shock of the Lin Biao affair. By 1973, however, the basic Cultural Revolution cleavage of old line Party administrators and radical critics again dominated political life and continued to do so until Mao's death. The struggle between the so-called "Gang of Four" and more pragmatic officials involved both bitter personal animosities and large ideological visions, and its intensity sent shock waves through all levels of the system. Throughout this struggle Mao remained a key figure, but a figure whose influence was more limited than at any time since the 1930s. This was in part owing to sheer physical deterioration. By 1972 Mao already found it extremely difficult to communicate and, as both Richard Nixon and Deng Xiaoping attest, by 1976 he was barely capable of more than grunts and groans.[113] In addition, as will be discussed further in the concluding essay, Mao was either unable or unwilling to choose decisively between the contending forces. While this may have been designed to enhance his position by playing off the two groups (and various intermediate forces in the elite), in the context of fierce factional struggle and his own disabilities it only further diluted his influence.

While Mao ultimately withheld endorsement of either of the major contending groups, the total available evidence suggests his strongest passions were with the radical position. Although he gave some support to the policies of stability and modernization advocated by the administrators around Zhou Enlai,[114] Mao's strongest endorsements were reserved for the programs of the radical forces. Thus the only *new* Mao quotations publicized in the 1973-76 period backed the rebellious and egalitarian themes of the Cultural Revolution, e.g., the 1973 call to "go against the tide," the 1975 demand that the eight-grade wage system "be restricted under the dictatorship of the proletariat," and the 1976 observation that the "bourgeoisie is right in the Communist Party."[115] In contrast, the best Zhou could do when unveiling the "four modernizations" at the 1975 National People's Congress (NPC) was to cite Mao's *1964* endorsement of this concept. Moreover, the fact that Mao not only did not appear at the Congress (he was well enough to meet Franz-Josef Strauss while the Congress was in session) or even send a message indicates less than wholehearted approval, and the virtual immediate launching of a campaign against "bourgeois right" in the wage system and other facets of Chinese society—none of which had been on the Congress agenda—suggests a quite different set of priorities.[116]

Whatever Mao's precise attitude toward the new modernization program, what is significant from our perspective is that it was now being advanced without Mao's authority, which instead was used to justify the onslaught against "bourgeois right." In a formal sense, the four modernizations derived their legitimacy from legal-rational considerations: they were sanctioned by the highest legal organ of the state at the January NPC, and over the following year, concrete policies were developed by a series of regular meetings involving the relevant specialized bureaucracies. But if the legal-rational authority of state bodies was used to bolster the modernization drive independently of, or even in conflict with, the charismatic authority of the leader, the political dynamics of the situation are better explained in traditional terms. At the heart of these developments stood the relationship between Mao and Zhou Enlai.

The interaction of Mao and Zhou in these years remains elusive. Theirs had long been a symbiotic relationship, and cooperation and mutual dependence had marked the Cultural Revolution period despite radical attacks on Zhou. Clearly, close cooperation also continued in some areas throughout 1972-75; foreign policy is an obvious example.[117] Yet on the overall thrust of domestic policy, as the above suggests, the two men undoubtedly had major differences. What is unclear is the exact political and authority relationship between Mao and his premier. By some post-Mao accounts Zhou was too much a "feudal premier" who would not stand up to the emperor.[118] Others, such as an inner-Party report by Liao Gailong, suggest a somewhat more assertive Zhou:

> Following Lin Biao's death . . . Comrade Zhou Enlai, supported by Comrade Mao Zedong, took charge of the work of the Central Committee [and] began to restore the Party's traditions, liberate cadres, rehabilitate and revive the national economy. He was credited with very big achievements. At the beginning Comrade Mao Zedong allowed him to do so. Later, he [Mao] became vexed because [Zhou] restored the original correct line. Thus, Comrade Mao Zedong criticized the resurgence of "right" deviationism. Later, he further initiated a struggle to criticize Lin Biao and Confucius to oppose Comrade Zhou Enlai.[119]

Ultimately, the two accounts may be compatible. It seems plausible that as a loyal minister Zhou would never *directly* oppose Mao. But given the ambivalent nature of Mao's views, his declining ability to monitor developments, and Zhou's own policy preferences, it is also likely that Zhou would attempt to use the opportunities available and shape a program at variance with Mao's deepest concerns. Mao, for his part, could be seen as reacting to objectionable policies without explicitly attacking Zhou because of the political costs that would have entailed,[120] his own partial sympathy with Zhou's objectives, and perhaps in gratitude for Zhou's loyalty and services over the years.

Whatever the relationship of Mao and Zhou, it is clear that Zhou's personal prestige was vital for the adoption of the four modernizations in 1975, and this prestige was to a substantial degree based on traditional factors. In terms of the CCP's own traditions, Zhou had unusual status as one of the Party's earliest and most important leaders. But particularly important was his style of leadership interaction. This has been especially apparent in the minicult of Zhou which emerged after Mao's death: the "esteemed and beloved" premier has been portrayed as a man exemplifying all the Confucian virtues of rectitude, moderation, cultivation, and kindness.[121] Of special significance was Zhou's role in protecting his high-ranking comrades during the Cultural Revolution. Even in early 1977, when the Cultural Revolution was officially still in favor, Zhou's righteous resistance to its excesses was hailed:

> The struggle came to a climax on August 11, 1967, when Chen Yi was brought to a public meeting for his alleged crimes. . . . When a group of thugs were about to make a physical assault on Chen Yi, Premier Zhou . . . ordered the guards to escort Chen Yi from the meeting hall, while he himself walked out in protest. This was the best he could do under the circumstances. . . .
>
> Lin Biao, Chen Boda and Jiang Qing then devised another scheme by forcing Premier Zhou to engage in exhausting talks [with a group of roughnecks] last[ing] 18 hours, during which the Premier neither ate nor slept. The[se] thugs even threatened to intercept Chen Yi's car and storm into the Great Hall of the People to seize Chen Yi. The Premier indignantly replied: "If you dare try, I'll do whatever I can to stop you!"[122]

Zhou had navigated the Cultural Revolution without tarnishing his loyalty to either the ruler or to his fellow ministers and comrades. In the 1970s the resultant prestige aided him in launching a program lacking Mao's explicit backing even as he still served the Chairman.

The significance of Zhou's personal influence was further demonstrated following his death in January 1976. Not only did the four modernizations now come under withering attack as Mao apparently concluded the new program had gone too far,[123] but Zhou's carefully arranged succession came immediately unstuck. At the 1975 NPC, Deng Xiaoping had been named senior vice-premier (as well as Party vice-chairman and PLA chief of staff), and Deng assumed the reins of government as Zhou's health worsened. Yet despite his impressive array of legal-rational authority Deng was pushed aside and subjected to intense media criticism. These attacks were based on Mao's charismatic authority, on the Chairman's conclusion that Deng "does not grasp class struggle. . . . [H]is theme of 'white cat, black cat' mak[es] no distinction between imperialism and Marxism."[124] In any case, Deng's "legal" position was ultimately dependent on Mao in the first place. Not only had the Chairman, undoubtedly at Zhou's urging, sanctioned Deng's rehabilitation in 1973, Mao also ratified the NPC personnel arrangements which placed Deng in charge of day-to-day government work.[125]

But if Zhou's prestige was no longer present to protect the four modernizations and Deng, traditional influences still worked to blunt Mao's authority. While Mao was able to have Deng removed from active duty and Hua Guofeng named as acting premier within a month of Zhou's death, no move was made either to strip Deng of his titles or to appoint Hua as full premier.[126] Indeed, some reports indicate that key Politburo members Ye Jianying and Li Xiannian made the very traditional gesture of leaving their offices in protest over the attacks on Deng.[127] It was only after the April Tiananmen incident when popular rioting shook the leadership that the Politburo closed ranks, formally named Hua premier, and stripped Deng of his posts. Nevertheless, resistance remained. Not only was Deng allowed to retain his Party membership despite Mao's strictures, but no sweeping purge of Deng's associates was allowed.[128] Moreover, Politburo members began to plot secretly with Deng. Xu Shiyou reportedly escorted Deng to South China following the Tiananmen incident, and over the next few months Deng met with various leaders, including Xu, Ye, and Wei Guoqing. With Mao's demise clearly impending, these leaders prepared for a military and political showdown with the "Gang of Four."[129] Thus as Mao's life ebbed away, some of the regime's highest officials conspired with the man he had recently declared unworthy; yet none of the conspirators were prepared to act against the dying leader himself.

Mao's authority had been weakened by a variety of factors. In addition to physical incapacity, his political judgment was clearly rejected by a majority of his colleagues; they saw Mao pursuing a course seriously detrimental to the performance of China's socialist system and opted for strikingly different policies. Mao's personality cult, while still significant, waned somewhat in this period, but as before this was not a major consideration within top CCP circles in any case. Moreover, the dangers involved in rejecting legality had been painfully brought home to the elite, which now sought to revive formal procedures to the extent possible. Even more significant were traditional concepts of the proper relationship between a monarch and his ministers—concepts which both strengthened Zhou's hand and gave some backbone to wavering Politburo members in the period following Zhou's death. Yet for all this, Mao's authority was still substantial—enough to unseat a powerful figure and undermine the legally sanctioned policies of the state. Revolutionary success over feudalism and national victory over imperialism (as well as resonance with the establishment of a new dynasty) remained a potent force despite the disasters of what would soon be known as the "ten bad years." It was still sufficient to keep Mao on the throne to the end and make his wishes a dynamic factor in Chinese politics, but not enough to command full obedience or prevent his comrades from planning a reversal of the course he had set in his last decade.

The Post-Mao Search for Legitimacy

By the time of Mao's death the communist regime faced a severe legitimacy crisis. As we have seen, from the late 1950s on, the confidence of major segments of society in the system had been shaken. In particular, the turmoil and shocks of the 1966-1976 decade not only weakened the support of many social groups but opened an ever-widening credibility gap for many ordinary CCP members and regime officials. To a certain extent the efforts of the post-Mao leadership to restore order in society and promote "stability and unity" within the elite alleviated the problem, but as the 1980s began, official sources increasingly spoke of crises of faith, confidence, and trust.[130]

These crises reflected not only the lingering disillusionment of the Maoist era but also problems generated by the emerging post-1976 policies. For those elements both in society and the bureaucracy who remained loyal to Mao's precepts, the policy directions of the new leaders often seemed dangerously "revisionist." More significantly, those alienated by the Maoist experience also had their confidence in the new leadership shaken by post-Mao developments. As contacts with the outside world grew, both populace and cadres became increasingly aware of superior living conditions not only in the capitalist West but also in regional states, including Taiwan. Particularly damaging to faith in the system was widespread bureaucratic corruption, a phenomenon owing to both opportunities created by the disruption of orderly procedures during 1966-1976 and to the determination of those who had suffered during the Cultural Revolution to gain compensation by any means possible. As a result of these and related factors, post-Mao society has been marked by open disbelief in the superiority of social- ism, widespread contempt for those wishing to join the Party, a view of officials as a self-seeking exploitative class, and pervasive political indifference. As indicated by the extensive official corruption, such cynical attitudes have deeply penetrated the Party and state structure as well. The net result has been that while the system has endured it has not regained the fundamental legitimacy of earlier days when, in Deng Xiaoping's exaggerated words, "The Central Committee uttered one word and the whole country acted accordingly."[131]

The post-Mao situation created authority problems within the top elite in a different sense. For this elite there were few real questions about the legitimacy of the regime of which they were the main benefi- ciaries. The prompt arrest of the "Gang of Four" within a month of Mao's death and the new emphasis on "stability and unity" within the leadership eliminated the most disturbing features of the system for this group as a whole. As time wore on, some members of the leadership had doubts about the "revisionist" nature of the unfolding policy line,[132] but there is little to indicate any strong sense in these circles that the Politburo and Central Committee majorities lacked the author- ity to make the decisions in question. The major problem at this level, a problem intensified by the diverse groupings of officials on the top bodies (see the final essay below), was to agree on who should be on those bodies as they were reconstituted after Mao, who should be the primary leader of the Party, what degree of authority that leader should have, and what principles should legitimate his position.

The Succession of Hua Guofeng. When Hua Guofeng was named CCP chairman shortly after the arrest of the "Gang of Four" in early October 1976, the decision was undoubtedly taken by the remaining members of the Politburo. Nevertheless, in the circumstances, it was a decision compatible with the immediate political needs of the top elite as a whole. The passing of a leader commonly produces an impulse for his successors to pull together and present a united face to both domes- tic and foreign audiences. This impulse was felt even more strongly than usual after the month-long delay while the final struggle against the "Gang" was concluded. Hua was the obvious choice for the posi- tion of leader at the time. Hua was acceptable both to the old line Party and state administrators with whom he had worked closely in the mid- 1970s and to those like himself who had risen dramatically as a result of the Cultural Revolution. Equally significant, Hua provided a desperately needed sense of continuity with the immediate past. Given that the regime had staked its claims to legitimacy over the preceding decade heavily in terms of Mao and his Thought, the fact that Hua could plausibly claim to be Mao's choice as successor was a strong plus. While it could be argued that Hua's link to Mao was no virtue in the eyes of major social groups who had suffered from the preceding decade of strife, clearly the connection was important for the many millions of Chinese who continued to hold Mao in esteem. In addition, Hua's formal appointment as the second ranking leader of the regime by the "Central Committee" during Mao's last months further made him the logical candidate. For considerations of continuity and stability, therefore, the leadership coalesced around Hua's appointment as new Party chairman. But this did not mean a grant of deeper legitimacy to Hua; nor could it remove doubts about his initial selection as successor.

Much remains uncertain about this initial designation. It apparently took place in April following the Tiananmen incident when Deng was formally ousted. Not only was Hua named premier, he was also chosen first vice-chairman of the CCP, a position never hitherto created. He thus stood clearly above all other Politburo members, the heir apparent. Who made the decision? Although a Central Committee plenum was not convened, it was formalized by a "Central Committee resolution," which said Hua's appointment was approved "unanimously on the proposal of our great leader Chairman Mao."[133] This could cover several possibilities. By far the most likely is that Mao simply selected Hua, with the Politburo giving its grudging consent under the pressure of events in Beijing's main square.[134] Much less likely but not totally implausible is that Mao preferred someone else[135] but in the face of Politburo resistance consented to accept Hua, who had played a major role in developing the policies of Zhou and Deng throughout 1975.[136] This in effect would have represented a compromise of sorts in which Mao not only gained Deng's removal but also the appointment of a man who upheld the Chairman's policies and prestige in the past,[137] while the Politburo majority secured the elevation of an experienced Party administrator. Whatever the reality, the April decision had the appearance of providing Hua with both hereditary charisma and traditional succession through Mao's "proposal," and legal-rational legitimacy through the Politburo and Central Committee actions. But these were shaky foundations at best, given doubts about the dying Mao's actual views[138] and his capacity to make a rational judgment, on the one hand, and the absence of a Central Committee plenum plus the extraordinary circumstances of the decision, on the other.

Although Hua's position as chairman was legally sanctioned—again in questionable fashion—by another "Central Committee resolution" in October 1976, the initial effort to bolster his legitimacy as leader relied heavily on charismatic and traditional themes. Here the perceived need to secure public support was particularly important. A claimed continuity with Mao was a major theme for both Hua and the regime as a whole; among the first acts of the new leadership were to announce a burial hall for the late Chairman and the publication of Volume V of his works.[139] With regard to Hua personally, great emphasis was placed on his being Mao's "worthy successor" and personal choice. The now famous note Mao assertedly gave Hua earlier in the year declaring that "With you in charge, I'm at ease" was widely reported,[140] with copies of Mao's disintegrating calligraphy and portraits of the scene also disseminated broadly. In addition to such hereditary charisma, Hua's own "exceptional qualities" received considerable attention. He was praised as the nation's "wise leader" and particularly hailed for decisive action in saving the Party from the clutches of the "Gang of Four." In addition, at the 1977 Party Congress where Hua finally gained proper legal-rational backing through formal election, Ye Jianying declared Hua the man capable of "lead-[ing] our Party . . . triumphantly into the twenty-first century" and thus of achieving the fundamental goal of socialist modernization.[141]

These claims formed the basis of a minicult of Hua which lasted well into 1978. Yet it is important to analyze further the content of Hua's cult. In many respects it more resembled the traditional themes of the posthumous praise of Zhou Enlai than the heroic terms still applied to Mao. Hua was portrayed as "loyal, selfless, open and straightforward, modest and prudent"—a human-sized characterization which followed almost word for word Deng's eulogy at Zhou's funeral.[142] Thus despite some charismatic claims, much of Hua's cult actually pointed to a leader of limited authority among his comrades. But Hua's immediate problem was less to expand his authority than to sustain support for his position as chairman.

Such support could not be taken for granted. While the asserted link to Mao attempted with mixed results to legitimize both Hua's position and that of the new leadership as a whole in the eyes of the populace, it could hardly convince the top elite. Although it is conceivable that some leaders saw Mao's presumed wishes as a legitimating factor,[143] even figures strongly loyal to Mao did not accept the late Chairman's

right to designate a successor. This view, which encompassed an assertion of legal norms of legitimacy, was strongly put by Politburo members Xu Shiyou and Wei Guoqing in February 1977:

> We have . . . the Party constitution and also the state constitution. They
> have set forth clearly the procedures for choosing the Party Chair-
> man. . . . Comrade Hua Geofeng came into office . . . without the prior
> convening of a national Party Congress, or even a plenary session of the
> Party Central Committee. This can only be seen as an arrangement made
> in the absence of any alternative as well as a consequence of the struggle
> against . . . the "Gang of Four." The entire Party and army and the
> people of the whole nation can accept this point. We need not emphasize to
> excess that Comrade Hua Guofeng's appointment . . . is based on the
> short phrase "With you in charge, I'm at ease" written by Chairman
> Mao. No matter how attractive the phrase is, it is at most an indication of
> Chairman Mao's personal intention and cannot be seen as a reflection of
> what the Party, the army, and the people have in mind.[144]

Although Xu and Wei were not challenging Hua's position in the
immediate context, they were raising a series of issues which underlined the uncertain nature of his legitimacy as leader. Apart from the
central questions of the validity of Mao's preferences and the absence
of proper legal procedures, another potential issue was the personality
cult, which so heavily emphasized Mao's imprimatur. If, as argued
above, Mao's cult had been divisive and unpersuasive within the top
elite, Hua's minicult could hardly carry much weight even among
leaders who genuinely admired his decisiveness in crushing the
"Gang." When Hua eventually was demoted from the chairmanship in
1981, the distaste for such cults among the leadership as a whole was
reflected in strong attacks on Hua's 1976-78 version. Yet at the time,
the issue seems to have been latent; there was little in the subsequent
attacks to indicate that major opposition to the cult had formed before
the December 1978 Central Committee plenum.[145] Indeed, it remains
uncertain precisely who pushed the personality cult. While Hua had an
obvious interest in enhancing his own image—and clearly contributed
to it through such devices as adopting a Mao-style haircut—it is by no
means clear that he acted alone in promoting the cult. Since Hua's link
to Mao was perceived as important for *regime* legitimacy, it is plausible
that other leaders were active in the venture and some—e.g., Vice-
Chairman Ye Jianying at the 1977 Party Congress—quite clearly gave
fulsome praise to Hua. In any case, from Hua's perspective, the point
of the cult was less to persuade the top leaders of his legitimacy in any
strict sense than to reiterate to them his political importance for the

stability of the system as a whole. And, of course, the more the cult was propagated, the seemingly more difficult it would be to remove Hua without threatening that stability. Yet by using (or allowing to be used) a personality cult, Hua was vulnerable to widespread sentiment that such devices really had little justification in a properly run socialist system.

Another issue, raised subsequently in Xu and Wei's statement, was the belief held widely in the elite that Deng Xiaoping had been wrongly dealt with by Mao in early 1976. As we have seen, this sentiment had clearly motivated both resistance to Mao's wishes and plotting outside formal Party councils in anticipation of the post-Mao struggle with the "Gang of Four." While those pressing Deng's case after the fall of the "Gang" asked only for his restoration to the leadership *body* rather than his designation as *the* leader, clearly there was widespread sentiment that the carefully arranged succession of Deng to Zhou's post (and by extension to Mao's) was the legitimate arrangement and that circumstances had made Hua something of a usurper.[146] The essentially traditional nature of Deng's claims will be examined in the following section; here it is enough to note that the substantial belief that Deng had been unjustly denied his due was yet another threat to Hua's position from the outset.

Given the revulsion within the elite over the lawlessness of the preceding decade, it was not surprising that the new leadership placed heavy emphasis on legality not only in society but within the Party as well. Irregular practices such as the use of the public security apparatus to handle inner-Party discipline were banned, while institutional approaches were revitalized as in the establishment of commissions for inspecting discipline.[147] Moreover, the long-standing Party norms which had been cast aside during the Cultural Revolution were resoundingly endorsed. Heavy stress was put on the need for inner-Party democracy. The 1977 Congress reaffirmed minority rights by calling on Party members to "say all you know and say it without reserve," and it further guaranteed both the right to criticize Party leaders and to reserve opinions once a decision was made. Furthermore, the Congress decreed that all decisions were to be made collectively and tendencies toward one man rule resisted.[148] Thus even in the early post-Mao period, despite the personality cult, legal-rational limits on the authority of the leader were strongly reaffirmed. Both charismatic and traditional appeals may have been accepted as necessary to muster support for the system as a whole, but the elite was in no mood to grant anything like the authority which had been so harshly turned against it in the 1966-1976 decade.

Looking back on the period of Hua's "wise leadership," it is clear that Hua represented the interests of some in the elite and was an acceptable stopgap for many others. But as suggested there was little sense within the elite as a whole that he had any unchallengeable right to the position of leader, much less any broad authority over the affairs of state. Not only did other leaders fail to perceive any genuine charisma—as opposed to talent—in Hua, but their experience with Mao's untrammeled charismatic mode of operation had left them deeply reluctant to cede such authority ever again. Synthetic cults similarly raised misgivings, although Hua's minicult was tolerated in view of larger perceived interests. Tradition both sustained and restricted Hua. He was sustained in the eyes of the elite less by any sense that Mao had a right to designate a successor than by a belief that to remove Mao's chosen heir would be a culturally unacceptable slap at the dead "dynastic founder."[149] But at the same time, Hua was restrained by those elements of tradition—reflected in the Zhou Enlai content of his cult—which called for consultation and consensus rule. Hua was similarly limited by the legal-rational rules, imperfect as they were, of collective leadership; yet as with tradition, he also gained support from this factor. As elected leader—and there could be no doubt on this score after the 1977 Party Congress—he had a certain right to the position of chairman which, if hardly decisive, at least provided some protection. Particularly in view of the absence of any clearly established procedure for removing a chairman, any action against Hua, although not excessively difficult politically, would be embarrassing in terms of legitimacy (see below).

In sum, although the various legitimating principles contained elements of support for Hua's position, the contrary pulls within them—as well as the more strictly political considerations discussed in the third essay below—emphasized the weakness of his position. But the most important factor undermining Hua was the return of Deng Xiaoping to an active leadership role in mid-1977. With Deng back in the Politburo, Hua's formal position as leader was quickly overshadowed by Deng's emergence as *de facto* leader. As the final essay analyzes in detail, Hua was reduced to seeking to retain his position in the leadership body. In the meantime, and in the post-Hua period as well, the real and formal positions of leader lay in different hands.

The Preeminence of Deng Xiaoping. After making the necessary self-criticism—necessary to mollify both those opposed to him and those feeling Mao's reputation must be upheld as a matter of propriety[150]—Deng was reelected to all the posts he had held at the time of Zhou's death by the August 1977 Party Congress. More importantly, it soon became apparent that Deng rather than Hua was the driving force behind the new modernization program. Even during the period of Hua's cult, according to the testimony of those who observed the two leaders together, Hua adopted a deferential attitude toward his older colleague.[151] Later, when Hua was removed from the chairmanship, the great majority of the elite wanted Deng to finally assume the formal position of leader,[152] although he refused for reasons to be examined later. At that time, the new chairman, Hu Yaobang, accurately summed up the leadership situation since Deng's reinstatement in mid-1977:

> . . . over the past years four comrades have been of major usefulness: [Ye] Jianying, [Deng] Xiaoping, [Li] Xiannian, and Chen Yun—especially Comrade Xiaoping. This is no secret. Even foreigners know that Comrade Xiaoping is the primary decision-maker in China's Party today. Sometimes they use another term, calling him the "primary architect." But whatever he is called, the meaning is the same.[153]

What was the basis of the elite's acceptance of Deng as the primary decision-maker? Clearly Deng's position rests on the support of a broad majoritarian coalition within the leadership as a whole (see the following essay, pp. 119ff, for an analysis of this coalition). Such support is based on the belief that strong—although not arbitrary—leadership is needed as China charts a new course in the post-Mao era and that Deng is the man to provide it. It has been and remains support which can be withdrawn in the face of policy failure or excessive damage to elite interests, but once given by such broad consensus, it conveys a sense of legitimacy to Deng in performing the leader's role of setting the agenda, mediating disputes, and providing overall direction. Given the strong elite interest in stability—and the absence of regularized mechanisms for a change in leadership—such support and concomitant legitimacy are unlikely to be withdrawn, barring severe failures or excesses. But the legitimacy granted to Deng is more that of position or role than that of authoritative command. Under the collective norms reasserted before Deng's reinstatement and strongly supported by him since his return, no leader can have unchecked authority. The period of Deng's leadership has been marked not only by assertions that decisions should be reached by consensus with divisive issues put off until agreement emerges, but by evidence that such an approach does generally prevail.[154] This, of course, does not mean that Deng (or other leaders) have no right to issue directives; in any collective arrangement, discretionary authority must be exercised to keep the system operating, and available information suggests that Deng has a considerable amount of such authority.[155] But in matters of general policy, Deng must prevail by persuasion, maneuver, or compromise rather than command—a situation also discussed more fully in the concluding essay.

Clearly, Deng's political support and hence legitimacy derive to a significant degree from performance considerations—his reputation as a dynamic official of great talents (the "living encyclopedia" as he was sarcastically referred to during the Cultural Revolution[156]). But this only goes part of the way toward explaining Deng's acceptance as leader. However exhalted his reputation or actual capabilities, neither could generate true charisma in the Weberian sense since Deng played only a supporting role in the revolutionary struggle. Moreover, legal-rational considerations, although bolstering Deng in the performance of specific roles—e.g., as PLA chief of staff—hardly support his claims as overall leader given the absence of the formal office. And a personality cult has largely been eschewed.

The key, then, lies in several considerations which have strong traditional aspects. First, as already indicated, Deng was seen as the rightful heir to Zhou Enlai, the official clearly designated by Zhou as his successor with the broad support of old-line Party and state administrators. Wall posters after Mao's death undoubtedly reflected deeply held elite opinions that Deng had been a heroic figure in defending Zhou's line and even "a living Zhou."[157] But beyond Zhou, and ultimately more significant, were Deng's links to Mao. Although twice purged by Mao, Deng's supporters could point to Mao's approval of Deng in personally sanctioning his rehabilitation in 1973. Moreover, part of the 1980 criminal indictment against the "Gang of Four"—ironically at a time when Hua's position was under attack as the result of an illegal "feudal" appointment—was the charge that the "Gang" had tried to dissuade Mao from naming Deng first vice-premier in 1974.[158] More fundamentally, Deng had unmatchable prestige as the leading survivor of that small band of men who had been identified as Mao's "close comrades-in-arms" before the Cultural Revolution.[159] Here the key factors were status and seniority—hallmarks of traditional legitimacy and Chinese political culture. Deng had achieved the highest status possible in the days when Mao had by and large fulfilled his duties as a just ruler, and that status was now convertible into a claim for leadership.

The traditional nature of Deng's support is further underlined by the nature of the elite conferring leadership on him. Up until 1966, there had been a substantial overlap between formal institutional power and personal influence based on prestige. That is, those who possessed informal influence because of their status as revolutionary leaders also monopolized the key bureaucratic positions of the regime. This reinforcement of traditional and legal-rational modes was cut asunder by the Cultural Revolution. Now, large numbers of honored revolutionaries were demoted or cast out of official positions altogether, while many high-ranking positions were filled by those with inferior status. Even after substantial rehabilitations, by the time of Mao's death a substantial corps of prestigious Communists were on the sidelines of political life, but they retained influence. Moreover, there was the sense that this larger elite had a rightful say in the reshaping of the leadership after the fall of the ''Gang of Four.'' Deng's reemergence cannot be explained in terms of the political interests of a Politburo majority in late 1976. More members of this rump Politburo had reason to fear Deng's return than to welcome it.[160] While the Central Committee undoubtedly included a larger proportion who would identify their interests with Deng's, in the circumstances of a ten-year erosion of institutional authority, it was the larger informal elite that was decisive. The measures finally worked out to restore Deng reflected the need of the Politburo to secure support from the influentials who had made the Chinese revolution; it was not a numbers game within a Central Committee containing many members who could not be taken seriously.[161] Those influencials, in turn, regarded the pre-Cultural Revolution period when Deng had both ranking position and status as the point of reference for getting China back on a proper course. Their support for Deng, then, reflected both the respect for seniority of Chinese tradition and a sense of proper status within the traditions and history of the CCP.

Uncertain Moves Toward Legal-Rationality. Although Deng's preeminence must be explained in traditional terms, part of his program strongly emphasizes the desirability of legal-rational norms both to promote societal modernization and to protect Party stability. As indicated earlier, much of the present analysis of Mao's arbitrary behavior focuses on China's feudal past and the lack of a tradition of legality. Moreover, although the CCP has had its own rules, the official verdict is that "for various historical reasons, we failed to institutionalize and legalize inner-Party democracy . . . , or we drew up the relevant laws but they lacked due authority."[162] To rectify this situation Deng has argued strongly that reliance on persons must be replaced by institutions and procedures:

> A sound system can prevent would-be evil doers from running amuck; under a bad system even good people will be unable to do things well and . . . may, in fact, move in the opposite direction. . . . If we do not improve the socialist system right now, people will ask why the socialist system cannot solve problems that the capitalist system can. . . . When Stalin seriously disrupted the socialist system, Comrade Mao Zedong said that such a thing could not have happened in the Western countries. . . . He [Mao] recognized that point, but because the question of system was not really solved . . . the ten years of great calamity brought by the "Great Cultural Revolution" came as a result. This lesson is a very poignant one. This is not saying that individuals do not have responsibilities; it is saying that the question of system is more fundamental, more comprehensive, and has a stabilizing effect and lasting nature.[163]

Deng's efforts to move the Chinese political system away from charismatic to legal-rational modes of legitimation have been wide-ranging, in some respects impressive, but ultimately flawed. In 1978 major steps were taken to undercut "religious" attitudes toward Mao and his ideas by advancing the slogan "practice is the sole criterion of truth," and by the end of the year the cults of Mao and Hua had been terminated.[164] The theme of legality has been reiterated even more strongly over the following four years, but China remains at a considerable distance from a genuinely legal-rational system. Deng has been thwarted by the constraints of Chinese culture, his own political needs, and the fundamental nature of socialist systems. These factors can be seen in the handling of three major issues: the historical verdict on Mao, the replacement of Hua by Hu Yaobang as CCP chairman, and the effort to impose constitutional restraints on authority.

The official evaluation of Mao Zedong has been one of the most intensely debated issues of recent years. The differing views toward Mao have reflected attitudes concerning policies favored by the late Chairman, calculations on how possible verdicts would affect individual careers, and deep feelings of loyalty or resentment based on personal experiences from the revolutionary period to the Cultural Revolution decade. Yet the formal verdict which finally emerged in mid-1981—a basically positive view of Mao as the great leader of the Chinese people whose personal brilliance more than once saved the Party despite serious errors over his last twenty years[165]—involved more than the balance of these forces; it reflected fundamental considerations of legitimacy as well. Here, it should be stressed, the critical factor was less legitimacy in the eyes of the masses than in the view of the elite itself. While concern with justifying the system to a population that had been exposed to decades of Mao glorification had been a major consideration following his death, by 1981 it was clear that broad sectors of society no longer held Mao's memory in any special esteem.[166] In contrast most of the top leadership still honored that memory.

In effect, the same considerations which sustained Mao's authority even through his most arbitrary periods were now supporting his posthumous reputation despite the attacks on feudal superstition. In part, cultural factors were again at play as reflected in Tan Zhenlin's complaint at the December 1978 Third Plenum about those who regarded criticism of Mao as "tantamount to being disrespectful . . . to the emperor . . . as well as a violation of Marxist-Leninist tenets."[167] The strong repugnance against dishonoring ancestors, particularly the founder of a dynasty, was further expressed in repeated statements by Chinese leaders that they would not do to Mao what Khrushchev had done to Stalin in the Soviet Union. Thus Xu Shiyou declared at the same plenum: "[I will be the first one to oppose imitating] the way Khrushchev moved Stalin's corpse out of Red Square to feed dogs, degraded him, and aired personal hatred of a dead person. . . ."[168] Even more important for the great bulk of the elite was that in their minds Mao still represented the Party and nation to which they had devoted their lives. Huang Kecheng, who had himself been unfairly dismissed by Mao along with Peng Dehuai at Lushan, forcefully stated this view: "For years, Chairman Mao has been . . . the symbol of the Chinese revolution—this tallies with the fact. To defame and distort him will only end in defaming and distorting our Party and our socialist motherland. . . ."[169] Despite the attempt to cut Mao down to size and declare his Thought the collective wisdom of the Party, such leaders could not separate Mao from the revolution which in their eyes legitimated the PRC. The rejection of Mao's arbitrariness notwithstanding, the reaffirmation of him as "the greatest national hero in Chinese history"[170] tacitly accepted the charismatic claims which had been the basis of Mao's authority. Mao remains forever legitimized by the victory of 1949.

Despite the overall positive evaluation of Mao, the critical aspects of the assessment had dire implications for Hua Guofeng. Even as the verdict was being drafted, attacks on Mao's "illegal, feudal practice" of personally designating successors were published in September 1980. By this time the Politburo was discussing alleged shortcomings in Hua's performance as leader and criticizing his earlier personality cult. By November Politburo pressure on Hua increased and he offered his resignation, suggesting that Deng assume the chairmanship. Although there was virtual unanimity in support of Deng, Deng himself declined the post and nominated his longtime protégé, Hu Yaobang, undoubtedly to bolster Hu's chances of eventually succeeding him. This move apparently met some opposition, but after a few days "everyone finally agreed."[171] (Although the post of chairman was abolished at the Twelfth CCP Congress in September 1982, Hu formally remains the top leader as Party general secretary and ranking member of the Politburo Standing Committee.)

The attacks on Mao's feudal ways and Hua's cult notwithstanding, the removal of Hua and his replacement by Hu left much to be desired from a legal-rational viewpoint. Not only were the decisive moves against Hua apparently carried out entirely within the Politburo rather than the Central Committee, which had the formal power to pass on such matters, but also, as in Mao's time, out-of-favor members of the Politburo were excluded from the proceedings.[172] Moreover, once the deed had been accomplished, confusion reigned as to precisely how it should be presented. Given the emphasis on legal-rationality and the absence of a Central Committee plenum, it was officially conceded that Hua was "still our chairman." But he was clearly on the way out, a fact lamely explained by Deng as the "kind of changes [which] happen in any country" rather than in terms of CCP procedures.[173] In addition, when the Central Committee finally demoted Hua in June 1981, it was not enough to vote him out of office. Instead, the historical document passing judgment on Mao also contained a section detailing Hua's alleged errors, and a brief press campaign attacking the former chairman followed. This not only contained echoes of traditional attitudes about the moral virtues of rulers, but followed the long-established precedent of communist regimes to denigrate those out of favor. Given the lack of binding procedures, such systems require a mythology of failure to justify leadership changes. Communist systems, moreover, prevent such procedures from emerging, given the basically cooptive nature of Central Committee membership. Although legally the Central Committee elects the Politburo and the leader, in fact—where institutions are not fractured by a Cultural Revolution—the Politburo and Party Secretariat basically select the Central Committee. With these institutional patterns reinforced by several years of emphasis on legal-rationality, Deng now forced a change in the chairmanship with scant regard for the formal authority of the Central Committee.

In pushing through Hu's elevation, Deng was clearly motivated by the desire to secure the succession of a loyal comrade who would carry forward his policies. But the apparent reluctance of the elite as a whole to accept Hu indicates not only Hu's political weakness but raises questions concerning the legitimacy actually conveyed. Reports of elite attitudes toward the leadership change indicate not only sympathy for Hua, whom many felt was being unfairly dealt with by Deng, but considerable doubts about Hu's claims. Some unfavorably compared Hu's achievements with Hua's role in crushing the ''Gang of Four''; others saw Deng imposing a member of his personal faction on the Party.[174] Deng was, in fact, to a substantial extent making the kind of personal choice of future leader for which Mao was being so bitterly criticized. But Deng had to persuade his Politburo colleagues to go along. In this, Hu's designation stands somewhere between that of Liu Shaoqi on the one hand and Lin Biao and Hua on the other. As in the case of Liu, the leader had secured the consent of the top elite in the choice of successor—but with much less conviction in the wisdom of the selection. The preference of significant numbers of PLA leaders is instructive: they reportedly would have preferred that Deng be the new chairman for reasons of seniority or that Hua retain the post because of his symbolic ties to Mao.[175] But if traditional factors fueled much of the discontent with the outcome, they ultimately supported the result. The appointment of Hu fundamentally was a concession to the demands of a leader who had the acknowledged status to fulfill that role. It reflected Deng's legitimacy rather than bestowing any broadly based legitimacy on Hu for the post-Deng era.

While making leadership changes in a highly personal manner, Deng continued to press for a tightening up of the rules governing the system. As indicated above, the major thrust of those efforts was to restrict arbitrary personal power and define precisely the authority of institutions. In 1982 this process resulted in new Party and state constitutions, yet the results were clearly ambiguous at best in legal-rational terms. This can be illustrated by examining some key components of the exercise: the elimination of an overconcentration of power by stressing collective norms; the attempt to eliminate the lifelong tenure of leaders; and the effort to construct institutional checks and balances. The emphasis on collective leadership, of course, has a long pedigree in CCP doctrine, if not always in practice. These values have been strongly asserted in the new legal documents but not fully reflected in their provisions, and more importantly, in the accompanying political arrangements. The clearest example of this in the new legal structure is the establishment by the state constitution of a Central Military Commission (CMC) to lead the armed forces. This commission, which is only briefly described in the document, is to be run by "the system of decision by its chairman"[176]—and clearly that chairman is meant to be Deng Xiaoping. Moreover, despite repeated emphasis on the need to separate leading Party and state personnel, explanations of the new Party constitution state that for the time being leadership of the Party MAC headed by Deng can overlap with that of the CMC.[177] Finally, in terms of appointments made at the 1982 Party Congress, the aged Deng was not only reconfirmed as head of the MAC and a Politburo Standing Committee member, he was also named chairman of the newly created Central Advisory Commission (CAC). In addition, the heads of other key Party bodies (the Secretariat and the Commission for Discipline Inspection) were now required to sit on the Politburo Standing Committee, and the premier of the State Council was also reaffirmed on that body by the new elections.[178] Thus the concentration of power at the top remains as strong as ever.

A more novel approach to the problem of excessive personal power has been a major drive since 1980 to end the established practice of leaders and bureaucrats generally staying at their posts for the duration of their lives. Considerable progress has been made particularly in replacing aged personnel in the State Council[179] and in persuading veteran leaders to give up their various posts and join the new advisory commissions. But what has emerged is considerably less sweeping than some of the earlier proposals: e.g., in August 1980 Deng declared that "no leadership positions should have an indefinite tenure."[180] When the new Party constitution was unveiled, however, it was evident that there would be important exceptions. New Politburo member Hu Qiaomu addressed the issue candidly:

> . . . [I]t is necessary that the central leading core of our Party has some veteran comrades who . . . are . . . good at handling various complicated situations and who enjoy high prestige in the Party and among the people for their great contributions. Only in this way can the maturity and stability of the leadership . . . be guaranteed. . . . Also only in this way

can the state maintain prolonged stability. . . . Therefore, after repeated conscientious discussions in the process of revising the Constitution of the Party, we finally decided not to set strict limits on the term of office for leading cadres. The term of office for each person will be decided according to his or her own situation.[181]

As in other contexts, the day was carried by seniority, prestige, and the belief that the fate of the Party outweighed any procedural considerations.

A similarly unsatisfactory outcome awaited Deng's efforts to establish institutional checks and balances. Again, Deng made far-reaching proposals in August 1980. He reportedly advocated setting up three parallel bodies—the Central Committee, a central disciplinary commission, and a central advisory commission—with clearly defined limits of authority which would "check, restrain, and supervise one another." If disputes were to arise among these bodies a joint conference would be held to thrash out differences. If that failed, a Party Congress would be convened to make a binding decision.[182] The three bodies were affirmed when the new Party constitution emerged two years later, but in a far looser form than originally advocated by Deng. The CAC and disciplinary commission were placed squarely under the leadership of the Central Committee, thus affirming the traditional locus of formal power. Also, the role envisioned is one of consultation and assistance rather than supervision and checking.[183] Yet the new CAC is not without political significance for traditional rather than legal-rational reasons. With the retirement of aged leaders, a new process of separating legal power and informal influence is under way. Leaders such as Xu Shiyou who have given up Politburo or Central Committee membership to join the new commission retain their status as revolutionary figures. In the transitional period ahead, their voices are likely to be far more influential than what might be assumed from a formal organizational table.

If the actual results of Deng's fascination with legal-rational notions have been disappointing, they have not been without effect. The repeated emphasis on avoiding arbitrariness has had an impact despite the inability of the leadership for systemic reasons to give it binding content. The PRC, like all communist systems, remains unable to deal with the question of power—of how to regularize procedures for the selection of not only the leader but the leadership as a whole. But larger forces have pushed the system in the direction of constraints, if not precise legal limits. Most importantly, the charismatic leader is dead, and no one else can make the same claims for obedience. Moreover, an elite which has suffered from the excesses of such a leader moves to prevent a repeat performance. This has been apparent in the post-Stalin Soviet Union and, following the somewhat individualistic leadership of Khrushchev, was particularly pronounced under the Brezhnev regime, where collective principles were reflected in broad consultation within the elite.[184] Yet, as Khrushchev's case and, in more restrained fashion, Deng's case indicate, considerable scope is still open to a strong leader.

In the Chinese case, the limits which do operate on the leader are both those of political calculation (see the concluding essay) and the sense of restraint generated not only by legal-rational stipulations but particularly by traditional notions of propriety. These provide no guarantees, yet Deng Xiaoping is restricted in action by concepts rooted in both Chinese culture and the particular traditions of the CCP, while at the same time his leadership is legitimized by those very forces. The legitimacy of the leader within the elite in China today has moved decisively away from a charismatic basis toward a mix of legal-rational and traditional considerations, with the traditions of the communist revolutionaries themselves providing the most potent support. As this founding generation dies off, the mix will inevitably be altered once again.

III
NORMATIVE AND PRUDENTIAL RULES UNDER AND AFTER MAO

This concluding essay analyzes the political strategies of leading figures in the CCP Politburo during Mao's rule and in the post-Mao
period.[1] It investigates the requirements for maintaining and enhancing
one's position during radically different periods of Mao's tenure—both
the pre-Cultural Revolution years of comparatively limited elite conflict and the turbulent 1966-1976 decade when politics often resembled, and in significant instances literally were, a life-and-death struggle. In the first period politics were essentially conservative despite
major innovations and radical policies; the name of the game was
retaining one's position and influence as opportunities for rapid advance were few and far between. In the latter decade, in contrast,
opportunities now opened up which led various figures to adopt high
risk strategies for advancement, while the bulk of the top elite initially
sought merely to survive the unprecedented upheaval and then maneu-
vered to prevent the dominance of those who had risen dramatically
during the Cultural Revolution. The post-Mao period has seen a shift to
more restrained politics where maintaining position or regaining power
lost after 1966 is central to political calculations. The politics of succession, and of resolving the accumulated tensions of 1966-1976, necessarily meant a more fluid situation than existed before the Cultural
Revolution, but the broad support for Deng Xiaoping as *de facto* leader
has allowed the elite to avoid the instability of a full-fledged succession
struggle.

In examining the strategies adopted by various leaders under these
changing circumstances, the following analysis focuses on two sets of
"rules"—one normative and the other prudential. Normative rules,
which include the leadership principles discussed under legal-rational

authority in the preceding essay, are those official guidelines laying out how elite politics should be conducted and what activities are beyond the pale. In a strictly formal sense these rules have changed little since the 1940s and were even reaffirmed in the Party constitutions of the 1966-1976 period. Nevertheless, as we have seen, the Cultural Revolution in practice negated existing norms; moreover, the CCP constitutions of 1969 and 1973 contained elements incompatible with the principles those documents reaffirmed. The persistent effort to restore traditional Party principles since Mao's death underlines the depth of the elite's commitment to these normative rules. While Mao had in effect suspended the norms during the last decade of his life, his successors moved rapidly to recreate an environment where accepted principles provided a more predictable basis for political calculation.[2]

Prudential rules—those rules of thumb about the types of behavior likely to result in success—are generally widely understood by leading participants in any established political system. These understandings are based on experience and practice; over time, high-level politicians and other actors learn what methods can build support and get things done. The rules which evolve are rooted in several sources—the institutional arrangements of the system (which in the Chinese case bear strong resemblance to those of the Soviet Union), the particular traditions of the dominant elite, and the prevailing political culture. Yet while implying an established pattern, prudential rules are usually more subject to change than normative rules in response to shifting social forces, unanticipated events, and new power configurations within the elite itself.[3] In the case of post-1949 China, where the fluctuating fortunes of normative rules have been so great, prudential considerations have necessarily undergone sudden and dramatic alteration at the critical junctures of the Cultural Revolution and the post-Mao transition. Nevertheless, the post-Mao moves to restore not only the normative rules but more generally major features of the pre-Cultural Revolution pattern of politics, as well as efforts of different actors to apply variants of earlier political strategies even during the 1966-1976 decade, point to the significance of identifiable prudential rules throughout the history of the PRC.

Normative Rules and Prudential Politics

In addition to collective leadership and minority rights, which are discussed in the second essay above, the CCP's normative rules of leadership behavior include several other principles of critical importance.[4] One of the most basic is Leninist discipline, the insistence that majority decisions and higher-level orders must be strictly implemented regardless of one's own views. Another is the ban on "factional" activities—the banding together outside normal Party channels to seek power or advantage for a particular subgroup within the elite at the expense of other groups. Finally, a fundamental normative rule common to all communist systems declares the institutional subordination of the military to civilian authority[5]—in Mao's words, "Our principle is that the Party commands the gun, and the gun must never be allowed to command the Party."[6]

Alongside these basic norms various prudential rules took shape as the new system developed after 1949. At the most general level these rules or requirements for political success correspond to those for Leninist regimes as a whole, and indeed for virtually all political systems. T. H. Rigby has called attention to three such basic requirements.[7] First, high-ranking politicians must be seen as capable of "delivering the goods" by those able to influence their fortunes, whether they be colleagues on formal bodies or in informal groupings, hierarchical superiors, or (in non-Leninist contexts) electors. The "goods" actually "delivered" may be quite diverse, but in the Chinese case they certainly include the capacity to take charge of troublesome programs, offer sound policy advice, and effectively administer large organizations. A second requirement is the development of a network of supporters, strategically placed political actors who identify their interests with those of the leading politician and will back him (or her) at times of conflict or crisis. Finally, Rigby's third rule emphasizes skill in forming alliances both within the peer group—i.e., the Politburo in the case at hand—and with officials standing outside one's primary organization. Here policy coalitions based on compromised, shared, or complementary goals play a particularly significant role.

These general guidelines must be refined considerably to take account of both Leninist structural and specifically Chinese considerations. Moreover, as prudential rules are elaborated, the tension between them and the official norms of the system quickly becomes apparent. Figure 2 schematically outlines the sources of tension.

Perhaps the most central prudential rule of PRC elite politics has been the need to retain the confidence of the leader. This was unquestionably the case during Mao's lifetime and to a large extent remains valid, albeit in more restricted form, for the period of Deng Xiaoping's preeminence. In this respect, being capable of "delivering

Normative rules   Prudential rules

1. collective leadership   1. don't cross the leader

2. minority rights   2. maintain broad alliances

3. Leninist discipline   3. "deliver the goods" even if
                                                violating directives is required
                                             4. protect institutional interests

4. ban on factions   5. maintain *guanxi** networks
                                             6. develop patron-client ties

5. civilian control of military   7. maintain PLA support

◄ ─ ─ ─ ► lines of tension

*Personal relations derived from some common experience or social interaction.

Figure 2. Sources of Tension between Normative and Prudential Rules

the goods'' has above all meant being perceived as such by the leader. But as already discussed in the preceding essay,[8] the dominant or at least preeminent role of the leader obiously clashes with the norm of collective leadership. Similarly, standing on one's right to dissent from majority decisions is politically risky. Apart from clashing with the theoretical insistence on the correctness of the Party line and the practical necessity of maintaining pressure for the implementation of that line, exercising the right to criticize approved policies risks the antagonism of the leader and/or the Politburo majority. A top-level figure cannot afford to be constantly in the minority but must be able to fashion a majority alliance on at least some policy issues.

The fundamental Leninist principle of strict implementation of Party policies also conflicts with the demands of political prudence in important respects. The pressure on leading officials to ''deliver the goods'' in their spheres of responsibility while coping with limited resources and restrictive regulations often necessitates bending or flatly violating approved directives.[9] Official policies, moreover, are usually of such generality as to leave a great deal to the discretion of responsible administrators, a situation which leaves them open to criticism or worse *either* if they are unable to adjust those policies sufficiently to produce results *or* if their adaptations draw the ire of those committed to the original guidelines. A related source of tension is created by the need for top politicians to protect the interests of "their" institutions. In communist regimes Politburo figures usually have primary responsibility for one institution or a cluster of related organizations. Given a shared interest in institutional well being, officials serving in such organizations normally provide strong support for effective Politburo patrons. The overzealous pursuit of institutional interests, however, violates not only specific prohibitions as in the hoarding of scarce resources but also the more general notion that narrow bureaucratic interests must take second place to the larger interests assertedly embodied in the overall Party line. In this case, furthermore, prudential considerations also militate against the unabashed promotion of bureaucratic goals. For while a top politician must generally be seen as an effective protector of his bailiwick to be taken seriously, ultimately the support of the leader, the Politburo collective, and the elite as a whole outweighs that of bureaucratic subordinates in determining career prospects.[10]

The requirement of building personal support comes into conflict with the ban on factions. Quite apart from crisis situations where some form of factional plotting outside official bodies may be unavoidable, even under ordinary circumstances the need to maintain an extensive network of relationships and cultivate patron-client ties is in tension with the formal prohibition. Here it is necessary to distinguish between links based on the structural features of Leninist systems and those derived from Chinese cultural considerations and the CCP's own history. In the former case, patron-client ties are firmly linked to organizational hierarchies. Such ties develop during bureaucratic careers, and the measure of a successful Politburo politician is the ability to promote former subordinates to key positions in major institutions. This has been *the* means of developing a personal following in the Soviet Union and a factor of significance in the Chinese case as well. Within the CCP, however, the looser culturally based notion of *guanxi*, i.e., personal relations derived from some common experience or social interaction, is at least as important. This has particularly been the case for the first generation revolutionaries who have dominated China since 1949; for them, shared revolutionary struggles created mutual obligations potentially outweighing formal institutional connections. In any case, the clash of the injunction against factionalism with personal networks in either sense is mitigated by the fact that such ties are generally more tacit than explicit.[11] Bonds of mutual support develop organically in the course of political life without pledges of eternal loyalty. But even a less than explicit network must be worked at if a leading politician is to have adequate backing; yet an overly assiduous effort can backfire by alarming other leaders and leaving one open to the charge of factionalism.

Finally, the normative insistence on Party control of the gun sits uneasily with the major role played by the PLA in Chinese politics and the need for ranking CCP figures to secure the support or at least tolerance of the military. To a certain extent the civilian leadership of any country with a large military establishment, hostile international environment, and weak constitutional order must strive to keep the army on its side. In the Chinese case, however, the special features of the revolution served to give the PLA a rightful place in key political decisions under the PRC. Unlike the Soviet Union where the army had been created out of the czarist officer corps and remained an object of suspicion for many years,[12] the protracted armed struggle which marked the CCP's rise to power placed military men at the center of the revolutionary process. Thus it is natural that active as well as past army leaders have been well represented on the Politburo and other key Party bodies since 1949.[13] In this sense, the political clout of the PLA has had less to do with its monopoly of the instruments of coercion (although this was a major factor during the Cultural Revolution decade) than with the fact that army leaders make up a large segment of the overall revolutionary elite. Civilian control, then, means the PLA is bound to accept the decisions of the Politburo on military as well as political affairs, but the presence of army leaders on top CCP bodies and more generally their revolutionary status allows them a voice on a broad range of policy issues. None of this necessarily undermines Party control, but the political importance of PLA leaders—although a real threat to civilian rule only in 1967-1971—has always been a factor which no prudent politician could ignore.

The tension between normative and prudential rules under the PRC derives from a number of considerations. Most fundamental, as indicated in the previous essay,[14] is the relative weakness of formal rules, especially as manifested in the dominant role played by Mao in spite of the norm of collective leadership. This weakness reflects both the Marxist critique of bourgeois democracy—the ideological position that *who* rules is more important than the *procedures* of rule—and the Chinese emphasis on the personal qualities of rulers. More fundamentally, as lifelong revolutionaries, CCP leaders have consistently placed higher value on protecting the revolution than on formal restraints. This was not only the explicit position of such an "organization man" as Liu Shaoqi;[15] it remains the view of the post-Mao leadership despite its pervasive concern with restoring organizational regularity.[16]

Finally, the failure to come to grips with the issues of conflict and power has weakened the CCP's normative rules. Apart from failing to create truly binding mechanisms for settling leadership differences, the whole structure of official norms is based on the myth of a unified Party. Forged at a time of considerable unity in the 1940s, these norms assumed a degree of consensus which would not always be the case. Thus collective leadership was compatible with Mao's authority since the Chairman and his colleagues were assertedly united behind "correct" policies. Minority views could be tolerated because those holding such opinions were assumed to dissent from discrete policies while remaining faithful to the overall "line." The failure to implement strictly official programs was seen as largely shortcomings of "work style" which could be overcome by rectification mechanisms. And factional behavior, while abhorrent, was viewed as the doings of the renegade few rather than reflecting systemic problems. Thus the formal normative rules are not only ambiguous and politically fragile in the best of worlds, but are particularly inadequate for times of enhanced conflict. The successful politician cannot place too much faith in them but must instead be highly sensitive to the dictates of prudence.

The above considerations notwithstanding, the basic fact remains that the stronger the normative rules—i.e., the greater the extent to which they are enforced—the stronger (more reliable) prudential guidelines will be as well. If certain types of behavior are clearly acceptable, and others unacceptable, then political figures can make strategic or tactical choices with enhanced confidence. But where normative rules are observed only erratically or not at all, the basis for prudential calculation correspondingly becomes more uncertain. This relationship becomes clearer as we examine the efforts of leading politicians to protect and advance their interests during different periods since 1949.

Elite Politics Under Stable Maoism, 1949-1965

The period from the founding of the PRC to the Cultural Revolution was one of remarkable political stability at the top despite some significant deterioration starting in the late 1950s. As discussed in the second essay,[17] the latter years saw the gradual erosion of normative rules, while the associated uncertainty also meant prudential rules could no longer provide as sure guidance for political activity as in the past. Nevertheless, the predominant stability of high-level politics over the entire period is demonstrated by the fact that of the twenty-two men serving under Mao as full Politburo members from 1949 to 1965, only two—Gao Gang (1954) and Peng Dehuai (1959)—were disgraced, while a third, Chen Yun (1957-58), was quietly eclipsed.[18] Notwithstanding the problems of the final seven to eight years, this suggests that prudential and normative rules were sufficiently engrained to provide a generally predictable political environment before the onset of the Cultural Revolution.

Stability and predictability were fundamentally owing to Mao's political style—a style which contrasted dramatically with that of Stalin. The pre-Cultural Revolution Mao for the most part lacked Stalin's sickly suspicion of his colleagues.[19] Rather than sowing mutual distrust and seeking to divide and rule, the Chairman created an atmosphere where Politburo members could on the whole collectively and openly thrash out problems. Power was indeed diffused under Mao but not by setting Politburo members at each other's throats. Instead, the presence in the top body of individuals with diverse institutional support both bolstered Mao's power by leaving him as the sole focus of loyalty and at the same time encouraged cooperative relations within the highest elite. While policy differences, conflicting organizational interests, and some personal friction existed among these leaders, Mao's insistence on unity, and their own interest in a stable regime, kept tensions within bounds.

Mao's commitment to a vigorous political process was underlined by his choice of closest collaborators. These men, listed in Table 1,[20] were long-standing leaders of talent and achievement with their own extensive political networks, rather than relatively junior officials like those who had formed Stalin's Politburos. Most were key figures in the new CCP hierarchy that Mao constructed around himself in the early 1940s, an effort which consciously drew together diverse constituencies into a unified leadership capable of winning the final struggle against the Guomindang. Although Mao subsequently added close personal supporters to the inner core when he elevated Deng Xiaoping and Lin Biao in the 1950s[21] (and in Lin's case promoted a man of uncertain administrative capabilities[22]), basically he proved willing to work with

Table 1

Mao's Closest Collaborators, 1949-1965

	Main revolutionary constituencies	Main institutional constituencies	Early relationship to Mao	Demonstrated administrative capabilities
Liu Shaoqi (1931-66)	early trade unions "white areas" New Fourth Army Yanan	Party apparatus	ally from late 1930s	yes
Zhou Enlai (1927-76)	Whampoa Academy Jiangxi Soviet Long March diplomatic missions	State Council	opponent in early 1930s, then ally	yes
Chen Yun* (1945-66, 1978-)	early trade unions Jiangxi Soviet Long March Yanan	economic administration	apparent ally from early 1930s	yes
Lin Biao (1955-71)	Jinggangshan Jiangxi Soviet Long March Yanan Fourth Field Army	military	close supporter since late 1920s	?
Deng Xiaoping (1955-66, 1974-76, 1977-)	Jiangxi Soviet Long March Second Field Army	Party secretariat	close supporter since early 1930s	yes
Peng Zhen (1945-66, 1979-)	"white areas" Jin-Cha-Ji base Yanan	Party secretariat Beijing local apparatus	apparent first contact mid-1930s, then ally	yes

Dates indicate periods of Politburo membership.
*Out of effective power by 1958, briefly active 1961-62.

and delegate substantial power to leaders who were significant figures in their own right. While the Chairman's ultimate authority was never challenged within this group, the dynamics of the situation allowed for a considerable degree of give and take within the parameters of broadly understood normative and prudential rules.

In this context top-level politics dictated two key prudential rules: do not alienate Mao and maintain basically harmonious relations within the Politburo as a whole. Given the overall personnel stability of this period, politics was essentially *conservative*: leaders generally sought to maintain their position and influence or at best make modest advances rather than initiate bold bids for sharply enhanced power. The initial post-1949 case of a disgraced leader, Gao Gang, illustrates how the key prudential rules were violated and also how closely these were related to normative rules.[23] Gao, in anticipation of Mao's physical demise, had quite clearly engaged in proscribed factional activity to prepare a bid for power. This apparently enraged Mao who, at least for others if not invariably for himself, insisted that the formal norms be obeyed. At the same time, Gao's activities rallied the opposition of the vast majority of the Politburo, including not only those who saw their individual positions threatened but the broader membership who were unwilling to risk the normative framework that had served the CCP so well.

The second case of political disgrace, that of Peng Dehuai, had some similar yet different lessons.[24] Here the foremost prudential rule of not alienating Mao was again violated, but in this case through Peng's attempting to assert the right of dissent by criticizing the Great Leap Forward at the 1959 Lushan meeting. As we have seen, for complex reasons including his intense personal identification with the Great Leap, the Chairman refused to accept Peng's criticism and instead forced his dismissal from all operational posts. The need for caution when Mao's demands clashed with official norms was quickly grasped by other leaders. Not only did key figures including Liu Shaoqi and Zhou Enlai join in the attacks on Peng despite their private agreement with his views, but responsible economic officials such as Politburo members Li Xiannian and Bo Yibo who had also come to Lushan prepared to criticize the leap changed their tune once Mao indicated his intolerance of criticism.[25]

The generally stable situation produced conservative interpretations of prudential guidelines in other respects. While Mao certainly expected his colleagues to "deliver the goods," he apparently did not have unreasonable expectations in this regard. Indeed, post-Mao leaders have complained that the overall bureaucratic system as it evolved under Mao made insufficient demands in terms of performance and that even incompetent officials could only be dismissed for blatant violations of law.[26] With respect to high-ranking leaders, while it seems that most had considerable administrative talent, it also appears that relatively few were dismissed for failing to produce. The stable environment, moreover, put less of a premium on risk-taking innovation than on competent administration. The most dramatic innovations in any case generally came from Mao himself, and while it was necessary to support him in such cases it did not, at least in the case of somewhat lower-ranking officials, necessarily work to one's advantage to carry out overzealously the Chairman's initiatives.[27] With regard to the highest echelons, the point is that responsible officials normally survived as long as they carried out the Party line regardless of their zeal or, within limits, lack of it. It is indicative that the greatest survivor of all, Zhou Enlai, was rarely known for his enthusiasm concerning bold domestic experiments.[28]

In terms of policy advocacy, a cautious game was also called for. Given the ban on factions, policy alliances had to be informal and shifting. The safest course, as revealed in the behavior of leading officials at Lushan, was to be sure to be on Mao's side. However, as Mao's position was often indeterminate and he looked to his colleagues for advice, other possibilities were also available. Here, apart from avoiding excessively sharp clashes within the Politburo, the prudent leader would seek as broadly based an alliance as possible. This could, as in the case of the 1956 economic retrenchment,[29] even persuade Mao to set aside his own preferences given the extent and expertise of an elite coalition favoring other views. Of course, taking positions contrary to Mao's might be dangerous as Peng Dehuai's largely individual criticism demonstrated, but it is important to emphasize that Peng's case was unique in its severity and that by and large the right to dissent was acknowledged if it wasn't pushed too far. Thus Zhou Enlai's apparent skepticism about the Great Leap did not significantly affect his position,[30] and it may even be that Chen Yun's quiet eclipse at the time of the leap was more owing to his own choice than Mao's fiat.[31]

Finally, the building of a base of support also demanded circumspection. In bureaucratic terms this meant protecting the interests of one's institutional constituency, but in a manner that was not too blatant. As suggested above, priority had to be given to satisfying Mao and the

Politburo collective. Thus when the Great Leap policies seriously weakened his governmental apparatus *vis-à-vis* the Party organization the skillful Zhou knew he had to go along, as did top PLA leaders when military spending was cut in 1956. Similarly, any overly blatant development or use of personal networks risked the ire of both Mao and one's Politburo peers. Such moves not only violated the rule against factionalism, but other leaders would see a political threat in too cohesive a group behind any central figure. Throughout the pre-Cultural Revolution period the leading echelons of the Party were staffed by the same coalition of disparate revolutionary groups Mao forged in the early 1940s—his Long Marchers, Liu Shaoqi's "white area" (underground) workers, and leaders of various base areas and armies. While the Long Marchers predominated, all significant groups were well represented, and a rough balance among them was maintained through 1965.[32] When filling new posts a prudent politician had to keep within bounds the natural desire to distribute patronage and respect the interests of other leaders through balanced appointments. In this regard it is suggestive that available evidence indicates General Secretary Deng Xiaoping, who of all top leaders presumably had the greatest day-to-day control of CCP personnel, did not significantly favor close former associates when vacant provincial Party secretarial posts were filled.[33] Of course, the occasional key patronage appointment—for example the 1952 posting of Hu Yaobang as Youth League secretary[34]—might in the long run be more important than promoting large numbers of associates, but under the conditions of 1949-1965 the game had to be played with considerable finesse.

The fundamentally conservative politics of the period were further reflected in the politics of succession. Mao's concern with continued stability after his death led him to designate Liu Shaoqi as his successor by the mid-1950s, if not earlier, and by 1960 saw him implementing a plan whereby he retreated to the "second line," leaving day-to-day affairs to Liu and others.[35] As argued in the preceding essay, these succession arrangements were more than the fiat of the charismatic leader; they were also broadly acceptable to the Politburo as a whole because they promised minimum turmoil after Mao's death and because Liu would clearly head a collective representing all of the regime's institutional and revolutionary constituencies. Given Mao's apparent commitment to these arrangements, there was little to be gained for other oligarchs in challenging Liu, although some jockeying for Mao's favor was inevitable. Indeed, as has been shown for other communist systems,[36] such a well-structured succession would have had good prospects of holding had Mao died before 1965-66.[37] Attacking Liu in a bid for power after Mao's passing would have been seen as rocking the boat—as well as violating the prohibition against factionalism. As long as Liu himself adhered to the rules and the Politburo as a whole believed his collective leadership was "delivering the goods," Liu's position would in all likelihood have been secure.

In the years immediately preceding the Cultural Revolution, however, a number of ominous signs appeared foreshadowing the sharp break from stable Maoism. Not only had Mao weakened the normative rules by his vindictive reaction to Peng Dehuai at Lushan, but others found the dictates of prudence leading them to violate organizational principles too. Thus Peng Zhen, wary of Mao's sensitivity on the issue, carried out a secret review of Great Leap errors in the early 1960s. There were also signs of incipient factionalism, especially in the group of radical ideologues led by Mao's wife, Jiang Qing, which began to carry out its own sometimes secret investigations of "revisionism" in the cultural sphere with at least the belated blessings of the Chairman. Perhaps most destabilizing was that Mao's planned retirement to the "second line" coincided with his growing distress over perceived revolutionary degeneration in Chinese society and the first dark thoughts about the culpability of his Politburo colleagues. In this context, the major problem for leading politicians was to determine the wishes of an ever more elusive Chairman. Now withdrawn from the ongoing policy process, intervening unpredictably, and articulating vague concerns but not clear plans of action, Mao left his leading associates in a quandary.[38] The key prudential rule of elite politics was still the need to stay in Mao's good books, but acting according to this principle was increasingly difficult.

The Rise and Fall of Lin Biao, 1966-1971

When Mao's forebodings finally exploded in the form of the Cultural Revolution, the result was to overturn both normative and prudential rules. Even so fundamental a norm as Leninist discipline was now denounced as reflecting a "slavish mentality" of simply obeying organizational decisions without scrutinizing them for ideological impurities, while factional behavior became rampant in all circles from student Red Guards to the highest Party bodies. Moreover, in an unpredictable situation where, as Chen Yi lamented, ''Everyone is in a panic and nobody knows when misfortune will befall him,''[39] many long-standing prudential rules could no longer provide effective guidance. Even the very structure of the regime was fundamentally altered as the Party organization, under virulent Red Guard attack, ceased to function in 1967 and was replaced by Revolutionary Committees dominated by the PLA. In this chaotic period the nature of the political game was transformed. Rather than a single game played by all top echelon figures, two very different games emerged. For the great bulk of the elite the game was one of survival, trying to avoid disgrace by deflecting criticism and taking refuge in personal networks built up over the years. For a minority in elite circles, on the other hand, it was a game of attack, an effort to advance rapidly by seizing on the vulnerability of others while professing commitment to the most radical strands of Mao's Thought.

The elite politics of the Cultural Revolution and its immediate aftermath can be well illustrated by the rise and fall of Lin Biao. Lin emerged dramatically in 1966 as Mao's new choice as heir apparent and disappeared even more unexpectedly in 1971 after assertedly dying while fleeing from an unsuccessful plot against Mao's life. The very selection of Lin as heir indicated how fundamentally the political game had changed. Although Liu Shaoqi also was undoubtedly Mao's personal choice, as we have seen he had been broadly acceptable to the various institutional and personal interests assembled in the Politburo while Lin in contrast was clearly imposed by the Chairman. Lin could hardly have been an impressive choice from the perspective of other Politburo members. Apart from the question the anointment of the minister of defense posed for Party control of the gun, Lin simply did not appear to be someone who could ''deliver the goods'' of successfully leading a complex political system. Not only was his experience largely limited to army affairs, but his administrative capacities had been called into question by repeated illness. For this reason Lin held no operational posts for most of the 1950s, and as his conflict with Luo Ruiqing (see above, p. 30) suggests, even as minister of defense after 1959 he seemingly played a minimal role in day-to-day PLA affairs. Indeed, this may have been the key to Mao's choice. Of all the leading figures of the CCP, Lin's *role* in the early 1960s was closest to that of the Chairman—both were aloof from operational matters, as a result were generally spared hard choices which compromised ideo-

Table 2

Breakdown of 9th CCP Politburo

	Central military	Regional military	Old-line Party and state administrators	Radicals
Standing Committee	†Lin Biao (VC)		Zhou Enlai	Chen Boda Kang Sheng
Full members	†Ye Qun (Mme. Lin) †Huang Yongsheng †Wu Faxian †Li Zuopeng †Qiu Huizuo	Chen Xilian Xu Shiyou	Li Xiannian Ye Jianying[a] Zhu De[b] Liu Bocheng[b] Dong Biwu[c]	*Jiang Qing (Mme. Mao) *Zhang Chunqiao *Yao Wenyuan Xie Fuzhi

VC = Central Committee vice-chairman.

†Lin's personal clique.

*Jiang Qing faction ("Gang of Four").

[a]Ye held military posts but was closely allied with Zhou's group.

[b]Zhu and Liu, although military men, were effectively retired and supported the old guard.

[c]Dong was effectively retired.

logical principles, and were prone to issuing vague slogans which in Lin's case were deeply flattering of Mao.[40] Lin, in the eyes of most top leaders, was undoubtedly a cipher on many key policy issues, lacked credibility as a leader, and from 1966 on by virtue of his role as a leading Cultural Revolution protagonist posed a threat to their basic interests. Quite clearly, then, to a substantial extent Lin Biao's position was dependent on Mao's continued support.

The end of the turbulent phase of the Cultural Revolution in fall 1968 left Lin politically strong but at the sime time vulnerable. Lin's strength can be seen in the Politburo chosen at the Ninth Party Congress in April 1969 (see Table 2). In terms of both factional ties and institutional support he was well placed in the new ruling group. Moreover, the possibility clearly existed for alliances with civilian "radicals" who had also ridden the Cultural Revolution wave to new heights. A danger remained, however, in the person of Zhou Enlai and the old-line officials he epitomized. This was less owing to Zhou's actual support on the new Politburo (many of the close colleagues Zhou had protected in 1966-68 were downgraded from Politburo to Central Committee status) than to the backing of the pre-Cultural Revolution elite as a whole and to the logic of the situation. For Mao, the Ninth Congress marked a

shift from destroying decadent ideologies to constructing a new puri-
fied order. Lin, the military man and Cultural Revolution phrase-
monger, was far less suited to fashioning concrete programs across the
entire board of Chinese public policy than a skilled administrator like
Zhou. Even the civilian radicals with their various schemes for promoting "newborn things" of the Cultural Revolution[41] were better prepared to deal with the new situation. Given his limited capacity for
"delivering the goods" of reconstruction, it is not surprising that Lin
reportedly "was not at ease [and] knew that he could not really become
the successor"[42] despite his strong Politburo following.

Lin's dilemma was further complicated by his dependence on Mao.
The need for the Chairman's continued approval left him with some
difficult choices. One possible strategy would have been to act cau-
tiously, follow Mao's lead, and rely on the strong position created by
the Politburo lineup, control over most key posts in the central military
apparatus, and his status as designated successor for the inevitable
struggle after Mao's passing. But given the strength of opposition
within the elite and the new conditions favoring Zhou, Lin opted for a
higher risk strategy of initiatives to bolster further his position while
the Chairman still lived. The main risk was that such efforts would run
afoul of Mao. As suggested above, apart from Mao's need for military
support during the Cultural Revolution, Lin was probably raised to the
heights largely because his relative inactivity allowed him to escape the
ire of an increasingly irascible Chairman. Now the active pursuit of
enhanced power raised the danger of some unanticipated clash with
Mao.

While much remains obscure, the broad outlines of Lin Biao's strategy can be reconstructed. Apart from trying to retain Mao's favor,
central features were protecting the interests of his institutional constituency, the PLA, and strengthening factional support—both areas
where Lin had demonstrated some vigor during 1966-68. And after the
Ninth Congress he tried to reach further by establishing alliances of
both a personal and policy nature. Given the legacy of Cultural Revolution strife, Lin's efforts were fraught with difficulty. Deep hostility
within the elite toward that experience severely weakened the appeal of
approaches based on institutional interests and policy alliances. Yet it
was only after Mao clashed overtly with Lin at the critical August-
September 1970 Central Committee Plenum, held once again at
Lushan, that Lin, in apparent growing desperation, made the most
dramatic departure from all previous rules of political conflict by

initiating plans for a military coup.[43]

The core of Lin's strategy was the effort to build up his own personal network. Mao's post-coup attempt remarks are particularly suggestive in this regard. By this account, policy issues were secondary to the extension of Lin's clique: Lin assertedly began the attempt to install a military dictatorship by "infiltrating" his partisans into key organs of state power and thus fortified *then* "broke ranks with the leadership on a number of domestic and foreign issues."[44] Such infiltration went furthest in the central PLA command structure—here Lin had been successful in placing his old Fourth Field Army colleagues in key positions, especially after the purge of Chief of Staff Yang Chengwu in March 1968. The process continued after the Ninth Congress with a particularly close-knit group formed around Lin's son, Lin Liguo, who was placed in a key operational position in the Air Force command in October 1969. The network was extended on a more limited basis to regional military commands and also to local political organs as the rebuilding of Party committees unfolded from 1969. Moreover, in Party rebuilding and political reconstruction generally, Lin assertedly hindered cadre rehabilitations in an effort to minimize the strength of old-line administrators and thus maximize the position of his group.[45]

All told, Lin's activities were an obvious violation of the ban on factions. In a sense, he had little choice but to rely on naked factionalism. As the main beneficiary of a movement profoundly inimicable to existing norms and threatening the great bulk of the elite, Lin could only continue the factional methods of the Cultural Revolution. These methods, however, produced a backlash from both Mao and the leadership as a whole. Thus when Mao launched his assault on Lin at the 1970 plenum it was in terms of Lin's conspiratorial methods, and after Lin's fall he singled out the need to uphold the norm proscribing factionalism as a key lesson of the affair.[46] At the same time, Lin's activities posed grave dangers to numerous other actors. Neither Politburo members outside his clique, veterans of other field armies generally, nor Mao were happy with the stranglehold Lin and his band of followers had developed over key levers of coercion.

Of nearly equal importance to Lin's strategy was securing his institutional base in the military. Even before the Ninth Congress Lin appealed to PLA interests by securing substantially increased defense spending.[47] Related to this, Lin adopted a foreign policy posture emphasizing military preparedness to cope with the threats posed by the American war effort in Vietnam and the Soviet buildup on China's northern borders. This position placed Lin in conflict with Zhou Enlai, who from late 1968 advocated a diplomatic approach to the United States in order to isolate the more dangerous enemy in Moscow.[48] Lin's emphasis in theory suited army interests since diplomatic solutions raised the possibility of cuts in military expenditures. Particularly revealing in this regard is that once in operational control of the PLA, Lin quickly became an advocate of the preparedness measures for which Luo Ruiqing ostensibly had been purged at the outset of the Cultural Revolution.[49] In calling for a military buildup rather than diplomatic efforts, Lin apparently sought to shore up the institutional support of the PLA and at the same time deny Zhou the center stage in national security policy.

Lin's attempts to secure military backing, however, were undercut by the crosscurrents of the Cultural Revolution. Ironically, this was a consequence of the rise of the PLA to replace the Party as the core institution of the regime in 1967; army officers quickly became dominant on the new revolutionary committees and subsequently on the reestablished local Party committees. While Lin's active promotion of this development undoubtedly won him the support of many ambitious military officers, the process was profoundly divisive within the PLA. The army did not enter the political arena of its own doing but rather was brought in by Mao over the objections of some top-ranking PLA officials. These military leaders were concerned with the costs of political involvement to PLA unity and *esprit de corps*, and they saw the army's primary defense role being undermined. Moreover, once PLA officers were placed in leading administrative positions they found themselves in much the same situation as their civilian Party predecessors. These officers not only resented the criticism of Red Guards and other radical elements, but after the Ninth Congress they generally sympathized with the moderate economic policies pushed by Zhou at the Center. Perhaps most detrimental to Lin personally was that despite his position at the top of the military hierarchy, as a leading Cultural Revolution protagonist he failed to protect regional army commanders when the local PLA came under violent Red Guard attack in mid-1967 at the urging of Jiang Qing's radical group. In contrast, the consistent support of Zhou Enlai earned the gratitude of the regional commanders. Thus Lin's efforts to secure his institutional base were severely compromised, and when Mao began to reassert the normative rule of Party control over the military following the Ninth Congress, the Chairman found a sympathetic audience within the army. Many, if hardly all, military men had no love lost for Lin Biao and were only too happy to return to their normal functions.[50]

The final aspect of Lin's strategy was to construct a policy program after the Ninth Congress which would appeal to Cultural Revolution radicals, China's "military-industrial complex," and Mao himself. This program was in sharp contrast to the moderate policies being forged by Zhou Enlai. The appeal to the radical camp—which succeeded in drawing Chen Bota to Lin's side but apparently did not make many further inroads—was based on radical policy premises and perhaps more significantly on the common threat from Zhou. Attacks on Cultural Revolution excesses led to a series of reversals for the radical camp—the Cultural Revolution Group which had been the organizational center of its power ceased to function by the end of 1969, leading provincial leftists were purged in late 1969-early 1970, and an investigation of the extremist Red Guard "May 16 Group" was undertaken in this same period.[51] The danger posed by these developments apparently was enough to solidify Chen's ties to Lin. But a broader target, as Harry Harding has skillfully argued, was the "military-industrial complex," and here policy content was crucial. While continuing to argue a foreign policy line presumably guaranteeing high military expenditures, Lin apparently advocated increased resource allocation to the industrial sector generally at a time when Zhou was calling attention to the need to bolster agriculture. The key to Lin's domestic program was to achieve agricultural growth by measures akin to those of the Great Leap rather than by material incentives as advocated by Zhou. As a result, in the first half of 1970 various areas implemented radical policies calling for restrictions on private plots and free markets, raising the unit of accounting above the production team, and mass mobilization to achieve a new leap forward in agriculture without additional resource allocations.[52] However attractive in theory, the appeal of this program, like the larger attempt to woo the PLA, suffered from Lin's Cultural Revolution legacy.[53] Industrial administrators, like regional PLA commanders, suffered from the radical thrust of 1966-68 and had found Zhou, not Lin, a sympathetic ally. Moreover, however much they may have desired increased appropriations, industrial officials were well aware of the disastrous results the last time a mass mobilization approach to agriculture was tried. And they undoubtedly felt Zhou rather than Lin was more capable of "delivering the goods" of economic recovery.

In the last analysis, the key remained Mao's support. The above policies had the virtue of appealing to Mao's presumed prejudices. Lin apparently calculated that the Cultural Revolution had glorified the Great Leap and attacked material incentives, and certainly that Mao was an unbending foe of American imperialism. But sadly for Lin, Mao viewed himself as a dialectician, and the Chairman's dialectic now called for a shift of emphasis to a more moderate program along the lines advocated by Zhou. The break seemingly did not originate over policy, however. Significantly, Mao's clear-cut espousal of Zhou's domestic policies and the opening to the United States only occurred *after* the August-September 1970 plenum[54] where the Chairman turned on Lin over quite different matters. The critical issue at the plenum according to Mao's subsequent account[55] was the alleged "surprise attack" by Lin and Chen Boda, who advocated restoring the position of chief of state and hailed Mao's "genius." Mao complained that he had told them on six occasions not to raise either matter and interpreted their actions as conspiratorial factional activity. While Mao was undoubtedly correct that their motive was to gain the state post for Lin if he declined it and to strengthen Lin's position as the successor to the "genius,"[56] the vehemence of Mao's reaction undoubtedly astounded Lin and Chen. Their likely calculation was that at worst a flattered Mao would simply shrug off the matter. Given the adulation Mao accepted without any sign of embarrassment in 1966-68, they must have regarded subsequent disclaimers about his "genius" as false modesty. But for Mao, perhaps distrustful of Lin's factional activities and disturbed by his emerging policy line, the "surprise attack" at Lushan (with all its echoes of an equally unpleasant surprise in 1959) served to focus distrust of his latest heir apparent.

Following the plenum, Lin's position became increasingly precarious. The rejection of his leftist agricultural policies and the victory of Zhou's diplomatic approach soon became clear. More ominous, Mao took several organizational measures which weakened Lin's hold over the PLA chain of command and his overall standing within the elite. Although apparently unsure initially how far Mao intended to push his recently kindled animosity, Lin nevertheless began to intensify secret activities; his growing desperation allegedly soon led to the drafting of military coup plans in March 1971. Finally, when Lin learned in early September of Mao's intent to pursue matters further, he set in motion a train of events leading to an abortive assassination plot and the ill-fated attempt to escape.[57] In the end, Lin Biao's failure was owing not only to breaking all the normative rules which had stood the CCP so well

before the Cultural Revolution—although this should not be underestimated—but also to the fact that the prudential rules he attempted to play
by were seriously compromised by the movement which had thrust him
to power. The crucial factor, however, was Lin's inability—though for
no want of trying—to fulfill the essential requirement of maintaining
Mao's support.

"Two Line Struggle," 1972/73-1976

After an initial phase marked by shock, an apparent unwillingness to
face difficult political questions, and an intensified drift toward Zhou's
moderate economic policies, the post-Lin Biao period by early 1973
was marked by deep conflict which in many ways suggested a "two line
struggle."[58] The polarizing issue was the Cultural Revolution itself.
From the start of 1973 the radicals around Jiang Qing, with Mao's
encouragement, launched a vigorous defense of the Cultural Revolution and warned against efforts to restore aspects of the pre-1966
system which they correctly saw in various policies advocated by the
old-line administrators. Moreover, Jiang's "Gang of Four"[59] both
pushed their pet reforms emphasizing egalitarian and participatory
values and repeatedly attacked official programs aimed at political
stability and economic development. Meanwhile, the old guard pressed
ahead with its plans for modernization, although occasionally retreat-
ing under radical fire, and strengthened its grip on the regime's administrative machinery. Reinforcing sharp ideological and policy differences were bitter memories of 1966-68: the fundamental nature of the
attack on the old guard's institutional and personal interests then meant
the game would again be a bitter zero-sum conflict. The terms of the
game, however, were decisively influenced by the physical deterioration of two men—Zhou, the administrators' patron, and above all the
enigmatic Mao. Thus Zhou's death in January 1976 was quickly followed by the ouster of the earlier rehabilitated Deng Xiaoping, while
the "Gang of Four" was ruthlessly crushed shortly after Mao's passing
in September of the same year.
    The balance of forces in the Politburo selected at the Tenth Congress
in August 1973 (see Table 3) if anything underestimated the overall
dominance of old-line administrators and exaggerated the radicals'
strength in the elite as a whole. A more accurate picture emerges from
appointments to operational posts. Not only were new provincial Party
secretaries overwhelmingly rehabilitated civilian officials including

Table 3

Breakdown of 10th CCP Politburo

	Old-line administrators	Regional military	Radicals	Others
Standing Com- mittee	Zhou Enlai (VC) Deng Xiaoping (VC)[a] Ye Jianying (VC)[b] Zhu De[b] Dong Biwu[b]		*Wang Hongwen (VC) Kang Sheng (VC) *Zhang Chunqiao	
Full members	Li Xiannian Liu Bocheng[b]	Li Desheng[c] Chen Xilian Xu Shiyou	*Jiang Qing *Yao Wenyuan	Hua Guofeng[d] Ji Dengkui[d] Wei Guoqing[e] Wu De[e] Wang Dongxing[f] Chen Yonggui[g]

VC = Central Committee vice-chairman.

*"Gang of Four"

[a]Elected to Central Committee at Tenth Congress, promoted to Politburo 1/74, promoted to Standing Committee and vice-chairman 1/75.

[b]See Table 2, p. 107.

[c]Demoted from Standing Committee and vice chairman 1/74.

[d]Central administrator, formerly local Party official.

[e]Local Party official.

[f]Commander Central Committee bodyguard unit.

[g]Former peasant cadre.

former first secretaries, but the new State Council appointed at the January 1975 NPC placed over 60 percent of ministerial positions in the hands of veteran administrators with experience in the pre-1966 central government apparatus. In contrast, only Zhang Chunqiao as second vice-premier and head of the PLA General Political Department plus a few lesser radicals received bureaucratic posts. This apportionment of power not only reflected the conviction of the old guard that the radical ideologues lacked the skills to "deliver the goods" of modernization, it also severely undercut the "Gang's" ability to produce tangible political benefits for possible allies. While such recently promoted officials as Hua Guofeng were unlikely allies in any case,[60] the lack of significant bureaucratic resources left the radicals with few means to satisfy the institutional needs of such relatively uncommitted leaders. Given the inability to mobilize such resources, the "Gang's" alliance efforts had to rely on ideological appeals, mutual Cultural Revolution involvements, and the opportunities and pressures of the moment, but at most this appears to have involved a few

Politburo members in occasional cooperation with specific radical programs.[61] In contrast, the old-line administrators not only possessed ample bureaucratic resources, but the very nature of their program encouraged pragmatic tradeoffs from which a broad alliance could be built.

A related organizational weakness was the inability of the radicals to penetrate deeply the PLA: while Lin Biao was able to link a leftist program to significant support within the military, the "Gang of Four's" backing was restricted to a relatively limited number of units and officers. Lacking broad ties of revolutionary experience to the PLA elite, even with Zhang Chunqiao as army political chief the radicals could make few inroads into an army leadership now (as of the 1975 NPC) firmly under the control of such well-connected figures as Defense Minister Ye Jianying and Chief of Staff Deng Xiaoping. The "Gang's" vulnerability in this respect was reflected in their abortive efforts to establish an urban militia independent of PLA command. The need to fall back on such tactics was not simply owing to the absence of old school ties to the army leadership or the inability to deliver governmental resources to the military. Much more fundamental was the widely shared distaste of the PLA elite as a whole for the radicals' role in the Cultural Revolution. If PLA commanders had resented Lin Biao's failure to protect them against leftist attacks in mid-1967 and subsequently, their hostility toward Jiang Qing et al. as the originators of such attacks was immeasurably greater. Indeed, although PLA leaders appeared willing to return to the barracks gradually after Lin's fall, this political disengagement seemed linked to their being satisfied that the old-line administrators held the upper hand in Beijing. Thus it is significant that the shakeup of regional military commanders in early 1974 coincided with the promotion of Deng Xiaoping to Politburo status, and that in all cases where PLA officers yielded local political power in this period it was to civilian Party officials of the old school. While ready to obey the normative rule that "the Party commands the gun," army leaders heeded the prudential lesson of 1967-68 that the radicals could not be trusted to respect their interests.[62]

Given the hostility of the administrative and military elites, the "Gang of Four" was forced to rely on Mao's patronage for their continued prominence and future prospects. The Chairman had raised them to their high positions, and it was only the Chairman, as the events of 1976 demonstrated, who could advance their cause in the struggle against the old guard. But the prudential requirement to obtain Mao's approval was clearly understood by both contending groups. Thus Deng Xiaoping, who became the leading figure in day-to-day operations following Zhou's hospitilization in mid-1974, repeatedly emphasized the need to send reports to Mao and request instructions from him when economic modernization plans were being drafted in 1975.[63] With both sides recognizing the importance of Mao's support, access to the Chairman became a crucial political resource which neither could monopolize or rely upon.[64]

The "Mao factor," with the Chairman as erratic as ever in his policy attitudes and perhaps consciously playing off the contending forces, was further complicated by his rapidly deteriorating health from 1973. Mao was now physically incapable of providing forceful direction and thus was increasingly vulnerable to manipulation by those who obtained access to his person. Moreover, with the end clearly in sight, the requirements of the post-Mao phase increasingly came to the fore with drastically different implications for the radicals and the old guard. For the old-line administrators the need was to outlast Mao while avoiding his ire, while the radicals required his intervention to strengthen their position if they were to have any chance of prevailing after his demise. Mao, however, refused to lean decisively to either side. Apparently dubious about the "Gang's" political skills and certainly antagonistic toward their factional activities, Mao underwrote the personnel arrangements of the 1975 NPC which strengthened the grip of the old guard. On policy matters, although sharing the administrators' concern with political stability and economic growth, as we saw in the preceding essay Mao's deepest predilection was for keeping alive the Cultural Revolution ideals advocated by the radicals. These preferences notwithstanding, the net result was to deny the "Gang of Four" the support necessary for a decisive breakthrough in their struggle with the old guard.[65] Even Deng's removal fell short of their needs.

With only sporadic backing from Mao and facing the entrenched hostility of the old guard, the "Gang of Four" was necessarily forced to adopt a high risk strategy of disruption. Apart from seeking to arouse Mao's distrust of the old guard and running the risk of his rebuff,[66] the radicals embarked on a course which flagrantly violated pre-1966 norms and deepened the animosity toward them. While the "Gang," with the Chairman's fluctuating support, attempted to revise the normative rules by infusing them with Cultural Revolution emphases on fidelity to Mao's Thought and mass criticism from below,[67] the effect was to challenge directly the fundamental principle of Leninist discipline. Using their substantial influence over the media, the radicals repeatedly if often esoterically encouraged resistance to official Party and state policies. In these circumstances, numerous radically inclined lower-level cadres simply refused to implement these policies while many more officials hesitated given the uncertain political situation. Thus the "Gang's" actions undermined the ability of the system as a whole to "deliver the goods" of orderly administration. Similarly, their encouragement of mass protest activity against the old guard led to economic and social disorder which was not only anathema to the administrators but unacceptable to Mao himself.

Beyond these measures the "Gang" relied on building and using its factional network. While the old guard maintained a firm grip on most bureaucratic organizations, both the ideological appeals of the Cultural Revolution and the self-interest of many rapidly promoted younger cadres provided the basis for a significant following. Thus the "Gang" attempted to infiltrate such followers into the bureaucratic empires of the opposition where they spied on the enemy, sabotaged official directives, and established their own secret communications network outside the formal channels monopolized by the old guard. The net result was an extremely tight factional setup which not only angered Mao for violating a cardinal norm but further incensed the old-line administrators who fully understood its threat.[68] Yet it is clear that the radicals had no alternative. Like Lin Biao, they had viciously attacked the interests of the elite as a whole during the Cultural Revolution, but unlike Lin they lacked major institutional assets, widespread contacts, or genuine revolutionary prestige. If Lin had been pushed into harsh factional politics by inclination or the logic of events, the "Gang of Four's" overwhelming political weakness left little option but to break the normative rules in this as in other regards if they were to have the slightest chance of survival.

If the "Gang of Four" was forced to play a risky game, the old guard also adopted a relatively high risk strategy. The major risk in addition to resisting radical initiatives which had at least Mao's partial backing was to push ahead with a comprehensive modernization policy in 1975 despite the Chairman's ambivalent attitudes. Under Deng Xiaoping's leadership, the administrators developed a far-reaching program, including many concrete proposals which inevitably clashed with Cultural Revolution values. Although Deng was careful to insist on consultation with Mao, and the Chairman had indeed called for concrete measures,[69] the uncertain nature of the venture was clearly revealed in

Deng's reported remark that "I am not afraid to fall a second time."[70] The fact that Deng's program was formulated openly in official Party forums in accord with the line adopted at the 1975 NPC provided important normative support for the old guard's position, but the administrators were not averse to illegitimate factional measures themselves given the danger posed by the "Gang." Thus some informal preparations were apparently undertaken in 1974-75 in addition to outright plotting, including plans for military force, after Deng's dismissal in 1976.[71] these measures notwithstanding, the old guard coalition was at best a loose arrangement of groups sharing old ties and common perspectives. Given the extensive *guanxi* built up over the decades, as well as control of major institutions, the tight factional arrangement of the radicals was not required. The coalition was motivated less by possible advantages for individual careers than by the desire to settle old scores, restore the reputation of veteran revolutionaries, and reestablish a predictable system which could "deliver the goods" of a strong and stable China.

The high risk nature of the game for both contending forces was underscored by the events of 1976. Deng's policies did indeed arouse Mao's suspicions, and following Zhou's death and the massive protests in Beijing's Tiananmen Square, the Chairman forced his purge. But rather than opening the way for the "Gang," Deng's demise resulted in Hua Guofeng's appointment as Zhou's and ultimately Mao's successor. Although the old guard was placed on the defensive by the onslaught against Deng, its control of the bureaucratic machinery had not been broken, and when the Chairman finally passed away in September the "Gang" was stripped of its most effective protection. The arrest of the radicals in early October was not only swift retribution for their repeated violation of normative rules, it also marked the end of a ten-year period where prudential guidelines had been severely distorted by Cultural Revolution tensions.

From Hua to Hu in the Age of Deng, 1976/77-1982

The purge of the "Gang of Four" was a decisive turning point. With Hua Guofeng now affirmed as Party chairman, a broad consensus quickly developed on enforcing social order, modernizing the economy along the lines of the 1975 program, and restoring the pre-1966 political system. The last requirement has led over the following years to extensive efforts to revive the normative rules which had been so badly fractured as a result of the Cultural Revolution, a process which strengthened prudential rules as well. But the legacy of the Cultural Revolution inevitably raised a series of divisive issues—the terms and timing of Deng Xiaoping's return to the leadership, the pace of rehabilitation of other victims of the 1966-1976 decade, the scope of the purge of the left, the symbolic treatment of the Cultural Revolution, the official verdict on the Tiananmen incident, and the broader attitude toward Mao. By the end of 1978, further issues came to the fore, including differences over the degree of political liberalization and the need to reassess economic policies. This reassessment led to a shift from relatively orthodox approaches to reforms involving decentralization, market mechanisms, and a revived private sector. The settling of these issues coincided with a decided shift in the balance of forces toward those led by Deng, who sought to break away from the rigid orthodoxies of the past, and in the process caused a breakup of the initial post-Mao coalition. Thus by early 1979 Wang Dongxing's "whatever" group, which opposed any questioning of Mao's symbolic status, was in full scale retreat, while by the end of 1980 Hua had been forced to offer his resignation. Finally, in mid-1981 Hu Yaobang, a long-standing Deng protégé, was appointed the CCP's new chairman.

The most basic source of division within the post-Mao coalition was contrasting Cultural Revolution experiences (see Table 4). Some leaders, most spectacularly Hua, were beneficiaries of the movement by virtue of obtaining top-level positions that almost certainly would not have come their way under normal circumstances. Thus whatever their personal feelings about the tensions and chaos of the period, they had little interest in denigrating either the Cultural Revolution or its progenitor, Mao. Moreover, as active politicians throughout the 1966-1976 period, these officials often took action to the detriment of other leaders, although Hua himself was not involved in the intense conflicts at the Center in 1966-68.[72] The Cultural Revolution victims, of whom Deng was the archetype and patron, had an almost totally negative view of the movement as well as bitter memories about specific actions of individual beneficiaries. Between the two groups stood the survivors of the 1966-68 period, officials led by Ye Jianying and Li Xiannian who generally had been severely criticized but whose status had variously risen or declined after 1968. As a group these survivors were harshly critical of the Cultural Revolution,[73] but they had fewer reasons for personal bitterness than the victims plus an interest in making the post-

Table 4

Breakdown of 11th and 12th CCP Politburos

	Cultural Revolution beneficiaries	Cultural Revolution survivors	Cultural Revolution victims
Standing Committee	(P) Hua Guofeng^a *(PS) Wang Dongxing^b	(M) Ye Jianying †(C) Li Xiannian (C) Chen Yun^e	(C) Deng Xiaoping (P) Zhao Ziyang^h †(C) Hu Yaobang^i
Full members	†*(M) Chen Xilian^c *(P) Ji Dengkui^c *(P) Wu De^c †(M) Li Desheng (BC) Chen Yonggui^d (BC) Ni Zhifu	†(M) Liu Bocheng^f †(M) Xu Xiangqian †(C) Nie Rongzhen †(C) Yu Qiuli †(M) Xu Shiyou^g †(P) Wei Guoqing^g †(C) Fang Yi †(D) Geng Biao^f (P) Peng Chong^f (C) Wang Zhen^e †(C) Deng Yingchao^e (Mme. Zhou Enlai) †(M) *Yang Dezhi*	(P) Ulanhu (M) Zhang Tingfa †(M) Su Zhenhua^j †(C) Peng Zhen^k †(P) *Wan Li^l* †(C) *Xi Zongxun^m* †(C) *Yang Shangkun* †(C) *Song Renqiong^n* †(C) *Hu Qiaomu* †(C) *Liao Chengzhi*

Italicized leaders added at 12th Congress 9/82.

*"Whatever" group.

†Significant pre-Cultural Revoltion career links to Deng Xiaoping.

Pre-Cultural Revolution posts:
(P) provincial Party, (C) central Party/state, (M) military, (PS) public security, (BC) basic-level cadre, (D) diplomatic

^{a}Demoted from chairman to vice-chairman 6/81, not reelected 9/82.

^{b}Demoted from vice-chairman to full member 12/78, relieved 2/80.

^{c}Relieved 2/80.

^{d}Chen held similar views but not linked to "whatever" group, not reelected 9/82.

^{e}Elected 12/78.

^{f}Not reelected 9/82.

^{g}Xu and Wei technically beneficiaries but both severely criticized 1967-68, Xu not reelected 9/82.

^{h}Promoted to full member 9/79, to Standing Committee 2/80, to vice-chairman 6/81.

^{i}Elected 12/78, promoted to Standing Committee 2/80, to chairman 6/81.

^{j}Died 2/79.

^{k}Elected 9/79.

^{l}Central state posts until 1958 assignment to Beijing Municipality.

^{m}Removed from power 1962, attacked in Cultural Revolution.

^{n}Regional posts in early 1960s.

Mao transition as smooth as possible. The key issue initially for all concerned was Deng's rehabilitation. Leading beneficiaries Wang Dongxing, Wu De, and Chen Xilian tried to block his return to power. The survivors, albeit with varying degrees of passion, called for Deng's reinstatement and helped arrange the compromise solution which simultaneously reaffirmed Hua's position.[74] In these maneuvers, Hua's role was problematic. Although accused in 1980-81 of having dragged his feet on the issue, in late 1976-early 1977 Hua was caught between conflicting pressures. While clearly desirous of bolstering his own position, Hua's deliberate pace is also explainable in terms of the Politburo opposition to Deng and the regime's larger need for continuity and stability at that juncture.[75] In any case, with Deng's formal return in July 1977 the leadership equation was transformed.

Analyses of post-Mao China which focus on an alleged succession struggle between Hua and Deng miss the point of this new equation. Whatever tensions existed between the two men, there could never be an equal struggle between them: in any showdown Deng would win, and both understood this from the outset. Despite Hua's formal position as chairman, many developments rapidly indicated that Deng was the *de facto* leader. Deng's policy initiatives generally became the official line, and personnel appointments, while not building up a narrow Deng clique, nevertheless repeatedly strengthened those committed to his course. Perhaps the most telling is that Deng could withstand policy setbacks without any real threat to his position. Thus in early 1979 he could take responsibility for the triple setback of disorders resulting from tentative democratization measures, the economic losses caused by overexpansion in 1977-78, and the mixed consequences of the war with Vietnam;[76] reverse his position by calling for a crackdown on dissent; and easily rebuff new attacks from Wang Dongxing and company.[77] Such policy shifts represent Deng's efforts to manage the political system rather than moves to outmaneuver opponents genuinely threatening his position. Under such circumstances the essential prudential role for other Politburo members has been to keep in Deng's good graces. Wang Dongxing et al. either didn't understand this rule[78] or their position was so compromised by events of the 1966-1976 period that they chose to ignore it, while Hua understood its requirements and sought to observe them but was ultimately unsuccessful.

Deng's position as *de facto* leader was assured for several reasons. As argued in the preceding essay,[79] the critical factor was his status as the leading survivor from Mao's pre-Cultural Revolution inner core. In a curious fashion Deng benefited both from being twice purged by Mao and by having been one of the late Chairman's "close comrades-in-arms." While his most ardent support comes from those who had also suffered at Mao's hands, more fundamental backing is derived from the wider elite whose members recognize Deng's long association with Mao in the revolution that represents their life work. Beyond this, in terms of the prudential rules discussed in this essay, Deng gained from a number of considerations, although in the strict sense he was not forging a strategy but rather reaping the benefits of earlier efforts. First, he was widely seen as capable of "delivering the goods." He had not only served as a key central leader throughout most of the post-1949 period and developed a rather awesome reputation as an administrator, he had also in 1975 shaped the basic economic program which the post-Mao leadership initially put into effect, a program which promised much to many bureaucratic interests. Hua could adopt that program as his own and announce it to official conclaves, but everyone knew Deng was the architect. Moreover, Deng's career both as an old revolutionary and as CCP General Secretary from 1956 to 1966 gave him an enormous network of contacts. The post-Mao Chinese elite was honeycombed with people who had significant ties to Deng and more broadly by officials who were accustomed to seeing him at the apex of authority. With institutional patterns weakened as a result of the turmoil of the Cultural Revolution decade, these broad contacts necessarily strengthened Deng, particularly in comparison with officials such as Hua who lacked similarly extensive networks and had to rely more on formal positions.

Given Deng's strong position, since mid-1977 if not earlier, prudent Chinese politicians have been careful to accommodate him, win his ear, and gain his support for their programs and interests. This situation, however, is considerably different from that which existed under Mao even before the Cultural Revolution. First, the normative rules—particularly the requirement for collective leadership—are far more binding. Deng not only lacks the charismatic authority which only a revolutionary leader like Mao can truly possess, but the lesson of Mao's abuses which Deng and his supporters have emphasized serves as a powerful bar to excessive individual power. Moreover, other leaders of nearly equal prestige—perhaps most notably Chen Yun[80]—sit with Deng on the Politburo and have their own extensive bases of personal and institutional support. In these circumstances, Deng has had to play according to prudential rules of respecting the interests of major actors, compromising on specific issues when necessary, painstakingly building a coalition behind his program, and placing his supporters in key positions without ignoring the claims of other groups. The need to trim sails was evident in Deng's early 1979 reversal and subsequent zigzags on the acceptable degree of political liberalization in the face of widespread dismay among orthodox officials, although it could be argued that Deng's own predilections also called for a crackdown.[81] The requirement of carefully building a consensus through compromise was seen in the sixteen-month process of drafting the historical resolution assessing Mao's contributions and faults, even if again one suspects the final outcome was fully compatible with Deng's personal position.[82] And the need to avoid overplaying one's hand in personnel appointments was demonstrated by the diversity of career affiliations of both the Party secretaries chosen when the central secretariat was reestablished in February 1980 and the Politburo members added since the 1977 Party Congress.[83]

For all these limits on his authority Deng has remained a powerful leader mediating a variety of interests rather than a vulnerable figure dependent upon any particular base of support. This and other features of post-Mao politics are apparent in the role of the PLA since 1976. Although initially presumed to be very powerful owing to playing a decisive role in crushing the ''Gang of Four'' and the substantial military representation on the new Politburo selected in 1977, army leaders have been unhappy with many of the policies adopted under Deng's leadership. In terms of resource allocations, defense spending has been restricted as military modernization has taken a backseat to economic development. Many officers, moreover, have been upset by personnel and professionalization reforms which have forced retirements and limited the PLA as a channel of upward mobility for rural youth. In addition, some PLA leaders have criticized various Party policies in nonmilitary areas, e.g., changes in agriculture which undermine soldiers' relatives, liberalization in society which both creates disciplinary problems within the army and damages its social prestige, and the downgrading of Mao.[84]

These grievances notwithstanding, there has been little serious challenge to Deng from the military. Instead, the normative rule that ''the Party commands the gun'' has been observed, with the army systematically completing the withdrawal from extensive political involvement which began after Lin Biao's fall. Consistent with this norm, military leaders have basically acted as a pressure group concerned with the PLA's institutional interests; they have not, for example, constantly sought to intrude into economic policymaking.[85] However, as members of the larger revolutionary elite, PLA leaders, as indicated above, have spoken out on developments in the ideological and political spheres. This, of course, is acceptable up to a point under the restored norms, but when that point is exceeded, as in an August 1982 *PLA Daily* article critical of liberal trends, swift disciplinary action follows.[86] From the perspective of Deng's prudential calculations, the army leadership remains an important constituency whose opinions and interests must be taken into account and sometimes mollified,[87] but that does not give it a veto over Party policy. Deng has demonstrated broad receptivity to the PLA's institutional requirements—particularly modernization— even while rejecting specific claims. Given Deng's overall interest in the well-being of the military, and the rule of civilian control, army leaders have generally limited their dissent to approved Party channels. Here, as with the CCP elite as a whole, Deng's position is secure as long as he remains sensitive to a wide range of interests, his policies "deliver" at least minimally satisfactory "goods," and he does not grossly overstep the norm of collective leadership.

If there have been constraints on even such a preeminent figure as Deng, what prudential considerations governed Hua, whose position was inherently weak? On some crucial counts there was relatively little Hua could do to bolster his status. In terms of "delivering the goods" it is unlikely that his brief period in Beijing would have provided more than a reputation as young man with a future. Aspersions about Hua's alleged failings as a leader have a rather hollow ring given the broad array of responsibilities he amassed under the old guard leadership in 1972-75,[88] but what is certain is that whatever his capabilities they were not recognized as being in the same league as Deng's. This, together with the aforementioned fact that Hua initially adopted Deng's 1975 program, meant that Hua's voice in Party councils could hardly be authoritative. Similarly, with regard to personnel, the limited provincial nature of Hua's long-term contacts severely restricted his opportunities for placing supporters in key positions. Thus in addition to the new Politburo, the extensive reshuffle of provincial leaders in the nine-month period *preceding* Deng's reinstatement saw the appointment of considerably more officials with clear-cut career ties to Deng than Hua.[89] Hua's long-standing associates were simply too few and too junior to be eligible for many powerful posts, while officials with sufficient seniority would at least have had dealings with Deng even when they lacked close personal links.

In terms of building alliances, Hua was faced with some unpalatable alternatives. If he aligned too closely with his "natural" constituency, his fellow Cultural Revolution beneficiaries, he would side with the weakest force within the elite and risk being caught up in resentments harbored against them by both the survivor and victim groups. But if he identified wholeheartedly with every aspect of Deng's policies he would be shorn of all independent support. A more appealing option was to deepen his ties with the survivor group, which supported him in the name of continuity and apparently had doubts about some Deng policies, but this group would surely ultimately back Deng as the leading figure of the old guard. In this context, moreover, Hua was handicapped by the fact that in contrast to Deng's case, bold initiatives involved major risks. While Deng, because of his status and the expectation of the elite as a whole that he would provide dynamic leadership, could launch innovations unwelcome to specific interests without seriously undermining his position, Hua's inherent weakness meant any innovative actions on his part threatened to anger groups he could ill afford to alienate. While Hua may have genuinely favored the more orthodox "Maoist" positions he tended to espouse in 1977-78,[90] his political situation required him to back existing approaches and placed him in the passive position of responding to Deng's initiatives (see below).

In these circumstances, Hua chose to play a cautious game which avoided overidentification with any group while at the same time trying to capitalize on his major assets—his apparent designation as successor by Mao and the regime's need for stability and unity. Indeed, Hua was in one sense fortunate that his personal needs to a substantial degree overlapped with these regime requirements, but in another sense he was vulnerable in that these requirements were largely transitional and clashed with the longer range need to come fully to terms with the Cultural Revolution. In this regard it is instructive that nearly all the charges which have been raised against Hua deal with the transition period before the December 1978 Third Plenum, which marked a clear break with Cultural Revolution symbolism.[91] Thus while Hua's cult of personality initially served to maintain the leadership's link to Mao following the traumatic events of 1976 as well as bolster his personal legitimacy, by 1980 it was under attack as a manifestation of the feudal attitudes which marred Mao's later years. The use of Cultural Revolution slogans in 1977-78, while in fact reversing the policies of that movement, served to cushion the shock of those reversals, but later such slogans were denounced as reflecting Hua's leftist ideology and contributing to the overambitious economic expansion program. And, as previously suggested, the measured pace of rehabilitations might have reflected a genuine need to work out acceptable compromises, but by 1980-81 it was pictured as a deliberate effort by Hua to prevent the righting of Cultural Revolution wrongs. On all these and other issues Hua was more caught out by changing circumstances than guilty of dogged resistance to the dominant trend.

In fact, Hua was quite cognizant of the prudential requirement of accommodating Deng, even at the cost of disowning his own positions and distancing himself from his "natural" allies. This can be seen with regard to the related charges that Hua promoted the "two whatevers" (whatever policy decisions Mao made, whatever instructions Mao gave) and tried to suppress discussions of the Deng-supported proposition that "practice is the sole criterion of truth." The actual cases were more complex. While Hua apparently coined the "two whatevers" in a draft speech in January 1977, the phrase was subsequently taken up by Wang Dongxing and others who were later dubbed the "whatever" faction. Hua appears to have remained aloof from their line, particularly after Deng's April 1977 letter criticizing the concept, and by the December 1978 plenum he was counseling Politburo member Chen Yonggui on the errors of Chen's "whateverist" views.[92] Similarly, while Hua assertedly temporized on the "criterion of truth" debate which promised to chip away at Mao's reputation and thus his own legitimacy, it was again Wang Dongxing who played an active role by banning articles on the "practice" question. When Hua did take action in the latter part of 1978 it was on the side of "practice": he countermanded Wang's suppression of a magazine carrying articles on the issue, lectured Wang against damaging stability and unity by his actions, and called for "emancipating the mind."[93] From the end of 1978, with the "whateverists" discredited, Hua had no choice but to step up further his cooperation with the dominant coalition and try to be a valued member of the team even though its policies were increasingly critical of the 1977-78 transition period.[94] Hua's dilemma was poignantly expressed at the 1980 NPC when, just as he was coming under sharp attack for his alleged past sins, he sought to identify himself with Deng's program by speaking out strongly in favor of economic and other reforms.[95]

But the die had already been cast. Whether because of doubts about Hua's commitment to the new program, a feeling that he had indeed tried to obstruct the rehabilitation of Deng and others, resentment over the events of 1976,[96] or simply the desire to install a more reliable successor, Deng now pressed home the attack on Hua and forced his resignation in favor of Hu Yaobang. Hua, accusations of fostering a personality cult notwithstanding, had largely observed the normative requirements of collective leadership and, given a weak hand, had not played the prudential game badly. Indeed, it could even be argued that Hua played a role of inestimable value in dampening tensions and facilitating a relatively smooth transition in the immediate post-Mao period. But whatever Hua's virtues, or skills as a politician, they could not withstand a determined Deng. As we have seen in the previous essay,[97] Deng's actions produced considerable resentment but no effective resistance. This was perhaps inevitable given the absence of binding normative rules governing the selection of successors. In such circumstances Politburo politicians found it prudent to heed the choice of the current leader, but only after satisfying themselves that unlike the case of Lin Biao the choice posed no threat to the larger interests of the elite as a whole.

Conclusions and Prospects

What conclusions can be drawn about normative and prudential rules in post-1949 Chinese politics on the basis of the foregoing analysis? Prudential rules in any system are necessarily fragile—they can only provide broad guidelines for political strategies which may be significantly altered at any time by changing circumstances. Even in the most stable situations, moreover, politics remains an art where both skill and luck are required for success regardless of how assiduously such rules are followed. In any case, the reliability of prudential guidelines is closely linked to the strength of normative rules. Normative standards not only claim to prescribe procedures which should be honored, but perhaps more importantly place restraints on political behavior by setting the parameters of what is acceptable. Where such norms have force politicians can evolve strategies within those parameters with some confidence of success and, more significantly, without risking all. But in cases where the norms are inoperative, the basis for political calculation is upset, prudential guidelines are less predictable guides to action, and the penalties for losing become much greater. Basically, effective normative rules make politics more conservative by circumscribing the options open to political leaders, forcing compromise, and reducing the stakes of the game.

This relationship between normative and prudential rules has been clearly manifest in the politics of the PRC. In the pre-Cultural Revolution years, normative rules functioned reasonably well despite definite erosion in the latter part of the period, and Politburo-level politicians could generally chart a safe course in the conservative politics which resulted. Before 1966, Mao's lieutenants could by and large get on with their jobs without running great risks or plotting against their colleagues. The 1966-1976 decade however, saw the norms fall by the wayside and a strife ridden, often lethal politics emerge. In this situation, leading politicians not only could not count on the protection of official Party principles, they were also thrown into a high risk game where strategies could backfire at any time. In this climate of bitterness, danger, and uncertainty the effectiveness of standard prudential ploys was severely eroded; thus Lin Biao's efforts to secure military backing through strong institutional appeals were only partially successful at best. More broadly, with the stakes now higher than ever before, leading politicians were driven in desperation to measures clearly proscribed by formal norms, including naked factionalism, planning for military action, and attempted assassination.

The key to this dramatic fluctuation of normative and prudential rules was, of course, Mao. The Chairman changed both sets of rules virtually at will. While engaging in various breaches of the norms before the Cultural Revolution—most notably in the attack on Peng Dehuai at Lushan—Mao had in theory and to a large extent in practice upheld official principles. The Cultural Revolution, in contrast, saw him effectively discard normative rules even though he later selectively championed the prohibition on factionalism with regard to Lin Biao and the "Gang of Four." Moreover, from the early 1960s on, Mao's increasingly erratic behavior made it extremely difficult to implement the central prudential rule of not crossing the Chairman. Even Lin Biao, who understood as well as anyone the need to cultivate the Chairman, in the end seriously miscalculated on how to maintain his goodwill. Ultimately, throughout Mao's lifetime, both the fortunes of individual leaders and the guidelines affecting political life were vulnerable to the visions and whims of the charismatic leader.

The death of Mao removed the major force which undermined both normative rules and the capacity of Politburo leaders to make relatively predictable prudential calculations. In certain senses the rules had come full circle. The elite's strong commitment to the normative rules which make politics a safer pastime resulted in their reassertion, including an emphasis on collective leadership that now limits Deng Xiaoping's still substantial power. With this reassertion many of the cautious prudential practices of the pre-1966 period have reappeared, including avoiding appointments overly weighted to any single group and careful consensus-building on contentious issues. Moreover, the absence of a charismatic Mao has produced an important reciprocal requirement to complement the still powerful prudential rule of the need to accommodate the leader: the leader must attend to the regime's major institutional interests and the views of the old revolutionary elite. Mao could grossly violate this requirement and remain supreme, but Deng is much more hemmed in by the key constituencies of "the system."

Despite the greater limits on Deng's authority, it is important to recognize that both normative and prudential rules still suffer from ambiguities and remain vulnerable to political circumstances and personalities. While the norms have been strengthened and institutional patterns reestablished, this is a relative condition which cannot obscure the fact that the ultimate question of power is not genuinely regulated by formal procedures. Thus Deng Xiaoping not only wields power without holding the ranking position in the CCP, even where he holds the relevant position—e.g., as head of the MAC overseeing military affairs[98]—power is derived more from his person than the office. Moreover, the capacity of even noncharismatic leaders in Leninist systems to go very far both in ignoring formal rules, damaging major institutional and elite interests, and pushing unsuccessful policies was amply illustrated by the case of Khrushchev.[99] Deng is in a somewhat analogous position in that many of his policies cut against ingrained interests and have been less than unmitigated successes, but he has been far more skillful in maintaining support by timely compromise and broad consultation. Clearly for Deng, as was the case for Khrushchev, there is a point in terms of damaging elite interests and failed policies beyond which he cannot go, but in the absence of binding procedures for removal from power, the capacity to bend normative rules and upset prudential calculations remains considerable.

What of the period after Deng? A long-term trend toward a more Soviet style politics where formal institutional positions and the tradeoff of organizational interests predominate seems inevitable. But it is important to realize that there will be a significant transitional period even after Deng when the peculiar consequences of the Chinese revolution and Mao's rule will remain a strong influence on the CCP elite. The key requirement before more institutionalized patterns take over fully is the complete passing away of the revolutionary elite. Until that time comes, ancient leaders too infirm to carry a full bureaucratic load will have strong voices in inner-Party councils. Only then will the *guanxi* of revolutionary peers be fully eclipsed by bureaucratic links.[100] Moreover, the turmoil of Mao's last decade greatly upset the "natural" precedence of leadership. The Cultural Revolution saw many figures of great seniority demoted or cast aside while those of little status were raised to great heights. While this situation has been corrected by post-Cultural Revolution and post-Mao rehabilitations to a large degree, the "natural" order is still disjointed owing to the political accidents of that decade. Not only has Deng's real leadership not been formally acknowledged, but other leaders—most notably Chen Yun—are recognized as in some sense having greater claims to leadership than the likes of Hu Yaobang.[101] Should Deng die before any or all of these leaders, their personal prestige is likely to outweigh the institutional powers Hu has been accumulating under Deng's patronage.

It would be rash to predict the succession to Deng for many reasons—not least the above-mentioned order of the old guard's departure. Some speculation, however, can shed light on the intermediate-range prospects of normative and prudential rules in a post-Deng China. First, the possibility of a genuine succession struggle must be acknowledged. While Deng has been widely perceived as the legitimate leader, it is unlikely that Hu Yaobang is generally seen as someone who can claim the mantle of successor as a matter of right. As argued in the previous essay, Hu's elevation was largely a concession to Deng rather than a broad consensus on Hu. In fact, Hu's very closeness to Deng will probably work against him in the long run. Rather than having independent prestige as someone capable of "delivering the goods" on his own initiative—as, for example, Premier Zhao Ziyang gained from his agricultural innovations in Sichuan during the early post-Mao period—Hu is largely regarded as Deng's protégé. In this role, while performing valuable services for Deng as a troubleshooter, Hu has often borne much of the resentment engendered by Deng's policies.[102] Such resentments, as well as those created by what important segments of the elite regarded as the shabby treatment of Hua Guofeng, will undoubtedly make Hu vulnerable after the passing of his patron. Of course, Hu could conceivably prevail, particularly if he has ample time to place old associates in key positions[103] and Deng's policies prove successful. The broad elite commitment to political stability could also work to Hu's advantage. But whatever the eventual outcome, in the absence of binding normative procedures the genuine succession struggle avoided after Mao's death may ensue. Yet it is almost certain that the norms will have an impact on any such struggle. The commitment to the norms, while perhaps not preventing a divisive conflict, is likely to keep it within bounds and limit the negative consequences for the losers and system as a whole. The naked factionalism and direct military intervention of the 1966-1976 period are improbable, and the relative humaneness of Hua Guofeng's fall would most likely be repeated.[104] The prudential rules of any conflict would increasingly center on "delivering the goods" of successful policies, forging bureaucratic alliances, and placing associates in key positions, although the presumed survival of at least some important figures from the revolutionary period will prevent an overly bureaucratized politics. While the very fact of a succession struggle would erode some norms and induce a more risk taking approach, the constraints created by major institutional interests and those of the elite as a whole will be heavily felt.[105]

Given the ultimately nonbinding nature of normative rules in the PRC, politics must remain significantly personalized in any circumstances. But the trend is clear: the scope of maneuver for leading political actors is gradually contracting as institutionalization proceeds. The founder of the system, the charismatic Mao, could in effect rewrite the rules at will. His unwanted successor, the old revolutionary Deng, can draw on a vast reservoir of revolutionary prestige and *guanxi* to bend those rules and govern without the full powers of office, but he must account for elite interests to a far greater extent than Mao. For Hu Yaobang or any other successor to Deng, the constraints of the rules and institutional interests of the system will be greater still. Unable to draw on the heroic legacy of the past to anything like the same degree, such politicians will increasingly shape their strategies around bureaucratic tradeoffs and policy outcomes. Nevertheless, the continuing influence of old revolutionaries and inherent flaws in the rules promise a special element of fluidity and unpredictability in Chinese leadership politics for the foreseeable future.

NOTES

Notes to Introduction

1. See Kenneth Lieberthal, *A Research Guide to Central Party and Government Meetings in China 1949-1975* (White Plains, N.Y.: International Arts and Sciences Press, 1976), pp. 3, 36.

2. This was a particularly pronounced feature at the 1956 Party Congress. See, e.g., Roderick MacFarquhar, *The Origins of the Cultural Revolution 1: Contradictions among the People 1956-1957* (New York: Columbia University Press, 1974), p. 124.

3. Most notably *Mao Zedong sixiang wan sui* [Long Live Mao Zedong's Thought] (2 vols., Taibei: 1967, 1969).

4. See the discussion of possible Politburo divisions over the 1957 Hundred Flowers movement in Frederick C. Teiwes, *Politics and Purges in China: Rectification and the Decline of Party Norms 1950-1965* (White Plains, N.Y.: M. E. Sharpe, 1979), pp. 247-57.

5. See Michel Oksenberg, "Sources and Methodological Problems in the Study of Contemporary China," in A. Doak Barnett, ed., *Chinese Communist Politics in Action* (Seattle: University of Washington Press, 1969), pp. 580-81.

6. See Michael Y. M. Kau, ed., *The Lin Piao Affair: Power Politics and Military Coup* (White Plains, N.Y.: International Arts and Sciences Press, 1975), pp. xxv-xxix, xliv-xlv and documents 5-12, 14-22.

7. Most notably the monthly *Zhengming* [Contention] which has supported the "reformist" policies generally associated with Deng Xiaoping.

8. It appeared in two parts in the Hong Kong journal of the United States Information Service (USIS), *Current Scene*, January and February 1974. Starting in 1973 a change in regulations governing USIS prevented the distribution of *Current Scene* within the United States.

9. See the discussion of changing fashions in the analysis of Chinese politics in Lucian W. Pye, *The Dynamics of Factions and Consensus in Chinese Politics: A Model and Some Propositions* (Santa Monica: RAND Report R-2566-AF, July 1980), pp. 41-45.

10. See particularly W. F. Dorrill's early analysis, *Power, Policy, and Ideology in the Making of China's "Cultural Revolution"* (Santa Monica: RAND Memorandum RM-5731-PR, August 1968), which refutes many of the "two line" assertions of PRC sources; and the Mao-centered argument of Michel C. Oksenberg, "Policy Making Under Mao, 1949-68: An Overview," in John M. H. Lindbeck, *China: Management of a Revolutionary Society* (Seattle: University of Washington Press, 1971).

11. See Richard M. Pfeffer's review of Richard H. Solomon's *Mao's Revolution and the Chinese Political Culture*, "Revolting: An Essay on 'Mao's Revolution,'" by Richard Solomon," *Bulletin of Concerned Asian Scholars*, December 1973. After attacking the "[anti-China] ideological zeal" of Solomon's psycho-cultural analysis, Pfeffer goes on to praise his "two line" mode of explaining the elite politics of the 1955-1964 decade (see pp. 48, 52-54).

12. See Ellis Joffe, *Between Two Plenums: China's Intraleadership Conflict, 1959-1962* (Ann Arbor: Michigan Papers in Chinese Studies No. 22, 1975), pp. 1-3.

13. See especially Lowell Dittmer, "'Line Struggle' in Theory and Practice: The Origins of the Cultural Revolution Reconsidered," *The China Quarterly* (*CQ*), No. 72 (1977); and Andrew J. Nathan, "Policy Oscillations in the People's Republic of China: A Critique," *CQ*, No. 68 (1976).

14. See Pye, *The Dynamics of Factions*; David M. Lampton, *The Politics of Medicine in China: The Policy Process, 1949-1977* (Boulder: Westview Press, 1977); and Benedict Stavis, *The Politics of Agricultural Mechanization in China* (Ithaca: Cornell University Press, 1978), for examples of these approaches. Although similar perspectives were advanced in the late 1960s and early 1970s and even such sophisticated analyses as those of Lampton and Stavis contain elements of the "two line" interpretation, the overall influence of the "two line struggle" model on scholarly writings was far greater at the start of the 1970s than by the end of the decade.

15. See, e.g., Robert Taylor, *China's Intellectual Dilemma: Politics and University Enrollment, 1949-1978* (Vancouver: University of British Columbia Press, 1981); and Louis T. Sigel, "On the 'Two Roads' and Following Our Own Path: The Myth of the 'Capitalist Road,'" *The Australian Journal of Chinese Affairs*, No. 7 (1982).

16. "Outline of 'Project 571,'" in Kau, *Lin Piao*, p. 92.

17. See the analysis in Michel Oksenberg, "The Political Leader," in Dick Wilson, ed., *Mao Tse-tung in the Scales of History* (London: Cambridge University Press, 1977), pp. 77-81, 91-95. In my view (see the third essay below), while Mao did consciously play off various colleagues against one another during his rise to power in the 1930s and from the mid-1960s on, "divide and rule" tactics were not a major facet of his leadership style from the time Mao consolidated his authority in the early 1940s until the immediate pre-Cultural Revolution period.

18. See his "The Changing Nature and Locus of Authority in Communist China," in Lindbeck, *Management of a Revolutionary Society*.

19. A variation on this perspective stimulated by the Cultural Revolution emphasizes the conflicting claims of the Party and leader to the mantle of legitimacy. See the relevant analyses in Stuart R. Schram, "The Party in Chinese Communist Ideology," in John Wilson Lewis, ed., *Party Leadership and Revolutionary Power in China* (Cambridge: Cambridge University Press, 1970); Benjamin I. Schwartz, "The Reign of Virtue: Some Broad Perspectives on the Leader and Party in the Cultural Revolution," in *ibid.*; and Leonard Schapiro and John Wilson Lewis, "The Roles of the Monolithic Party under the Totalitarian Leader," in *ibid.*

20. See T. H. Rigby's essays, "A Conceptual Approach to Authority, Power and Policy in the Soviet Union," in T. H. Rigby, Archie Brown, and Peter Reddaway, eds., *Authority, Power and Policy in the USSR* (London: Macmillan, 1980); and "Introduction: Political Legitimacy, Weber and Communist Mono-

organisational Systems," in T. H. Rigby and Ferenc Feher, *Political Legitimation in Communist States* (London: Macmillan, 1982).

21. "Getting Ahead and Along in Communist China: The Ladder of Success on the Eve of the Cultural Revolution," in Lewis, *Party Leadership*.

22. See Parris H. Chang, "Provincial Party Leaders' Strategies for Survival during the Cultural Revolution," in Robert A. Scalapino, ed., *Elites in the People's Republic of China* (Seattle: University of Washington Press, 1972); and Richard Baum, "Elite Behavior under Conditions of Stress: The Lesson of the 'Tang-ch'üan P'ai' in the Cultural Revolution," in *ibid.*

23. See, e.g., Parris H. Chang, "Who Gets What, When and How in Chinese Politics—A Case Study of the Strategies of Conflict of the 'Gang of Four,'" *The Australian Journal of Chinese Affairs*, No. 2 (1979).

Notes to Chapter I

1. "Comments on a Letter' (July 26, 1959), in *Chinese Law and Government* (*CLG*), Winter 1968-69, p. 51.

2. "Letter to Chiang Ch'ing" (July 8, 1966), in *Issues & Studies* (*IS*), January 1973, p. 96.

3. Editorial note to *Socialist Upsurge in China's Countryside* (1956), in Stuart R. Schram, *The Political Thought of Mao Tse-tung* (revised and enlarged edition, New York: Frederick A. Praeger, 1969), p. 351.

4. See especially the account of Mao's struggle against the "three 'left' lines" in "Resolution on Certain Questions in the History of Our Party" (April 20, 1945), *Selected Works of Mao Tse-tung* (*SW*), Vol. III (Beijing: Foreign Languages Press, 1965), pp. 177-225.

5. "Talk at the Conference on the Question of Intellectuals Called by the Center" (January 20, 1956), in Jerome Ch'en, ed., *Mao Papers: Anthology and Bibliography* (*MP*) (London: Oxford University Press, 1970), p. 21.

6. *Quotations from Chairman Mao Tse-tung* (Beijing: Foreign Languages Press, 1966), pp. 118-19 (emphasis added).

7. See, e.g., "The Question of Agricultural Cooperation" (July 31, 1955), in *Communist China 1955-59: Policy Documents with Analysis* (*PDA*), with a foreword by Robert R. Bowie and John K. Fairbank (Cambridge, Mass.: Harvard University Press, 1965), p. 96.

8. This was apparent in warnings that higher-level work teams only play a supportive role in the conduct of mass movements and do not supplant the leadership of basic-level cadres who have closer links to the masses. See Mao's editorial note to *Socialist Upsurge*, in Schram, *Political Thought*, pp. 321-22.

9. "Some Questions Concerning Methods of Leadership" (June 1, 1943), *SW*, III, 118.

10. See, e.g., Mao's 1965 interview with André Malraux in Jerome Ch'en, ed., *Mao: Great Lives Observed* (*Mao*) (Englewood Cliffs: Prentice-Hall, Inc., 1969), pp. 121-23, where he declared, "broad layers of our society are conditioned in such a way their activity is necessarily oriented toward revisionism," and "humanity left to its own devices . . . re-establish[es] inequality."

11. See the original version of "Some Questions Concerning Methods of

Leadership" in *Jiefang ribao* [Liberation Daily], June 4, 1943 (cited in Schram, "The Party in Chinese Ideology," p. 179).

12. Schram, "The Party in Chinese Ideology," pp. 178-79.

13. In "Agricultural Cooperation," p. 94, Mao noted the failure of Party leaders to keep up with the masses but went on to stipulate the careful measures cited below, p. 17.

14. In his "Talk at the Central Work Conference" (October 25, 1966), in *MP*, p. 43, Mao pointed out that while directives issued through organizational channels had failed to elicit much response, the chaotic Red Guard movement had forced people to take notice of the problems he wished dealt with. In February 1967, however, Mao attacked a proposal to abolish "chiefs" as "extreme anarchy" and "most reactionary." See "Chairman Mao's Speech at His Third Meeting with Chang Ch'un-ch'iao and Yao Wen-yüan," in *Joint Publications Research Service* (*JPRS*), No. 49826, p. 44.

15. "Talk in Hangchow" (December 21, 1965), in *Mao*, p. 105.

16. See Mao's "Sixty Articles on Work Methods (Draft)" (January 31, 1958), Article 22, in *MP*, pp. 64-65.

17. *Peking Review* (*PR*), July 17, 1964, p. 21.

18. See, e.g., "On Some Important Problems of the Party's Present Policy" (January 18, 1948), *SW*, Vol. IV (Beijing: Foreign Languages Press, 1961), pp. 181-189.

19. *Mao*, p. 72.

20. In his October 1953 "Speech at the Third Conference on Mutual Aid and Cooperation Convened by the Central Committee," Mao warned that "if rural positions are not occupied by socialism, they would necessarily be occupied by capitalism." *Current Background* (*CB*), No. 897, p. 38.

21. See Mao's "Preface to *Socialist Upsurge in China's Countryside*" (December 27, 1955), in *PDA*, p. 118; his editorial note to the same volume in Schram, *Political Thought*, pp. 322-23; and "Opening Address at the Eighth National Congress of the Communist Party of China" (September 15, 1956), *Eighth National Congress of the Communist Party of China*, Vol. I (Beijing: Foreign Languages Press, 1956), p. 7.

22. "Talk at Core Group Meeting in Peitaiho" (August 9, 1962), in *JPRS*, No. 52029, p. 22.

23. *Speech at the Chinese Communist Party's National Conference on Propaganda Work* (Beijing: Foreign Languages Press, 1966), pp. 2-3, 25.

24. Mao expressed this view in "Talk at Reception for Our Country's Students and Trainees in Moscow" (November 17, 1957), in *CB*, No. 891, p. 26; and the introductory note to "Sixty Articles on Work Methods," p. 57. Only in 1962 did he flatly say the ideological and political efforts of 1957 had been insufficient. See "Talk at Core Group Meeting," p. 23.

25. In his July 1955 call for more rapid development of cooperativization, Mao stipulated: "Whenever a number of cooperatives have been established in a province or county there must be a time when we can stop for a check up before we go on to set up some more. The idea of never allowing any pause, any rest, is all wrong." "Agricultural Cooperation," p. 102.

26. *Ibid.*, p. 97.

27. See "Ten Great Relationships" (April 1956), in *Mao*, p. 70.

28. See "The Greatest Friendship" (1953), in *Mao*, pp. 119-20.

29. "On the Correct Handling of Contradictions Among the People" (February 27, 1957), in *PDA*, p. 286.

30. A major premise of Mao's argument for increasing the rate of agricultural cooperativization was that otherwise polarization of the rural rich and poor would develop. See "Agricultural Cooperation," p. 103.

31. See "Correct Handling of Contradictions," p. 284, where Mao discusses the balance among state, agricultural cooperative, and individual peasant interests.

32. See, e.g., "The Bourgeois Orientation of *Wen Hui Pao*" (June 14, 1957), in *MP*, p. 56.

33. See Mao's remarks at the July 1959 Lushan meeting where he responded to criticisms of the Great Leap by saying: ". . . in 1958 and 1959 I should take main responsibility, it is I who am to blame. In the past responsibility was on others . . . but now I am to blame for I really have taken charge of a great many things." "Speech at the Lushan Conference" (July 23, 1959), in *The Case of Peng Teh-huai: 1959-1968* (Hong Kong: Union Research Institute, 1968), p. 25.

34. "Speech to the Supreme State Conference" (January 28, 1958), in *CLG*, Winter 1968-69, pp. 10, 12.

35. "Speech at the Eighth Plenum of the Eighth Central Committee" (August 2, 1959), in *Case of Peng*, p. 30.

36. "Sixty Articles on Work Methods," Article 21, as translated in Stuart R. Schram, "Mao Tse-tung and the Theory of the Permanent Revolution," *CQ*, No. 46 (1971), p. 227.

37. "The Origin of Machine Guns and Mortars, etc." (August 16, 1959), in *CLG*, Winter 1968-69, p. 74. In 1962 Mao noted that many leading comrades were startled at his view that class struggle still existed, a further tacit admission that Mao had not placed major emphasis on class struggle in his thinking during the Great Leap period. See "Remarks on August 6, 1962," in *JPRS*, No. 52029, p. 19.

38. "Ten Great Relationships," pp. 83-84. The words quoted, which give a more graphic expression of Mao's meaning than his actual 1956 words, are taken from *Hongqi* [Red Flag], June 1, 1958, in Schram, *Political Thought*, p. 352.

39. "Speech to the Supreme State Conference," p. 11. Cf. Schram's discussion in *Political Thought*, p. 91.

40. *Hongqi*, No. 10, 1958, in Schram, *Political Thought*, pp. 352-53.

41. "Speech to the Supreme State Conference," as translated in Schram, "Mao and Permanent Revolution," p. 226. Cf. Schram's discussion in *ibid.*, pp. 231ff.

42. "Sixty Articles on Work Methods," Article 22, as translated in *ibid.*, p. 228.

43. "Speech at the Chengtu Conference" (March 22, 1958), in *JPRS*, No. 49826, p. 47; and "Talk at the Conference of Heads of Delegations to the Second Session of the Eighth Congress" (May 18, 1958), in *CB*, No. 888, p. 9.

44. See "Speech at the Lushan Conference," pp. 16-18, 22-24.

45. For a discussion of this shift in economic strategy, see Franz Schurmann, *Ideology and Organization in Communist China* (Berkeley: University of California Press, 1966), pp. 76-90, 101-104.

46. See Mao's description of himself in "Speech at the Lushan Conference," p. 23. In a post-Cultural Revolution interview with Couve de Murville, Mao did use

the term "center-leftist" to describe himself; see Ross Terrill, *800,000,000: The Real China* (Boston: Little, Brown, 1972), p. 68.

47. "Letter to Brigade Leaders" (November 29, 1959), in *MP*, p. 9.

48. "Speech at the Tenth Plenum" (September 24, 1962), in *CLG*, Winter 1968-69, pp. 86-87.

49. See "Talk at a Central Work Conference" (September 1965), in *MP*, p. 102.

50. "Speech at the Tenth Plenum," pp. 90, 92. There is some confusion in Mao's use of "class struggle" here. In his first reference to its different nature from work he adopts a broad usage—"the struggle between Marxism and revisionism." When speaking of the need not to jeopardize work, however, he refers to public security work against enemy sabotage, a much narrower usage.

51. "Talk at Expanded Central Committee Meeting" (January 30, 1962), in *JPRS*, No. 52029, pp. 13-14.

52. Mao in 1965 as quoted by André Malraux. *Mao*, pp. 121, 123.

53. See, e.g., "Talk with the Guinean Educational Delegation" (August 8, 1965), in *CB*, No. 888, p. 15.

54. "Instruction on Literature and Art" (June 27, 1964), in *MP*, p. 97.

55. See, e.g., "Conversation with Nepalese Educational Delegation" (1964), in *MP*, pp. 21-23.

56. See, e.g., "Courses and Examinations" (March 10, 1964), in *MP*, p. 97.

57. In "Summary of a Talk with Mao Yüan-hsin" (July 5, 1964), in *CB*, No. 888, p. 14, Mao cited the example of teachers using their status to deny students printed lecture notes, thus preserving the traditional lecture format and hiding their limited competence which would be revealed through discussion classes.

58. See "Instruction on Public Health" (June 25, 1965), in *MP*, pp. 100-101; "Talk at Core Group Meeting," p. 22; and "Comment on Comrade Ch'en Cheng-jen's Report on his Squatting Point" (January 29, 1965), in *MP*, p. 100.

59. See "Maniacs of the New Era," in *Selections from China Mainland Magazines (SCMM)*, No. 602, p. 8. It is also worth noting that Liu's revised 1962 edition of *How to Be a Good Communist*, which was accused during the Cultural Revolution of being an attempt to denigrate Mao, actually added quotations from the Chairman.

60. See "Chiang Ch'ing's Speech at the Enlarged Meeting of the Military Affairs Commission of the Central Committee" (April 12, 1967), in *IS*, July 1970, p. 88; and "Circular of the Central Committee" (May 16, 1966), in *MP*, p. 107.

61. See *Jinggangshan* and *Guangdong wenyi zhanbao* [Jinggang Mountains and Guangdong Literary Combat Bulletin], September 5, 1967, in *Survey of China Mainland Press (SCMP)*, No. 4046, p. 4.

62. For example, concerning the 1959 replacement of Mao by Liu as chief of state, Mao proposed his retirement in late 1957 as the Great Leap Forward was taking shape, a time of undoubted strength. See "Sixty Articles on Work Methods," Article 60, p. 75.

63. "A Minister of Foreign Affairs Like Me," in *Facts and Features*, March 20, 1968 (cited in Lowell Dittmer, "The Cultural Revolution and the Fall of Liu Shao-ch'i," *Current Scene*, January 1973, p. 8).

64. "Self-Criticism at the Work Conference of the Center" (October 23, 1966),

in *SCMM*, No. 652, p. 23.

65. See "The Confession of Wu Leng-hsi," translated and annotated by Parris H. Chang, in *CLG*, Winter 1969-70, pp. 78-79.

66. See Michael Yahuda, "Kremlinology and the Chinese Strategic Debate, 1965-66," *CQ*, No. 49 (1972), pp. 68-71.

67. New China News Agency, Beijing, September 23, 1967, in *CB*, No. 843, p. 5.

68. "A Collection of Chou Yang's Counterrevolutionary Revisionist Speeches," in *SCMM*, No. 646, pp. 4-6.

69. "Collection of Ch'en I's Speeches," in *SCMM*, No. 636, p. 29.

70. "Speech at Enlarged Central Committee Meeting" (January 30, 1962), in *JPRS*, No. 50792, pp. 44-45.

71. "Speech at Group Leaders Forum of the Enlarged Conference of the Military Affairs Commission" (June 28, 1958), in *CLG*, Winter 1968-69, p. 15.

72. "Talk at an Enlarged Central Work Conference" (January 30, 1962), in Stuart Schram, ed., *Mao Tse-tung Unrehearsed, Talks and Letters: 1956-71* (Harmondsworth: Penguin Books, 1974), pp. 164-65. (This translation has been substituted for the less accurate one used in the original article.)

73. *Wenge fengyun* [Cultural Revolution Storm], No. 4, 1967, in *SCMM*, No. 635, p. 10.

74. See "Report on the Question of the Errors Committed by Lo Jui-ch'ing" (April 30, 1966), in *IS*, August 1969, pp. 88-89.

75. In his talks with local leaders immediately before Lin's demise, Mao attacked the notions of "peak" and "genius." See "Summary of Talks with Responsible Comrades of Various Places during Inspection Tour" (mid-August-September 12, 1971), in *IS*, September 1972, pp. 67-68.

76. In addition to the above quotations, see "Talk at Expanded Central Committee Meeting," in *JPRS*, No. 52029, p. 9.

77. As the Cultural Revolution unfolded in 1966, Mao's comments about individuals frequently manifested resentment of imagined personal slights and suspicion of motives and character. See, e.g., "Speech at Central Committee Work Report Meeting" (October 24, 1966), in *Mao*, pp. 93-94.

78. In his July 1966 "Letter to Chiang Ch'ing," p. 95, Mao indicated he was disturbed by some of Lin's theories.

79. In his interview with Lord Montgomery, reported in *South China Morning Post*, October 17, 1961.

80. "Sixty Articles on Work Methods," Introduction, p. 57. Although the fact that Article 23, presumably the one written by Liu, dealt with rules and regulations and has been cited as evidence of Liu's preoccupation with order, a close reading of this section produces a different impression. Liu, in fact, emphasized the impermanence of rules and the need to revise or abolish them in response to new situations created by mass initiative. Indeed, the masses were to be "encourage[d] . . . to break those rules and regulations which restrict the development of productive forces." At this time, it seems there was a close compatibility of views between Mao and Liu.

81. *Heilongjiang ribao* [Heilongjiang Daily], June 14, 1967 (cited in Tang Tsou, "The Cultural Revolution and the Chinese Political System," *CQ*, No. 38 (1969), p. 75).

82. Wang Guangmei (Mme. Liu) at her "first trial" in April 1967 said: "The Chairman entrusted Liu Shaoqi with many things and held him responsible when trouble occurred." "Three Trials of Pickpocket Wang Kuang-mei," in *CB*, No. 848, p. 11.

83. "Talk at Central Work Conference" (October 25, 1966), in *Mao*, p. 96.

84. Mao's August 1966 big character poster, "Bombard the Headquarters," in *MP*, p. 117, cited the 1962 "right deviation" together with differences over the conduct of the Socialist Education Movement and Cultural Revolution as evidence that a "bourgeois dictatorship" had been set up.

85. "Self-Criticism at Central Work Conference" (October 23, 1966), in *CLG*, Winter 1970-71, pp. 283, 289.

86. See Chen Boda's "Speech at Central Work Conference" (October 25, 1966), in *CB*, No. 651, p. 6.

87. "Report on the Errors Committed by Lo Jui-ch'ing," p. 97.

88. "Self-Criticism at Central Work Conference" (October 23, 1966), in *IS*, June 1970, pp. 95-96.

89. "Talk at Core Group Meeting," p. 27.

90. "Talk at the General Report Meeting" (October 24, 1966), in *Mao*, p. 95.

91. See Deng Xiaoping's "Self-Criticism," p. 288; and Chen Boda's "Speech at Central Work Conference," p. 5.

92. See, e.g., the discussion of Tao Zhu's rural experiments in Guangdong in "Tao Chu Is the Khrushchev of South China," January 14, 1967, in *CB*, No. 824, pp. 12-13, 16-17.

93. Chen Yi's statement in *Renmin ribao* (*RMRB*) [People's Daily], November 13, 1955 (cited in *PDA*, p. 3).

94. "Speech on the Party's General Line for the Transition Period," in *CB*, No. 897, p. 30.

95. Liu Shaoqi, "Self-Criticism at Central Work Conference" (October 23, 1966), in *IS*, June 1970, p. 94; and Kenneth R. Walker, "Collectivisation in Retrospect: The 'Socialist High Tide' of Autumn 1955-Spring 1956," *CQ*, No. 26 (1966), pp. 21, 29.

96. Frederick C. Teiwes, "Provincial Politics in China: Themes and Variations," in Lindbeck, *Management of a Revolutionary Society*, pp. 140-42.

97. Walker, "Collectivisation," p. 30.

98. "Agricultural Cooperation," pp. 95-97, 102.

99. Teiwes, "Provincial Politics," pp. 142-43; and Walker, "Collectivisation," pp. 34-43.

100. In addition to provincial officials, a number of central leaders on the economic front recanted their errors and enthusiastically endorsed Mao's initiative in fall 1955. See Walker, "Collectivisation," p. 33.

101. The following is based on a series of articles in *Nongye jixie jishu* [Agricultural Machinery Techniques], August-September 1967 and September 1968, in *SCMM*, Nos. 609, 610, 613, 630, 633; and "The Conflict between Mao Tse-tung and Liu Shao-ch'i over Agricultural Mechanization in Communist China," *Current Scene*, October 1, 1968.

102. "Talk at Expanded Central Committee Meeting," in *JPRS*, No. 52029, p. 13.

103. In "Speech at the Chengtu Conference," as translated in Schram, "Mao and Permanent Revolution," p. 237, Mao noted that while there had been relative unity on fighting Japan and the Guomindang and on land reform, a variety of views appeared on cooperativization.

104. In his December 1955 "Preface to *Socialist Upsurge*," p. 118, Mao declared "right conservatism" concerning production the main danger facing the Party.

105. "Speech at the Chengtu Conference," as translated in Schram, "Mao and Permanent Revolution," p. 237.

106. Roderick MacFarquhar, "Communist China's Twenty Years: A Periodization," *CQ*, No. 39 (1969), p. 60.

107. In his "Letter to Wang Chia-hsiang" (August 1, 1959), in *CLG*, Winter 1968-69, p. 53, Mao noted that Khrushchev and "skeptics within the Party" opposed the Hundred Flowers, the people's communes, and the Great Leap Forward— all Chinese innovations.

108. "Talk at Expanded Central Committee Meeting," in *JPRS*, No. 52029, p. 13.

109. See Schurmann, *Ideology and Organization*, pp. 195-208.

110. See Frederick C. Teiwes, "The Purge of Provincial Leaders 1957-1958," *CQ*, No. 27 (1966), pp. 16-19, 28-29.

111. See Liu's "The Present Situation, the Party's General Line for Socialist Construction and Its Future Tasks" (May 5, 1958), in *PDA*, pp. 416-38; and above, note 80.

112. See the discussion of Henan First Secretary Wu Zhipu in Teiwes, "Provincial Politics," pp. 130, 140.

113. Li Jingquan, the first secretary of Sichuan and a Politburo member, reportedly attacked Mao's letter of late April 1959, which warned provincial officials to be more realistic in their work, as a manifestation of retreat and conservatism. Radio Chengdu, April 8, 1968.

114. See Frederick C. Teiwes, "The Evolution of Leadership Purges in Communist China," *CQ*, No. 41 (1970), pp. 126-29. Roderick MacFarquhar, "On Photographs," *CQ*, No. 46 (1971), pp. 98-99, provides evidence that Liu together with Zhou Enlai were the main supporters of Mao at Lushan in the absence of other Party leaders.

115. "Talk at Expanded Central Committee Meeting," in *JPRS*, No. 52029, pp. 12, 14. Mao's comments on the question of bungling, and also his admission that some cadres had been mistreated and apologies were in order (*ibid.*, p. 3), suggest that the major Cultural Revolution charges against Liu's speech at the same meeting—that he blamed the failures of the Great Leap primarily on human errors and called for an extensive rehabilitation of people dismissed in 1959—while true did not reflect a substantial divergence from Mao's own position.

116. "Talk at Expanded Central Committee Meeting," in *JPRS*, No. 50792, pp. 49-50.

117. See especially "Revised Draft Regulations for Work on Rural People's Communes" (September 1962), available in Chinese and translation at the East Asian Institute, Columbia University.

118. For example, Mao called for cutting school classes in half and sending all doctors except a few recent graduates to the countryside. "Spring Festival Instruc-

tion on Education" (February 13, 1964), in *MP*, p. 93; and "Instruction on Public Health," p. 101.

119. "Talk at a Central Work Conference," in *MP*, p. 102.

120. "Thirty-three Leading Counterrevolutionary Revisionists," March 1968, in *CB*, No. 874, pp. 19, 42. During the Cultural Revolution both Mao and his supporters stated that his views were frequently misunderstood. See, e.g., Mao, "Talk at the Central Work Conference" (October 25, 1966), pp. 42-43; and Lin Biao, "Speech at the Eleventh Plenum of the Eighth Central Committee" (August 1966), in *JPRS*, No. 49826, p. 17.

121. See *Heilongjiang zhongyiyao* [Heilongjiang Chinese Traditional Medicine], February 5, 1966, in *SCMM*, No. 596, p. 17.

122. See Donald J. Munro, "Dissent in Communist China: The Current Anti-Intellectual Campaign in Perspective," *Current Scene*, June 1, 1966, p. 14; and Neale Hunter, *Shanghai Journal: An Eyewitness Account of the Cultural Revolution* (New York: Frederick A. Praeger, 1969), p. 114.

123. See Munro, "Dissent in China," pp. 7ff.

124. "Conversation with the Nepalese Educational Delegation," p. 22. See also "Talk at the Central Work Conference" (October 25, 1966), p. 43.

Notes to Chapter II

1. Max Weber, *The Theory of Social and Economic Organization*, ed. with an introduction by Talcott Parsons (New York: The Free Press, 1964), pp. 324-25.

2. *Ibid.*, p. 124.

3. Cited in Johnson, "Changing Nature and Locus of Authority," p. 44.

4. See Rigby "Introduction," pp. 7-8, for a related discussion of this question.

5. See above, p. 3.

6. The term is taken from Oksenberg, "The Political Leader," p. 98.

7. "Caesarism in China," *Encounter*, December 1976.

8. See *Social and Economic Organization*, pp. 324-25, 327, 341, 360.

9. This does not exclude tactical efforts to mobilize specific groups. For example, a plausible explanation of the "democracy wall" episode of 1978 is as an effort by Deng Xiaoping to secure popular support for his programs, but Deng's basic claims to leadership were directed at the elite.

10. *Social and Economic Organization*, p. 382.

11. An additional problem of analysis is the danger of seduction by the CCP's explicit statements attempting to legitimate the regime. While these are of course relevant, they are not the same thing as the actual basis upon which legitimacy is granted. This is particularly the case with regard to the top elite since public statements are often directed at wider and less sophisticated audiences. See especially the discussion of the Cultural Revolution period below.

12. *Social and Economic Organization*, pp. 68ff, 363ff, 382.

13. Cf. Rigby, "A Conceptual Approach," pp. 15-16.

14. See the forceful statement of this position in Johnson, "Changing Nature and Locus of Authority."

15. *Social and Economic Organization*, p. 358.

16. *Ibid.*, pp. 65-67, 359ff.

17. Lenin's propensity to break the rules is discussed in an unpublished manuscript by Graeme Gill "The Nature of Leadership in Pre-1917 Bolshevik Political Culture."

18. Cited in Bertram D. Wolfe, *Three Who Made a Revolution: A Biographical History* (Harmondsworth: Penguin Books, 1964), p. 411. See also the statement of the former Menshevik, Potresov, in *ibid.*, p. 294.

19. This is discussed by Gill, "Nature of Leadership."

20. See Adam B. Ulam, *The Bolsheviks: The Intellectual and Political History of the Triumph of Communism in Russia* (New York: Collier Books, 1965), p. 470.

21. While the time of Mao's attainment of unchallenged leadership cannot be given with precision, the official date of January 1935 seems much too early. At best, it would appear that Mao shared leadership responsibilities with Zhang Wentian following the Zunyi Conference. A more realistic date would be about the time of Mao's defeat of Wang Ming on the issue of united front policy in late 1938. Certainly Mao's ascendancy was complete by 1943 when he was formally elected Chairman of the Central Committee and Politburo, other top leaders began to praise his theoretical contributions, and first mention was made of the "Thought of Mao Zedong." See Raymond F. Wylie, *The Emergence of Maoism: Mao Tse-tung, Ch'en Po-ta, and the Search for Chinese Theory 1935-1945* (Stanford: Stanford University Press, 1980), ch. 8.

22. See *Social and Economic Organization*, p. 359.

23. *Mao Tse-tung: The Man in the Leader* (New York: Basic Books, 1976), pp. 23-24, 34, 35. For a firsthand, if intensely negative, view of Mao's aloof posture in Yanan, see Peter Vladimirov, *The Vladimirov Diaries—Yenan China: 1942-1945* (Garden City, N.Y.: Doubleday and Company, 1975), p. 365.

24. *White House Years* (Boston: Little, Brown and Company, 1979), p. 1058.

25. See *Vladimirov Diaries*, pp. 58-59, 68; and Pye, *Mao Tse-tung*, pp. 55-57, 235-36.

26. *The New York Times* (*NYT*), December 11, 1978, p. A2.

27. See *Social and Economic Organization*, p. 360.

28. On the representative function of charisma, see Martin E. Spencer, "What Is Charisma?" *British Journal of Sociology*, September 1973. I am indebted to Lowell Dittmer for this reference.

29. See above, pp. 28, 37.

30. One of the phrases used during the rectification campaign of 1942-44; cited in Stuart Schram, *Mao Tse-tung* (Harmondsworth: Penguin Books, 1967), p. 233.

31. On the cults of Malenkov, Khrushchev, and Brezhnev, see Rigby, "A Conceptual Approach," pp. 15-16. For Hua, see below, p. 79.

32. For a useful discussion of the content of the Stalin and Mao cults, see Graeme Gill, "Personal Dominance and the Collective Principle: Individual Legitimacy in Marxist-Leninist Systems," in Rigby and Fehér, *Legitimation in Communist States*.

33. From *Pravda*, December 21, 1939 (cited in *ibid.*, p. 99).

34. *Khrushchev Remembers: The Last Testament*, translated and edited

by Strobe Talbott (Boston: Little, Brown and Company, 1974), p. 193.

35. Edgar Snow, *The Long Revolution* (New York: Random House, 1971), p. 205.

36. See above, pp. 26, 27; and below, pp. 67-68, 69, 80-81.

37. Nevertheless, one should hestiate before writing off the legitimizing function of the personality cult within the top CCP elite. It is at least arguable that some of the more marginal members of the Central Committee in particular, finding Mao a remote figure, developed an intensified sense of awe as a result of long-term exposure to claims about his "exceptional qualities."

38. See Rigby, "A Conceptual Approach," pp. 18ff; and *Social and Economic Organization*, pp. 35, 50, 185.

39. See Gill, "Personal Dominance," pp. 99-100.

40. The case of Stalin is an exception but one which underlines the distinction. To the extent Stalin had genuine charisma it was largely owing to his giving shape to socialist institutions—a truly creative and historic accomplishment. Most subsequent leaders of socialist states in the largest sense could only follow in Stalin's footsteps, notwithstanding some substantial modifications. Thus goals achieved along a more or less well-charted course lacked the Stalinist aspect of innovative solutions to a crisis. Moreover, with increasing economic and social complexity, the goals pursued depend increasingly on skills associated with bureaucratic rationality rather than charisma.

41. Similarly, successful task performance in economic development draws nationalist support which in turn enhances the legitimacy of a leader who can claim credit for such accomplishments.

42. The analogy was used by Mao in a February 1942 lecture in Yanan; see Boyd Compton, trans., *Mao's China: Party Reform Documents, 1942-44* (Seattle: University of Washington Press, 1966), p. 21.

43. Cf. Wang Gungwu, "The Chinese," in Wilson, *Mao in the Scales of History*, p. 289.

44. *NYT*, November 28, 1978, p. A5.

45. *Social and Economic Organization*, p. 328.

46. See *ibid.*, pp. 329ff, 392.

47. Weber was ambiguous on this score. While he stated that elected officials exercise legal-rational authority (*ibid.*, p. 330), his sketchy treatment of democratic legitimacy and elective processes tends to emphasize charismatic factors. See *ibid.*, pp. 73-74, 386ff.

48. Cf. Rigby, "A Conceptual Approach," pp. 11-13.

49. See the sections of the various constitutions on organizational principles and central organs in *Collected Works of Liu Shao-ch'i, 1945-1957* (Hong Kong: Union Research Institute, 1969), pp. 103-108; *Eighth National Congress*, I, 151-57; *The Ninth National Congress of the Communist Party of China (Documents)* (Beijing: Foreign Languages Press, 1969), pp. 119-23; *The Tenth National Congress of the Communist Party of China (Documents)* (Beijing: Foreign Languages Press, 1973), pp. 67-71; and *CQ*, No. 72 (1977), pp. 922-23. On the abolition of the chairmanship, see *Beijing Review* (*BR*), No. 39 (1982), p. 17.

Ironically, the state constitutions of 1975 and 1978 did grant the CCP chairman significant power as commander of the armed forces. See *The Constitution of the People's Republic of China* (Beijing: Foreign Languages Press, 1975), p. 22; and

The Constitution of the People's Republic of China (Beijing: Foreign Languages Press, 1978), p. 15. This stipulation, however, further emphasizes the weakness of legal-rational norms since it was directed at the previous fiction that the chairman of the state (a position vacant since the Cultural Revolution) was commander-in-chief, and since by 1978 Deng Xiaoping had displaced Chairman Hua Guofeng as *de facto* leader.

50. See the inner-Party report of Liao Gailong, "Historical Experiences and Our Development" (October 25, 1980), Part II, in *IS*, November 1981, p. 92.

51. For an extended analysis of Party organizational norms in the pre-Cultural Revolution period, see Teiwes, *Politics and Purges*.

52. See the Yanan period essays by Mao and Liu Shaoqi in Compton, *Mao's China*, p. 241; *CLG*, Spring 1972, p. 39; and *Collected Works of Liu 1945-57*, pp. 57-58.

53. See Liu Shaoqi "On the Intra-Party Struggle" (1941), in Compton, *Mao's China*, p. 236.

54. Cited in *CLG*, Spring 1972, p. 45.

55. See Ulam, *The Bolsheviks*, pp. 360ff, 465ff.

56. See above, p. 26 (emphasis added).

57. Cf. Graeme Gill, "The Soviet Leader Cult: Reflections on the Structure of Leadership in the Soviet Union," *British Journal of Political Science*, April 1980, pp. 176-79, on the Soviet case.

58. Of course, Hua's case was made easier by the fact that he was not the real leader by the time of his ouster. See below, pp. 87-89.

59. *Social and Economic Organization*, p. 341.

60. See *Ibid.*, pp. 60-61, 328, 341-42.

61. *Ibid.*, p. 360.

62. Although often referred to as the "right to rebel," this was in fact a duty. See Wang Gungwu, *Power, Rights and Duties in Chinese History* (Canberra: The Australian National University, 1979), p. 10.

63. See Wang Gungwu, "Feng Tao: An Essay on Confucian Loyalty," in Arthur F. Wright and Denis Twitchett, eds., *Confucian Personalities* (Stanford: Stanford University Press, 1962).

64. See Harold L. Kahn, *Monarchy in the Emperor's Eyes: Image and Reality in the Ch'ien-lung Reign* (Cambridge, Mass.: Harvard University Press, 1971), ch. 12.

65. These and many other "limits" on imperial authority are detailed in the rather extreme account of Franklin W. Houn, *Chinese Political Traditions* (Washington: Public Affairs Press, 1965), ch. III.

66. See John King Fairbank, *The United States and China* (3rd ed., Cambridge, Mass.: Harvard University Press, 1971), p. 57. In addition, from the Han on the Confucian tradition was reshaped to emphasize an increasingly absolutist version of loyalty to the throne. See Wang, *Power, Rights and Duties*, pp. 13-14.

67. Cited in Houn, *Chinese Political Traditions*, p. 65.

68. Cited in *CB*, No. 851, p. 30.

69. Snow, *Long Revolution*, p. 170; and *BR*, No. 37 (1981), p. 18.

70. See Liao, "Historical Experiences," Part II, p. 91. Cf. Oksenberg, "The

Political Leader," p. 99; and Stuart R. Schram, "To Utopia and Back: A Cycle in the History of the Chinese Communist Party," *CQ*, No. 87 (1981), p. 433.

71. See *BR*, No. 14 (1980), pp. 2, 11-20.

72. Lowell Dittmer, "Bases of Power in Chinese Politics: A Theory and Analysis of the Fall of the 'Gang of Four,'" *World Politics*, October 1978, p. 29.

73. The following paragraph owes much to Michael Yahuda.

74. See reports of peasant discontent in J. Chester Cheng, ed., *The Politics of the Chinese Red Army: A Translation of the Bulletin of Activities of the People's Liberation Army* (Stanford: Hoover Institution Publications, 1966), pp. 13, 190-91.

75. On the Tiananmen incident, see *PR*, No. 15 (1976), pp. 4-7.

76. See *Peng Dehuai zishu* [Peng Dehuai's Autobiography] (Beijing: Renmin chubanshe, 1981), pp. 257-58.

77. Above, pp. 32-34.

78. See Teiwes, *Politics and Purges*, chs. 6-7.

79. See the claims of the December 1958 Central Committee communique in *PDA*, p. 485.

80. See the statements collected in Gill, "Personal Dominance," pp. 99-100.

81. E.g., Liu Shaoqi's 1951 address to a Beijing rally in *Collected Works of Liu 1945-57, p. 253.*

82. See MacFarquhar, *Origins 1*, pp. 100-102.

83. "Legal-rational" norms began to erode from late 1957-early 1958 when policy issues (along with organizational matters) became involved in an unfolding provincial purge and Mao reportedly ceased to attend regular Politburo meetings. See Teiwes, *Politics and Purges*, ch. 8; and Liao, "Historical Experiences," Part II, p. 90. However, the 1959 Lushan meetings were clearly the watershed in terms of Mao violating Party rules.

84. The most significant exceptions were Bo Yibo, who lost the finance portfolio in 1953 over differences on tax policy but resumed work in an important economic capacity the next year, and Deng Zihui, whose moderate approach to agricultural cooperativization apparently resulted in a brief reduction of his powers in the rural sphere in late 1955. See Teiwes, *Politics and Purges*, pp. 114-15, 344n; and MacFarquhar, *Origins 1*, pp. 18-19.

85. The only major purge up to this point, that of Gao Gang and Rao Shushi in 1954-55, was essentially unrelated to policy issues. See Teiwes, *Politics and Purges*, ch. 5.

86. See MacFarquhar, *Origins 1*, pp. 86-90, 241-49; and above, p. 38 and note 83.

87. For a detailed analysis of developments at Lushan, see Teiwes, *Politics and Purges*, ch. 9.

88. *CB*, No. 851, p. 13; and *Case of Peng*, p. 36.

89. See *Miscellany of Mao Tse-tung Thought (MMT)*, in *JPRS*, No. 61269, pp. 176, 180-81.

90. Radio Chengdu, August 31, 1967, in *News from Chinese Provincial Radio Stations*, No. 223, p. Q9. Cf. above, note 113 to Chapter I.

91. *CB*, No. 851, p. 19.

92. Tom Fisher, "'The Play's the Thing': Wu Han and Hai Rui Revisited," *The*

Australian Journal of Chinese Affairs, No. 7 (1982). See also Teiwes, *Politics and Purges*, pp. 476-79.

93. Peng reportedly declared in 1962 that "I want to be a Hai Rui," although Mao apparently did not draw the conclusion that "Hai Rui is Peng Dehuai" until late 1965. See Lowell Dittmer, *Liu Shao-ch'i and the Chinese Cultural Revolution: The Politics of Mass Criticism* (Berkeley: University of California Press, 1974), pp. 62, 69ff.

94. "Yeh Chien-ying's Talk at the Third Plenum of the Eleventh CCP Central Committee" (December 1978), in *IS*, May 1980, p. 77.

95. See *JPRS*, No. 50792, pp. 2ff; *MMT*, pp. 359; and above, p. 26.

96. *BR*, No. 9 (1981), p. 14; and above, pp. 26, 27.

97. *MP*, pp. 98, 99.

98. See MacFarquhar, *Origins 1*, pp. 153-55.

99. Here and subsequently (below, p. 78) I have used the more familiar term "hereditary charisma" rather than the more strictly correct "designated charisma." See Weber, *Social and Economic Organization*, p. 365.

100. Nevertheless, Mao's contribution to the recovery program was recognized within the elite. See Liao "Historical Experiences," Part I, in *IS*, October 1981, p. 86. In addition, this report also indicates the importance of nationalism in bolstering Mao at this juncture by praising his leading role in the Sino-Soviet dispute. *Ibid.*, p. 85.

101. See Edward E. Rice, *Mao's Way* (Berkeley: University of California Press, 1972), pp. 251-54.

102. *IS*, February 1972, p. 106.

103. For a similar judgment, see Oksenberg, "The Political Leader," p. 99.

104. See Wang, "The Chinese," pp. 294-95. Of course, there were some profoundly antitraditional aspects of the Cultural Revolution such as the public humiliation of officials by young students.

105. See, e.g., the pamphlet "Chairman Mao's Successor—Deputy Supreme Commander Lin Piao," in *CB*, No. 894.

106. *Ninth National Congress*, p. 113.

107. Not only were many PLA leaders purged during the Cultural Revolution, but the army's national defense role was undermined by its involvement in maintaining civil order. This, however, was offset to a degree by increased defense expenditures; see below, pp. 109-111.

108. For the case of Liu Shaoqi, see Dittmer, *Liu*, pp. 94ff, 114-17.

109. See *BR*, No. 37 (1981), pp. 18, 21; Liao, "Historical Experiences," Part I, p. 92, Part II, p. 98; *IS*, September 1969, pp. 105-106; and Dittmer, *Liu*, pp. 153-55. Dittmer argues that Mao made some concessions which checked the excesses of the movement, but the denigration of major figures continued and the basic nature of the Cultural Revolution was unaltered.

110. In the early stages of the Cultural Revolution Chen Yi on several occasions cited Mao's magnanimous handling of opponents; *SCMM*, No. 635, pp. 12, 14. That confidence in the Chairman was not totally misplaced is suggested by post-Mao reports of his interventions to right wrongs done to veteran comrades during the movement. See *BR*, No. 21 (1980), p. 19.

111. "Hsu Shih-yu's Talk in a Group Discussion at the Third Plenum of the

Eleventh CCP Central Committee'' (December 1978), in *IS*, May 1980, p. 79.

112. This assessment is based not simply on denunciations of Lin as one who constantly waved the red book and shouted *"wan sui"* (long live) but also on Lin's activities before the Cultural Revolution. See above, pp. 27, 30.

113. See *NYT*, May 13, 1977, p. A8, November 27, 1978, p. A9.

114. While Deng Xiaoping came under heavy attack in 1976 for giving Mao's directives on stability and unity and promoting the national economy equal status with class struggle, the existence of such directives indicates that Mao was not totally opposed to the concerns of Party administrators. See *China News Analysis* (*CNA*), No. 1032 (1976), p. 6. Most importantly Mao approved the personnel arrangements which placed the administrators in key state posts (see below).

115. *Tenth National Congress*, p. 48; and *PR*, No. 14 (1975), pp. 7-8, No. 19 (1976), p. 16.

116. See Kenneth Lieberthal, "China in 1975: The Internal Political Scene," *Problems of Communism*, May-June 1975, pp. 6-9.

117. This was the clear perception of American policymakers; see Kissinger, *White House Years*, pp. 1088-89.

118. Personal communication based on conversations held in Beijing during 1980. The view of Zhou as subservient to Mao is also supported by foreign statesmen who saw the two together. See, e.g., Tanaka's remark that "Zhou is a nobody before Mao," reported in Ross Terrill, *Mao: A Biography* (New York: Harper & Row, 1980), p. 372.

119. "Historical Experiences," Part II, p. 98. The official CCP verdict, "Resolution on Certain Questions in the History of Our Party Since the Founding of the People's Republic of China" (June 27, 1981), in *BR*, No. 27 (1981), pp. 22-23, is more circumspect about the Mao-Zhou relationship. While acknowledging some differences between the two, the Resolution claims the attacks on Zhou during the Lin Biao-Confucius campaign were the work of Jiang Qing and company and that Mao criticized their activities.

120. Cf. Mao's reported 1976 statement concerning the dead Zhou that "the people will surely oppose any attack on Zhou En-lai"; Terrill, *Mao*, p. 418.

121. Cf. Fox Butterfield's perceptive articles in *NYT*, November 18, 1976, and January 8, 1977.

122. New China News Agency, Beijing, January 8, 1977, in *Survey of People's Republic of China Press*, No. 6263, pp. 184-85. See also Luo Ruiqing's discussion of Zhou's sheltering of He Long; *PR*, No. 11 (1978), p. 30.

123. Actually, the attacks began in late 1975 during the terminal stages of Zhou's illness. See *CNA*, No. 1028 (1976), pp. 2-7.

124. *PR*, No. 23 (1976), p. 16.

125. See Terrill, *Mao*, pp. 373-74, 391-92; and "Resolution on History Since the Founding," p. 23.

126. It is, of course, possible that at this stage Mao did not ask for Deng's formal dismissal. See the report to this effect in *IS*, August 1977, p. 66.

127. See the accounts in *NYT*, November 18, 1976, p. 18; and Parris H. Chang, "Mao's Last Stand?" *Problems of Communism*, July-August 1976, pp. 11-12.

128. See *CNA*, No. 1039 (1976), pp. 1-2, No. 1054 (1976), p. 2.

129. "Chang P'ing-hua's Speech to Cadres on the Cultural Front" (July 23,

1978), in *IS*, December 1978, pp. 93-94.

130. See Alan P. L. Liu, "Political Decay on Mainland China: On Crises of Faith, Confidence and Trust," *IS*, August 1982.

131. "On the Current Situation and Tasks" (January 16, 1980), in *Foreign Broadcast Information Service: People's Republic of China* (FBIS:PRC), March 11, 1980, Supplement p. 23.

132. Perhaps the most genuine holder of such doubts at the apex of power was Chen Yonggui, the peasant cadre who had been brought into the Politburo in 1973. See Chen's remarks at the December 1978 Third Plenum in *IS*, May 1980, pp. 82-84.

133. *PR*, No. 15 (1976), p. 3.

134. Hua himself offered the version of a Mao initiative and Politburo response in explaining both his April appointment and earlier designation as acting premier; *BR*, No. 42 (1979), p. 9. It is also consistent with subsequent attacks on the "feudal" nature of Hua's elevation.

135. According to some reports, the "Gang of Four" claimed that Mao in his last days tried to designate Jiang Qing as CCP chairman and Zhang Chunqiao as premier. *Hong Kong Standard*, January 19, 1977.

136. See *NYT*, January 8, 1977; *IS*, July 1981, p. 28; and Kenneth Lieberthal, "The Politics of Modernization in the PRC," *Problems of Communism*, May-June 1978, p. 8.

137. For example, by strongly pushing agricultural cooperativization in the mid-1950s and resisting efforts to close Mao's birthplace in the early 1960s. See Michel Oksenberg and Sai-cheung Yeung, "Hua Kuo-feng's Pre-Cultural Revolution Hunan Years, 1949-66: The Making of a Political Generalist," *CQ*, No. 69 (1977), pp. 12-16; and *IS*, March 1976, p. 81.

138. Although characterized as "rumors," official documents report doubts that Mao actually did designate Hua. See "Suggestions regarding Certain Current Issues Made by the PLA Canton Military Region Party Committee and the Kwangtung Provincial Party Committee of the CPC" (February 1, 1977), in *CLG*, Spring 1977, p. 78. It would be unusual if such "rumors" did not have some credibility within the elite given the highly restricted access to Mao in his last years (see below, note 64 to the third essay). Indeed it remains unclear through what channels Mao conveyed his reported selection in April, and some reports claim that Mao's letter to Hua, "With you in charge, I'm at ease" (see below), was only produced by Hua after Mao's death. See *IS*, June 1978, p. 35.

139. *PR*, No. 42 (1976), pp. 3-4.

140. See, e.g., *PR*, No. 45 (1976), pp. 5-6.

141. *PR*, No. 35 (1977), p. 11, No. 36 (1977), p. 24.

142. See Fox Butterfield's report in *NYT*, November 18, 1976, p. 18. In contrast, the story circulated among Party members of Mao's purported selection of Hua emphasized the differences between the two chairmen. According to this story, Hua several times declined to be acting premier on the grounds he lacked the qualifications and his knowledge of Marxism-Leninism was too low. Mao allegedly replied that this was the reason for his selection because "a man who knows his own weaknesses will not boast . . . and will always make progress." *Ibid.*, November 10, 1976, p. 11.

143. This presumably could have been the case for the so-called "whateverist"

group led by Wang Dongxing, who argued that all of Mao's directives had to be carried out and opposed Deng's rehabilitation on the ostensible grounds that Mao had ordered his purge. See Wang's self-criticism in *IS*, October 1980, pp. 90-97; and the final essay below, pp. 121, 126. It is likely, however, that the political implications of Hua's leadership and Deng's return for their own positions were a greater influence on the "whateverists'" actions than any sense of the authoritative nature of the departed Mao's wishes. Moreover, to the extent Wang believed it was necessary to uphold Mao's wishes he apparently argued less in terms of the binding authority of those wishes than in the more traditional sense of avoiding damage to the late Chairman's prestige. See *IS*, October 1980, p. 92.

144. "Suggestions regarding Current Issues," pp. 77-78. While this document was issued in the name of Guangzhou and Guangdong authorities, Politburo members Xu and Wei were the leading officials of the relevant organizations.

145. While official discussions at the time of Hua's demotion revealed that Deng had criticized the "whateverist" view soon after it was articulated in 1977 (see below, p. 126), I have found no claims that Deng or any other leader directly opposed Hua's cult before late 1978.

146. Although I have found no direct evidence of this view within the elite, it was vehemently asserted in a January 1977 Beijing wall poster and surely shared if perhaps in more modulated form by many leaders. See *CLG*, Spring 1977, pp. 69-72.

147. See Lieberthal, "Politics of Modernization," p. 4; and *PR*, No. 35 (1977), p. 12.

148. *PR*, No. 35 (1977), p. 55, No. 36 (1977), pp. 27, 33.

149. For evidence of elite concern over Mao's reputation, see above, note 143; and below, p. 87.

150. See "Teng Hsiao-p'ing's Speech to the Ad Hoc Forum of the Third Plenary Session of the Tenth CCP Central Committee" (July 20, 1977), in *IS*, pp. 74-78, which followed an earlier letter acknowledging mistakes. Although not without implied criticisms of Mao, this talk not only admitted shortcomings, affirmed Mao's greatness, and positively evaluated the Cultural Revolution, it also attacked Liu Shaoqi as the "capitalist-roader" of Mao's demonology.

151. See *Los Angeles Times*, March 6, 1978, p. 3, September 17, 1978, p. 11; and *NYT*, March 9, 1978.

152. "Comrade Hu Yao-pang's Speech to the Closing Session of the Plenum" (June 29, 1981), in *IS*, December 1981, p. 75.

153. *Ibid.* Of course, it is impossible to know that this was the case from the moment of Deng's return to the Politburo, and in any case the precise extent of his influence, as any politician's, has varied with events. Nevertheless, both foreign observers and "Chinese sources" viewed Deng as performing the leading executive role well before the December 1978 plenum which is now viewed as the watershed between left-influenced errors conveniently blamed on Hua and the current correct line. See *NYT*, June 1, 1978, p. 8; Lieberthal, "Politics of Modernization," p. 10; and the sources above, note 151.

154. See Wang Renzhong's report on the operations of the Party secretariat, *Hongqi*, No. 5 (1982), in *FBIS:PRC*, March 1, 1982, p. K8; and Michel Oksenberg, "Economic Policy-Making in China: Summer 1981," *CQ*, No. 90 (1982), p. 175.

155. See, e.g., the account of Deng's July 1981 talk with leading cultural offi-

cials where his call for a harder line toward writers quickly led to a propaganda conference and other measures reflecting Deng's views. *Zhengming*, October 1, 1981, in *FBIS:PRC*, October 28, 1981, pp. W1-11.

156. "Selected Edition on Liu Shao-ch'i's Counter-revolutionary Revisionist Crimes" (April 1967), in *SCMM*, No. 651, p. 5.

157. See the January 1977 wall poster in *GLG*, Spring 1977, pp. 69-72; and the November 1978 poster in *BBC Summary of World Broadcasts: Far East*, November 22, 1978, 5975/B11/1-3.

158. *The Indictment Against Lin Biao-Jiang Qing Cliques* (Hong Kong: Ta Kung Pao, November 1980), pp. 9-10.

159. Chen Yun and Peng Zhen of this group also survived. However, Chen had not played an active role since 1962 while Peng was not rehabilitated following his Cultural Revolution disgrace until 1979.

160. See the breakdown of the Politburo elected in 1973 below, p. 114. Of this group, only eleven were not dead, inactive, or purged by late 1976. Of these, seven (Hua, Wang Dongxing, Ji Dengkui, Wu De, Chen Xilian, Li Desheng, and Chen Yonggui) as Cultural Revolution beneficiaries had reason for concern over Deng's rehabilitation, and several led by Wang actively opposed Deng. See below, p. 121.

161. Of the Central Committee elected in 1973, about 40 percent were "mass representatives" of little consequence in the communist movement as a whole. See Thomas W. Robinson, "China in 1973: Renewed Leftism Threatens the 'New Course,'" *Asian Survey*, January 1974, p. 3.

162. "Resolution on History Since the Founding," pp. 25-26.

163. "A Speech at the Enlarged Meeting of the Politburo of the Central Committee" (August 18, 1980), in *IS*, March 1981, pp. 93-94.

164. On the "practice" issue, see Brantley Womack, "Politics and Epistemology in China since Mao," *CQ*, No. 80 (1979). On the curbing of cults and other aspects of individual authority by the December 1978 plenum, see *PR*, No. 52 (1978), p. 16; and *CNA*, No. 1146 (1979), p. 6, No. 1153 (1979), p. 3.

165. See "Resolution on History Since the Founding," especially pp. 10-13, 29-35. A broadly positive result was foreordained by instructions from "Central Committee leaders" to the committee drafting the resolution that Mao's historical position be affirmed. *BR*, No. 30 (1981), p. 6.

166. For example, see the claim in the February 1982 issue of *Zhengming* that "the masses have . . . sobered up from their superstitious faith in individual personalities. . . ." *Inside China Mainland* (Taibei), May 1982, p. 7. Indeed, it could be argued that attacks on Mao were desirable to win the support of alienated groups.

167. "T'an Chen-lin's Talk in a Group Discussion at the Third Plenum of the Eleventh CCP Central Committee" (December 1978), in *IS*, May 1980, pp. 80-81.

168. "Hsu Shih-yu's Talk," p. 79. See also Deng's interview with Oriana Fallaci in *The Guardian Weekly*, September 21, 1980, pp. 17-18.

169. *BR*, No. 17 (1981), p. 22.

170. "Hu Yaobang's Speech" (July 1, 1981), in *BR*, No. 28 (1981), p. 12.

171. See *Zhengming*, February 1, 1981, in *FBIS:PRC*, February 2, 1981, pp. U1-3; *Ming Pao* [Clarity Daily] (Hong Kong), June 26, 1981, in *FBIS:PRC*, June 26, 1981, pp. W1-2; and *RMRB*, September 18, 19, 1980.

172. Full member Chen Yonggui and alternate Seypidin reportedly were not informed of the meetings. *Zhengming*, February 1, 1981, in *FBIS:PRC*, February 2, 1981, p. U2.

173. As reported in *The Sydney Morning Herald*, February 14, 1981.

174. See *Zhanwang* [Outlook] (Hong Kong), May 16, 1981, in *FBIS:PRC*, May 22, 1981, p. W6; *Zhengming ribao* [Contention Daily] (Hong Kong), July 6, 1981, in *FBIS:PRC*, July 9, 1981, pp. W4-5; and *Zhengming*, December 1, 1981, in *FBIS:PRC*, December 9, 1981, pp. W2-3. Complaints among cadres of Deng's factional behavior at the time of Hua's forced removal were reported in a personal communication from a former resident of Beijing.

175. *Zhengming*, August 1, 1981, in *FBIS:PRC*, August 14, 1981, p. W6.

176. *BR*, No. 19 (1982), pp. 42-43. Decision by individual leaders was also sanctioned for the premier and ministers, a more defensible provision given the declared administrative as opposed to policy function of the State Council. *Ibid.*, p. 41.

177. *BR*, No. 39 (1982), p. 17.

178. *BR*, No. 38 (1982), pp. 6, 15, 20.

179. See the report on the reorganization of the State Council in *BR*, No. 11 (1982), pp. 5-6.

180. "Speech at Enlarged Meeting of Politburo," p. 92.

181. *BR*, No. 39 (1982), p. 29.

182. See Liao, "Historical Experiences," Part III, in *IS*, December 1981, pp. 95-98.

183. *BR*, No. 39 (1982), p. 17.

184. See Jerry F. Hough, "The Brezhnev Era: The Man and the System," *Problems of Communism*, March-April 1976, pp. 3-6, 13.

Notes to Chapter III

1. The following discussion focuses on the strategies of various key Politburo leaders, but many of the conclusions are also applicable to China's "800 rulers" as a whole (see above, p. 3).

2. On the vicissitudes of normative rules during the Cultural Revolution decade and since Mao's death, see Teiwes, *Politics and Purges*, pp. 619-33.

3. The vulnerability of prudential rules in even highly institutionalized systems can be illustrated by recent American politics. The election of President Reagan in 1980 and the early legislative successes of his administration violated the longstanding rule of thumb about the need to occupy the middle ground. More narrowly, the fate of Secretary of State Haig indicates that a political style that was spectacularly successful in one Republican administration was self-defeating in another.

4. Besides the principles examined here, in *Politics and Purges* I discuss two further norms dealing with the discipline of erring comrades: disciplinary measures should generally be lenient and aim at reform; and such measures should be implemented by official Party bodies with any mass participation subject to strict control. Upon reflection, I believe that the latter norm has been far less formal and more ambivalent than other CCP organizational principles, but that prior to the Cultural

Revolution it was widely accepted at least with regard to the top elite.

5. Martial law in Poland since late 1981, as well as the role of the PLA during the Cultutal Revolution, are so exceptional as to underline the significance of this rule.

6. *SW*, Vol. II (Beijing: Foreign Languages Press, 1965), p. 224.

7. See "Khrushchev and the Rules of the Soviet Political Game," paper presented to the annual conference of the Australasian Political Studies Association, Canberra, August 1980, pp. 1-4. The remainder of this paragraph is based on Rigby's account but somewhat modified. Moreover, I have not included a fourth "rule" advanced by Rigby, that of the need to take risks. While agreeing that risk taking is a common feature of politics and giving attention to this aspect in the following accounts of various conflicts in post-1949 China, in many cases successful politics involves the avoidance of risks. This is my view of the great bulk of pre-Cultural Revolution PRC leadership politics in particular.

8. See above, pp. 56-57.

9. Cf. T. H. Rigby, "Politics in the Mono-Organizational Society," in Andrew C. Janos, ed., *Authoritarian Politics in Communist Europe: Unity and Diversity in One-Party States* (Berkeley: University of California Press, 1976), pp. 34-49. For a discussion of this conflict as it affected lower-level Chinese officials, see Teiwes, *Politics and Purges*, pp. 117-20.

10. For a discussion arguing the primacy of the Politburo collective over sub-Politburo institutional interests in the Soviet case, see Myron Rush, "The Soviet Military Build-up and the Coming Succession: A Review Essay," *International Security*, Spring 1981, pp. 170-71.

11. For further discussion along these lines, see Pye, *Dynamics of Factions*, pp. 8, 10-15.

12. See the comparative study by Jonathan R. Adelman, *The Revolutionary Armies: The Historical Development of the Soviet and the Chinese People's Liberation Armies* (Westport: Greenwood Press, 1980).

It should also be noted that the Chinese revolutionary experience departed from traditional notions of the superiority of *wen*—the literarily accomplished civilian official— over *wu*, the military official, although the Confucian *wen* could don the *wu* mantle in times of need. Of course, the *wen/wu* distinction reinforced the notion of the Party controlling the gun.

13. In terms of Politburo representation, PLA leaders made up roughly one-quarter of Politburo members before the Eighth Party Congrss in 1956, one-third of the full members selected at the 1956 Congress, 45 percent of the 1969 Ninth Politburo, one-sixth of the 1973 Tenth Politburo, one-third of the 1977 Eleventh Politburo, and one-fourth of the 1982 Twelfth Politburo. See MacFarquhar, *Origins 1*, p. 165, and below, pp. 107, 114, 120.

This high level of representation contrasts strikingly with the Soviet case, where career military officers have served on the Politburo only in extremely rare instances.

14. See above, pp. 55-58.

15. See Liu's 1939 essay, "Self-Cultivation in Organization and Discipline," *CLG*, Spring 1972, p. 27.

16. Thus the Tiananmen riots of April 1976 (see above, p. 63) are now upheld as a "revolutionary act" despite being in clear defiance of legal authority at the time. These riots, due to popular anger over slights to the memory of Zhou

Enlai, indicated support for veteran Party officials in their struggle with Cultural Revolution radicals. See also above, pp. 85ff.

17. See above, pp. 65ff. For a more extended discussion, see Teiwes, *Politics and Purges*, Part III.

18. An alternate Politburo member (one of six), Zhang Wentian, was also disgraced with Peng in 1959. Chen Yun was subsequently active during the 1961-62 economic crisis but again faded into the background once the crisis passed. On Chen's earlier eclipse, see below, note 31.

Central Committee positions and key bureaucratic posts were also comparatively stable throughout the pre-Cultural Revolution period, although notably less so from 1958.

19. A problem of timing arises here since, as suggested in the first essay (above, p. 29), Mao did begin to lose confidence in his Politburo colleagues sometime in the early to mid-1960s (c. 1962-65/66). Similarly, such actions as allowing his wife to carry out independent activities on the cultural front in this same period, while not "dividing and ruling" the Politburo, did indicate a willingness to set up antagonistic groups within the larger elite, and the increasing prominence of Lin Biao by the end of the period could be seen in "divide and rule" terms. My general feeling is that while such trends were incipient throughout the early 1960s, it was only in late 1965-early 1966 that they became a pronounced feature of Mao's approach to his top colleagues.

20. This listing includes all members of the pre-1956 secretariat and the post-1956 Politburo Standing Committee except Zhu De, who did not play a key operational role for most of the post-1949 period. In addition, it includes Peng Zhen, who held a series of crucial Party and state posts throughout the 1949-1965 period and by 1964 was identified as a "close comrade-in-arms" of Mao.

21. Both were closely linked to Mao during the Jiangxi Soviet in the early 1930s, and in Lin's case his association dated from the Jinggangshan base area in the late 1920s. A distinction must be made between Lin and Deng, however. Lin already had independent prestige as a gifted military commander by the early 1930s, while Deng's rise to prominence—although reflecting genuine talent—was more closely tied to Mao's patronage.

22. See above, p. 30; and below, pp. 106-107.

23. For detailed analysis, see Teiwes, *Politics and Purges*, ch. 5.

24. For detailed analysis, see *ibid.*, ch. 9.

25. See above, p. 66; and Teiwes, *Politics and Purges*, p. 420.

26. See Hua Guofeng's speech to the 1980 National People's Congress, *BR*, No. 38 (1980), p. 22. Here the focus is on middle and lower echelon bureaucrats, but the problem undoubtedly affected higher officials as well.

27. An examination of data on the 1955 collectivization drive and the Great Leap Forward suggests that the provinces most enthusiastic in implementing these policies had relatively unstable Party leaderships. See Teiwes, "Provincial Politics," pp. 167-74.

28. The apparent exception was Zhou's backing of the Hundred Flowers experiment. See MacFarquhar, *Origins 1*, pp. 218-19, 232, 235-36, 238-40.

29. See *ibid.*, pp. 86-90, 122-29; and above, p. 37.

30. For a contrary view, see MacFarquhar, *Origins 1*, pp. 88, 312, 315.

31. In *Politics and Purges*, pp. 342-46, I concluded that Chen had been down-

graded although not formally disciplined by Mao as a result of his opposition to the Great Leap policies. This conclusion, however, unlike all others in that study, was based entirely on contextual evidence and not on official or Red Guard attacks on Chen which were notable by their absence. A contrary interpretation, stimulated by a private communication from a former resident of Beijing, is that Chen voluntarily stepped aside rather than be saddled with the implementation of policies he believed wrong. This version, of course, is consistent with the traditional notions discussed in the second essay above, pp. 59-60.

32. The most extensive data on balanced representation of different revolutionary groups concerns civil war field armies in the post-1949 regional military structure; see William Whitson, "The Field Army in Chinese Communist Military Politics," *CQ*, No. 37 (1969). Whitson, however, draws conclusions about alleged conflict and balance of power politics among these armies which I find unsupportable.

33. See Frederick C. Teiwes, *Provincial Party Personnel in Mainland China 1956-1966* (New York: Occasional Papers of the East Asian Institute, Columbia University, 1967), p. 20. Contrast Deng's apparent restraint with Khrushchev's appointment of many former subordinates in the Ukraine and Moscow to leading central and provincial posts during 1953-55; Rigby, "Khrushchev," p. 20.

34. This appointment took place before Deng became CCP General Secretary. The supposition of Deng's patronage is based on the fact that Hu came with Deng to Beijing from Sichuan in mid-1952 as well as on their earlier close career ties.

35. See MacFarquhar, *Origins 1*, pp. 152-56. Of course, Mao's retreat in the early 1960s (cf. above, p. 29) also reflected his dismay with the collapse of the Great Leap, but the origins of the "second line" scheme were clearly in the effort to provide for a smooth succession.

36. Myron Rush, *How Communist States Change Their Rulers* (Ithaca: Cornell University Press, 1974), pp. 295-98, demonstrates that in a surprising number of cases the ranking Party figure not only succeeded to the number one post but was also able to consolidate his leadership, a tendency significantly enhanced where the former ruler had unequivocally designated him as heir.

37. Here again (cf. above, note 19) the question of timing is crucial. By 1964-65 it is likely that Mao's disenchantment with Liu was leading to second thoughts about the succession arrangements, a situation which to the extent perceived by other Politburo members would have undermined the smooth succession forecast here. The evidence for such a development is not only Lin Biao's increasing prominence in 1965, but also suggestions that Peng Zhen was being seen as a possible successor at about this time. See above, p. 30; and Teiwes, *Politics and Purges*, pp. 503-504.

38. See above, pp. 24-25, 29, 40-41. For further detail on these and other destabilizing aspects of the immediate pre-Cultural Revolution period, see Teiwes, *Politics and Purges*, pp. 491-92, 495-506, 572ff, 592-96.

39. "Collection of Ch'en I's Speeches," p. 25.

40. See above, p. 27. Of course, another plausible reason for choosing Lin was Mao's need for PLA backing while he launched a massive attack on the Party organization and its leaders. Yet Mao's concern with the future of the revolution and the need for committed revolutionary successors suggests that considerably more than a tactical alliance was involved in the selection of Lin.

41. For example, educational reforms and model operas.

42. Zhou Enlai to a delegation of American newspaper editors, quoted in *NYT*, October 12, 1972.

43. While the manner in which evidence of Lin's coup plans has been presented is highly suspect and the substance often incredible, the various documents issued after his disappearance and information released during the 1980 trial of his associates are on balance persuasive that some such plot existed.

44. Mao quoted in *NYT*, July 28, 1972.

45. See *IS*, June 1972, pp. 2-4; *Indictment*, p. 27; and Harry Harding, "Political Trends in China since the Cultural Revolution," *The Annals*, July 1972, p. 73.

46. See Ying-mao Kau and Pierre M. Perrolle, "The Politics of Lin Piao's Abortive Military Coup," *Asian Survey*, June 1974, pp. 566-67.

47. The link between Lin and the increase in military spending is further suggested by the fact that such spending dropped significantly after his fall. See Sydney H. Jammes, "The Chinese Defense Burden, 1965-74," in Joint Economic Committee, Congress of the United States, *China: A Reassessment of the Economy* (Washington: U.S. Government Printing Office, 1975), pp. 460-64.

48. The precise nuances and timing of the foreign policy debate involving Lin, Zhou, and Mao remain unclear. In a provocative study, Thomas M. Gottlieb, *Chinese Foreign Policy Factionalism and the Origins of the Strategic Triangle*, RAND Report R-1902-NA, November 1977, argues that the debate between Lin and Zhou dates from 1966 and that Lin's position included a relatively soft posture toward the Soviet Union. In my view, this places Zhou's advocacy of a diplomatic probe much too early and that any softening of Lin's posture toward Moscow occurred after he had clashed with Mao on other matters at the 1970 Lushan meetings. Cf. Michael B. Yahuda, *China's Role in World Affairs* (London: Croom Helm, 1978), pp. 220-24.

49. See Harry Harding and Melvin Gurtov, *The Purge of Lo Jui-ch'ing: The Politics of Chinese Strategic Planning*, RAND Report R-548-PR, February 1971, especially pp. 52ff.

50. See the excellent analysis of Ellis Joffe, "The Chinese Army after the Cultural Revolution: the Effects of Intervention," *CQ*, No. 55 (1973), especially pp. 452-55, 460-64.

51. See *ibid.*, pp. 470-71; and Philip Bridgham, "The Fall of Lin Piao," *CQ*, No. 55 (1973), p. 432.

52. See Harding, "Political Trends," pp. 71, 74-75.

53. In a different sense Lin's appeal to the radical group was also flawed by Cultural Revolution developments—in this case by his support of PLA officers over mass representatives in the staffing of the emerging political structures. Cf. *ibid.*, p. 75.

54. Efforts to curb rural radicalism under the rubric of "Mao's economic policies for the countryside" gathered force after Lushan; see Dennis Woodward, "Rural Campaigns: Continuity and Change in the Chinese Countryside—The Early Post-Cultural Revolution Experience (1969-1972)," *The Australian Journal of Chinese Affairs*, No. 6 (1981), pp. 105ff. As for foreign policy, the situation is less clear since it is unthinkable that the diplomatic probes toward Washington starting in late 1968 were undertaken without Mao's approval. Nevertheless, Mao's position in this period shifted in response to events, and his public reaction to the American invasion of Cambodia in spring 1970 was harsh. It might have been the case that Mao was influenced by the arguments of both Zhou and Lin in this period, or even play-

ing them off against each other. In any case, it was only in October 1970 when Mao appeared with the American writer Edgar Snow and then at the end of the year when he told Snow that Nixon would be welcome in China that Mao publicly signaled his personal commitment. See Kissinger, *White House Years*, pp. 687-702.

55. Mao's recorded views on the events at Lushan are collected in Kau, *Lin Piao*, pp. 55-68.

56. There may have been an additional anti-Zhou motive. Bridgham, "Fall of Lin Piao," p. 434, asserts that Lin and Chen directed attacks at Zhou and others responsible for drafting the new state constitution which deleted the post of chief of state and references to Mao's "genius."

57. See Kau and Perrolle, "Politics of Lin Piao's Coup," pp. 561-62; and *Indictment*, pp. 27-31.

58. For this period some essential features of the "two line struggle" model criticized in the first essay did apply—politics were highly polarized, with two diametrically opposed policy orientations closely linked to identifiable elite groupings engaged in clear and sharp conflict. This situation differed from that in 1966-1971 where Lin Biao's program was both less clearly articulated and more opportunistic. The "two line" model, however, did not totally apply in that Mao was not fully committed to either side of the struggle and also because of the presence of intermediate groups between the opposing forces.

59. Mao allegedly coined the term to refer to Jiang, Zhang Chunqiao, Wang Hongwen, and Yao Wenyuan. See *PR*, No. 35 (1977), pp. 26-27.

60. Although Hua and similar officials were in an ambivalent position toward the old-line administrators given their rapid promotions over members of that group, they were sharply differentiated from the radicals both by their broad pre-1966 bureaucratic careers and by virtue of having themselves been subjected to attacks during the Cultural Revolution. Such officials must also be distinguished from even lower-ranking cadres who rose much more rapidly, often as a result of attacking their superiors. These "helicopters," to use Deng Xiaoping's phrase, were more inclined to side with the "Gang of Four." Of course, the dividing line between the two types is fuzzy in both concept and practice.

In the case of Hua, mutual antipathy with the radicals is indicated by the "Gang's" reported attacks on him at the time of his 1976 promotions. See *Indictment*, p. 10.

61. On possible cooperation between the "Gang" and Chen Xilian, Wu De, Ni Zhifu, and Li Desheng, see Earl A. Wayne, "The Politics of Restaffing China's Provinces: 1976-1977," *Contemporary China*, Spring 1978, pp. 126-27.

62. See Ellis Joffe and Gerald Segal, "The Chinese Army and Professionalism," *Problems of Communism*, November-December 1978, pp. 1-5; Dittmer, "Bases of Power," p. 53; and John Bryan Starr, "China in 1974: 'Weeding Through the Old to Bring Forth the New,'" *Asian Survey*, January 1975, p. 12.

63. See, e.g., *IS*, September 1977, p. 76.

64. Apparently only three personal aides and more significantly Mao Yuanxin, the Chairman's nephew who had links to the "Gang," had unrestricted access. Jiang Qing reportedly had to arrange appointments to see Mao from early 1973, while Zhou Enlai met with him very infrequently after entering the hospital in 1974. See Terrill, *Mao*, pp. 385-87; and Ting Wang, *Chairman Hua: Leader of the Chinese Communists* (Hong Kong: University of Queensland Press, 1980), p. 106.

65. See Terrill, *Mao*, pp. 374-75, 381-84, 386, 392-95, 417; *Indictment*, pp. 9-

10; Merle Goldman, "Teng Hsiao-p'ing and the Debate over Science and Technology," *Contemporary China*, Winter 1978, pp. 62-64; and above, pp. 72-73.

66. The Chairman reportedly took umbrage at the "Gang's" efforts to sow suspicions about Zhou. See *PR*, No. 35 (1977), pp. 26-27, No. 10 (1978), p. 9.

67. See Teiwes, *Politics and Purges*, pp. 624-26.

68. On the "Gang's" factional activities, see *Indictment*, pp. 18, 24; *IS*, July 1978, pp. 99-102; and Kenneth Lieberthal with the assistance of James Tong and Sai-cheung Yeung, *Central Documents and Politburo Politics in China* (Ann Arbor: Michigan Papers in Chinese Studies, 1978), pp. 33ff.

69. See *IS*, July 1977, p. 112, September 1977, p. 64.

70. *RMRB*, February 29, 1976.

71. See Wang, *Chairman Hua*, pp. 114-15; and above, p. 75.

72. It is useful to contrast Hua, who only arrived in Beijing in 1971, with those who were active in the capital during the Cultural Revolution. In particular, consider Wang Dongxing, whose tasks as head of the security detail for Central Committee headquarters included arresting and holding in custody such top leaders as Deng Xiaoping. See Parris H. Chang, "The Rise of Wang Tung-hsing: Head of China's Security Apparatus," *CQ*, No. 73 (1978), pp. 130-32. As for Hua, he was perhaps most compromised by his part in the suppression of the Tiananmen riots.

73. The 1981 "Resolution on Party History" cited Ye and Li along with Xu Xiangqian and Nie Rongzhen for their sharp criticism of Cultural Revolution excesses during the "February Adverse Current" in 1967. See *BR*, No. 27 (1981), p. 22; and above, p. 70.

74. See Parris H. Chang, "Chinese Politics: Deng's Turbulent Quest," *Problems of Communism*, January-February 1981, pp. 2-3; and *CLG*, Spring 1977, pp. 52-53.

75. Hua's calculations remain unknown, and it is of course plausible that he considered an effort to keep Deng out of the leadership. Nevertheless, as early as December 1976—three months before the terms of Deng's return were approved—Hua was already consulting with Deng on policy matters. See *IS*, December 1978, p. 103.

76. See the purported text of a March 1979 talk where, in a manner reminiscent of Mao at the 1959 Lushan meeting, Deng declared, "This time I seem to have triggered a disaster"; *Inside China Mainland*, May 1979, p. 1. Even if this text is not genuine, it is nevertheless clear that Deng was closely identified with all three of the policies then in trouble.

77. See *IS*, October 1980, p. 96.

78. With regard to Wang Dongxing, a story making the rounds in Beijing in 1979 claimed that after his initial rebuffs Wang read *Romance of the Three Kingdoms* in search of clues on how to handle Deng but was too stupid to absorb its lessons.

79. See above, pp. 84-85.

80. Apart from a personal reputation as an honest and unassuming leader and status as one of Mao's "close comrades-in-arms," Chen has great prestige as the architect of the successful economic policies of the early and mid-1950s and of the recovery measures of 1961-62. See *Zhengming ribao*, July 13, 1981, in *FBIS:PRC*, July 15, 1981, pp. W2-5.

81. One does not have to adopt the cynical view that Deng simply sanctioned such ventures as "democracy wall" to encourage attacks on Wang Dongxing et al. and scrapped them once his purposes were served to believe that this old-line Party man concluded the disorders accompanying liberalization had reached an unacceptable level by early 1979.

82. On the drafting process, see *BR*, No. 30 (1981), p. 5. Deng, as a close collaborator of Mao's before the Cultural Revolution and a victim during that movement, undoubtedly was well pleased with a formula that affirmed the late Chairman's enormous revolutionary achievements while criticizing the errors of his later years.

83. While the vast majority of new secretaries had some significant ties to Deng over the full course of their careers, only two of eleven had primary links to him in the pre-Cultural Revolution period. Others had primary links to such active figures as Li Xiannian and Peng Zhen as well as to various deceased leaders. Similarly, of the thirteen individuals added to the Politburo since 1977, only four could be classified as close associates of Deng.

84. For an extensive catalog of PLA complaints, see Richard D. Nethercut "Deng and the Gun: Party-Military Relations in the People's Republic of China," *Asian Survey*, August 1982.

85. See Joffe and Segal, "Chinese Army and Professionalism," pp. 5-9, 15; and Oksenberg, "Economic Policy-Making," p. 192.

86. See *Inside China Mainland*, November 1982, pp. 1-7, for documents on this affair. In this case the *Jiefangjun bao* [PLA Daily] self-criticism of September 27, 1982, distinguished between having the right to different opinions about decisions already made which could be aired "in certain processes [to] raise questions," on the one hand, and the impermissible practice of "publish[ing] or broadcast[ing] statements which contradict Party Center decisions" in official organs, on the other; *ibid.*, p. 6.

87. For example, in the 1981 case of the "liberal" army writer Bai Hua it is arguable that pressure from leading PLA figures brought about a harsher response than the CCP's literary hierarchy desired, although it is again plausible that this reflected Deng's own preferences. See *Zhengming*, October 1, 1981, in *FBIS:PRC*, October 28, 1981, pp. W4-10.

88. Hua's responsibilities in the State Council under Zhou and Deng included such diverse and critical areas as public security, agriculture, and science and technology. Wang, *Chairman Hua*, pp. 79-82. Moreover, American and Australian diplomats who dealt with Hua in 1978-1980 were impressed with his growing competence.

89. See Wayne, "Politics of Restaffing," pp. 150-51. Wayne overstates possible links to Hua by including such tenuous criteria as being of the same generation; his hard data show five appointees with definite links to Deng compared with only one with ties to Hua.

90. For an analysis arguing Hua's more orthodox views in 1977-78 in contrast to Deng's greater willingness to introduce change, see Lieberthal, "Politics of Modernization," pp. 8-14.

91. I have found only one quasi-official source concretely suggesting Hua's opposition to the Third Plenum line—a report of a Hunan meeting where Hua was charged with hindering the implementation of agricultural responsibility systems; *Ta kung pao* [Impartial Daily] (Hong Kong), August 25, 1981, in *FBIS:PRC*, August

27, 1981, p. W1. For broader but vaguer charges of opposition to Third Plenum policies in the procommunist Hong Kong press, see, e.g., *Zhengming*, June 1, 1981, in *FBIS:PRC*, June 3, 1981, p. W4.

92. See *RMRB*, July 21, 1981, in *FBIS:PRC*, July 22, 1981, p. K5; and *IS*, February 1979, p. 39, May 1980, pp. 83-84.

93. See *Zhengming*, February 1, 1981, in *FBIS:PRC*, February 2, 1981, p. U2; *IS*, October 1980, pp. 93-95; and *Inside China Mainland*, March 1981, p. 16.

94. It is, of course, impossible to know the extent of such cooperation, but I am impressed by the absence of charges against Hua for the post-1978 period in the 1981 historical resolution and other official statements. However, see above, note 91, for suggestions of post-Third Plenum errors.

Also note the case of the 1980 PLA political work conference where Western analysts (e.g., Nethercut, "Deng and the Gun," p. 697) have interpreted Hua's use of the Maoist slogan "promote proletarian ideology and eliminate bourgeois ideology" as a counteroffensive against Deng. But while it is plausible that Hua used the occasion to strengthen his standing with PLA leaders, Deng's own account indicates that he too approved the slogan at the time; *IS*, March 1981, p. 98.

95. See Hua's speech to the NPC in *BR*, No. 38 (1980), especially pp. 15-16, 19-24. In this talk Hua was speaking as an individual rather than conveying an official report and used the first person when endorsing reform measures.

96. Apart from assuming the premiership, which had been earmarked for Deng, Hua had also been in charge of the campaign to criticize Deng and shared responsibility for suppressing the Tiananmen riots, although his overall course on these matters had been cautious and moderate. See Wang, *Chairman Hua*, pp. 101-108.

97. See above, pp. 87-89.

98. When Hua Guofeng was forced to step down as Party chairman he also gave up the chairmanship of the MAC, which had previously been concurrently held by the Party leader. Deng apparently wished this post to go to new Chairman Hu Yaobang but relented in the face of military opposition. This suggests that PLA leaders were happy to take orders from Deng, as they in fact had when he did not hold the MAC post, but balked at being under Hu who lacked the requisite revolutionary status. See *Zhengming*, February 1, 1981, in *FBIS:PRC*, February 2, 1981, p. U3; and above, p. 89.

99. After becoming the preeminent Soviet leader in 1957, Khrushchev undermined the role of the Central Committee, dismissed longtime supporters from key positions, damaged almost all major bureaucratic interests, and produced dramatic policy failures such as the installation of ballistic missiles in Cuba. Yet Khrushchev was able to rule in this vein for fully seven years before he was ousted as the result of a conspiracy among his colleagues. See Rigby, "Khrushchev," pp. 33-35.

100. Bureaucratic careers in China, as in the Soviet Union, tend to limit officials to specific bureaucracies or functional systems. Thus for the great bulk of officials personal ties are organizationally circumscribed. But for old revolutionaries, whose activities gave them great mobility in the pre-1949 period, a large and diffuse network of contacts is more the norm.

101. See the report that Deng and Chen suggested "younger and more vigorous comrades assume the posts of Party Chairman and Premier of the State Council even though they themselves are more experienced and enjoy high prestige"; *BR*, No. 9 (1982), p. 3. Concerning Chen, see also *Zhengming*, February 1, 1981, in *FBIS:PRC*, February 2, 1981, p. U5. Of course, such measures reflect a genuine need to place younger figures in grueling administrative positions, but the point

here is that politically more influential leaders other than just Deng are now formally outranked by comparatively junior officials.

102. Hu has taken the lead on a number of important issues—e.g., the "criteria of truth" debate, criticism of Mao, and the "liberal" line toward intellectuals—and has often put the case for Deng's policies in stronger terms than Deng himself. Hu finds himself in a predicament similar to that of Hua Guofeng (see above, p. 125) in that his statement of innovative positions produces potentially damaging resentment, whereas Deng can, within limits, assert similar views without threat to his position. The difference, of course, is that Hua's position led him generally to eschew such initiatives, while Hu's dependence on Deng required him to play the gadfly role.

103. As, for example, in the November 1982 appointment of Wu Xueqian, an old colleague in the Youth League central apparatus, as minister of foreign affairs.

104. Note also the post-Stalin Soviet practice of pensioning off failed leaders such as Khrushchev.

105. The emphasis placed on institutional interests here does not alter the argument concerning the primacy of the Politburo collective (see above, p. 97). While the perspectives of Politburo members will be increasingly shaped by their bureaucratic experience, once on the leading body they will be subject to its internal discipline, and leadership politics will revolve around compromising various interests within the context of the peer group. Cf. Rush, "The Coming Succession," p. 172.

INDEX

ABOUT THE AUTHOR

A graduate of Amherst College, Frederick C. Teiwes received his Ph.D. in political science from Columbia University. From 1969 to 1976 he first taught at Cornell University and then held a research appointment at The Australian National University. Since 1976 he has been on the faculty of the University of Sydney where he is a Reader in Government.

Mr. Teiwes has written widely on various aspects of Chinese affairs, particularly provincial politics and elite analysis in addition to Party disciplinary methods. His works include *Provincial Party Personnel in Mainland China* (1967), *Ssu-Ch'ing: The Socialist Education Movement* (with Richard Baum, 1968), *Provincial Leadership in China* (1974), *Elite Discipline in China* (1978), and *Politics and Purges in China: Rectification and the Decline of Party Norms 1950-1965* (1979).